PROFITS OF PEACE

PROFITS OF PEACE

The Political Economy of
Anglo–German Appeasement

SCOTT NEWTON

CLARENDON PRESS · OXFORD

1996

Oxford University Press, Walton Street, Oxford OX2 6DP

Oxford New York
Athens Auckland Bangkok Bombay
Calcutta Cape Town Dar es Salaam Delhi
Florence Hong Kong Istanbul Karachi
Kuala Lumpur Madras Madrid Melbourne
Mexico City Nairobi Paris Singapore
Taipei Tokyo Toronto
and associated companies in
Berlin Ibadan

Oxford is a trade mark of Oxford University Press

Published in the United States
by Oxford University Press Inc., New York

British Library Cataloguing in Publication Data
Data available

Library of Congress Cataloging in Publication Data
Newton, Scott, 1956–
Profits of peace : the political economy of Anglo-German
appeasement / Scott Newton.
p. cm.
Includes bibliographical references (p.   ) and index.
1. Great Britain—Politics and government—1936–1945.   2. Great
Britain—Economic conditions—20th century.   3. Great Britain—
Foreign relations—1936–1945.   4. Great Britain—Foreign relations—
Germany.   5. Germany—Foreign relations—Great Britain.   I. Title.
DA586.N49   1996
327.41043'09'043—dc20   95-30149
ISBN 0–19–820212–1

1 3 5 7 9 10 8 6 4 2

Typeset by Graphicraft Typesetters Ltd., Hong Kong

Printed in Great Britain
on acid-free paper by
Biddles Ltd.,
Guildford and King's Lynn

Acknowledgements

I would like to thank my research assistant Patricia Clark and Mike Earde for their invaluable and tenacious investigations on my behalf. Vince Moss was an unpaid but fertile ideas man. Hugh Thomas provided me with a host of fascinating insights into the intelligence war, 1939–45: historians should note that the gradual declassification of documents in Britain, the United States, and elsewhere has provided supporting evidence for some remarkable (and disturbing) information. Andrew Rosthorne was the source of many helpful tips. Robin Ramsay, the late James Rusbridger, Alan Spence, and John Zametica all furnished me with plenty of interesting and important material. My three interviewees, Kenneth de Courcy, the late Adrian Liddell-Hart, and Sir Peter Tennant, very kindly allowed me to copy (or even gave me copies of) original documents in their possession.

I owe a special debt to friends and colleagues who have contributed their own thoughts and advice over the last six years. I would like to single out Peter Cain, Bill Fuller, Meirion Hughes, Rhodri Morgan, MP, Dilwyn Porter, Robert and Helen Stradling, and Alice Teichova.

Duncan Cameron, Dave Eves, Lionel Guest, Terry and Ann Hawkes, Alun and Lynne Hutchings, Phil John, Steve Latham, Charles Newton, Margaret Newton, Nick Schroeter, and Richard and Judy Shields all provided intellectual and moral support and encouragement.

Richard Shields was also extremely generous with his time and computing expertise. Chris Goldoni made sure I would never go short of discs. My wife, Maria, helped me with the translation of Italian material into English; Jordi Larios performed the same service when it came to the Spanish documents.

I would like to thank my Head of Department, Professor John Percival, for his ready provision of generous support from the research fund. I am most grateful to the British Academy, whose small grant of £920 financed not only travel but also the services of my research assistant.

It is, finally, my wife whom I should thank above all. She has lived with this project for six years and without her constant love and companionship through hectic times it would never have seen the light of day. I hope the end result is worthy of her.

Contents

List of Tables

Introduction

Historiography and Argument

Historians today generally use the term 'appeasement' to characterize the attempts of British governments in the 1930s, and above all the administration of Neville Chamberlain (1937–40), to preserve world peace at a time of deepening international crisis. Appeasement has been seen at least in its European context[1] as a diplomatic initiative whose fundamental purpose was to accommodate German territorial and economic grievances arising from the Versailles Treaty. It has therefore been the practice of most commentators on the subject to treat it as an aspect of interwar British foreign policy. Representative texts, drawing on published and unpublished collections of private and official British and German archives, are A. J. P. Taylor, *The Origins of the Second World War* (1961); Ian Colvin, *The Chamberlain Cabinet* (1971); Keith Middlemas, *Diplomacy of Illusion* (1972); Simon Newman, *March 1939: The British Guarantee to Poland* (1976); Andrew Crozier, *Appeasement and Germany's Bid for Colonies* (1988); and Richard Lamb, *The Drift to War 1922–1939* (1989). The most substantial recent volume in this tradition is D. C. Watt's *How War Came* (1989). Here Anglo-German relations are discussed as one, albeit critically important, aspect of a mounting international crisis simultaneously viewed from the perspectives of contemporary civil servants and politicians in Moscow, Paris, Rome, Warsaw, and Washington DC.

There have been alternative approaches, particularly since the early 1970s, but these have been fairly limited in number. Thus, J. A. Gallagher explored appeasement as a facet of Imperial strategy in *The Decline, Rise and Fall of the British Empire* (1982). He argued that in the 1930s British governments sought to reduce the level of tension in Europe so that they could retain the freedom (and the resources) to contain the escalating diplomatic and military challenge presented by Japan in East Asia.

(Unless otherwise stated, place of publication is London for all titles.)

[1] See e.g. S. E. Endicott, *Diplomacy and Enterprise* (Manchester, 1975) and Ann Trotter, *Britain and East Asia* (Cambridge, 1975), for Chamberlain's attempt to reach a *détente* with Japan.

Gallagher's work relied heavily on chief-of-staff sources: Treasury and Foreign Office papers, however, suggest that the British attempted to reach an accommodation with the Japanese in the Far East after 1935, and only with reluctance came round to the view that confrontation might be inevitable.

Another route into the subject of appeasement was found in the study of economic diplomacy. In 'Economic Appeasement and the German "Moderates", 1937–39' (*Past and Present*, 56, 1972), C. A. MacDonald set Chamberlain's efforts to reach an Anglo–German accommodation in the context of attempts to revive international trade. His argument followed from B. J. Wendt's *Economic Appeasement: Handel und Finanz in der Britischen-Deutschland Politik* (1971), which maintained that the National Governments sought to reduce international tension and ensure recovery from the depression by integrating Germany into a liberal-capitalist global community led by Britain. This interpretation has been challenged by Gustav Schmidt in *The Politics and Economics of Appeasement* (1986)—but unfortunately for the strength of the case here the discussion stops in 1937, well before appeasement reached its climax. In consequence some of the most significant episodes in both Wendt's and MacDonald's histories of the search for economic *détente* are not seriously explored by Schmidt at all.

Other historians have argued that financial policy was at the root of appeasement. George Peden in *British Rearmament and the Treasury, 1932–9* (1979)[2] suggested that Treasury caution over rearmament derived not so much from anti-Keynesian dogma as from concern that a rapid and intensive buildup would both divert resources away from investment in productive industry and exhaust Britain's reserves of gold and dollars. The Treasury argued that 'finance was the fourth arm of defence'. British strategy was drawn up on the assumption that it would take three years to defeat Germany if the worst came to the worst; it was believed that the 'profligacy' being urged on the government by Churchill and the hawks around him would leave Britain unable to survive this long. Peden's concentration on the Treasury's pragmatism does not, however, do justice to the depth of its ideological investment in economic orthodoxy, an investment appreciated by Richard Shay Jr. in *British Rearmament in the 1930s: Politics and Profits* (1977). Shay's monograph focused

---

[2] See also two articles on the subject by Peden: 'Keynes, the Economics of Rearmament and Appeasement', in W. Mommsen and L. Kettenacker (eds.), *The Fascist Challenge and the Policy of Appeasement* (1983), and ' "A Matter of Timing": The Economic Background to British Foreign Policy, 1937–9', *History*, 69 (1984).

on the determination of the Baldwin and Chamberlain administrations to avoid the challenge to the balanced budget which inevitably followed from the escalating world crisis of the 1930s, a thesis viewed sympathetically by Brian Bond (*British Military Policy between the Wars*, 1979).

Despite the near-saturation coverage of appeasement there remain lacunae in the treatment of the subject. First of all, little effort has been made to relate appeasement as a foreign policy to the domestic politico-economic background from which it was developed, notwithstanding some gestures in such a direction by Peden and Shay. Yet does not any foreign policy reflect the efforts of the nation-state to shape an international environment congenial to its own preservation, or rather to the preservation of the prevailing economic system and social order within its borders?[3] Maurice Cowling's *The Impact of Hitler* (1975) does show an appreciation of this point—but his study concentrates on the world of Westminster. There is no analysis of the socio-economic context in which the politicians operated. So although we are led to understand that the 'actors' in this particular drama of high politics believed that appeasement was a strategy for the defence of the *status quo*, it never becomes clear exactly *how* appeasement is supposed to achieve this purpose. The methodological deficiencies of Cowling's approach are not present in *Crisis and Deconstruction* (1993), the second part of *British Imperialism*, the two-volume survey by P. J. Cain and A. G. Hopkins. These authors argue that the policy reflected the efforts of the British financial establishment to protect the 'gentlemanly order' which sustained it from the destabilizing impact of total war. However, their discussion of appeasement of necessity forms only a small part of an analysis which covers the period between 1688 and 1990.

Secondly, although Anglo-German peace-feelers have recently received some attention, notably from John Costello (*Ten Days that Saved the West*, 1991),[4] few studies published to date have argued that *the policy of appeasement itself* was continued beyond the outbreak of war with the support of the government until Chamberlain's resignation on 10 May 1940, and quite unofficially thereafter. Indeed, the consensus among

---

[3] The magisterial, two-volume survey by P. J. Cain and A. G. Hopkins, *British Imperialism* I: *Innovation and Expansion, 1688–1914* and *British Imperialism* II: *Crisis and Deconstruction, 1914–1990* (both 1993), operates from this perspective. It has been applied to post-war European reconstruction by Alan S. Milward, *The Reconstruction of Western Europe 1945–51* (1984).

[4] See in addition to John Costello, *Ten Days that Saved the West* (1991), the work of Richard Lamb, *The Ghosts of Peace 1935–1945* (Salisbury, 1987) and Peter Padfield, *Hess: The Führer's Disciple* (1992).

historians is that appeasement was abandoned in 1939, although whether in March (with the invasion of Czechoslovakia) or in September (with the invasion of Poland) is a matter of dispute. Yet the evidence clearly points to its continuation well into the war. This book will attempt to fill in these lacunae, and in so doing to demonstrate the interrelationship between the two 'missing dimensions' in the historiography of appeasement.

The argument, in brief, is that between 1921 and 1940 the dominant alliance in Britain was founded on a coalition between a ruling élite centred on the Treasury, the Bank of England, and the City of London and an expanding middle class whose wealth was based on personal savings and on the growth of the tertiary sector. In terms of politico-economic ideology this hegemonic group, based at the popular and the political level on a fusion between the Conservative and pre-1914 Liberal parties, was committed to the defence of free enterprise and the limited state against the internal threat of socialism and the external menace of Bolshevism. It was in the interests of this coalition to eschew unorthodox finance, associated in particular with Lloyd George, Oswald Mosley, and J. M. Keynes, and to work for the construction of a liberal international trade and payments system in which sterling would be the leading reserve currency. In 1925 these objectives were apparently achieved when Chancellor of the Exchequer Churchill returned Britain to the gold standard at the pre-1914 parity. This project was supported by many industrialists who after 1918 believed themselves to be facing an unenviable choice between government interference and militant trade unionism on the one hand and severe pressure on costs of labour and capital on the other. But the price in terms of lost export markets and domestic unemployment was high, and after 1929 deflation at home was reinforced by the disintegration of the world economy. The financial crisis of 1931 ultimately drove Britain off gold and modifications were made to the liberal strategy in and after 1931, with the introduction of a floating exchange rate, protection, and imperial preference in response to the global economic emergency.

Through the adoption of protection, imperial preference, and government-assisted rationalization, notably of ageing sectors in the home economy such as coal, textiles, and iron and steel, the City–Bank–Treasury establishment was able to retain the support of industrial capitalists anxious for the preservation of domestic and international markets. But the break with free trade was also essential to the preservation of the financial system. Imperial preference guaranteed exports in Britain to debtor countries such as Australia, India, and Canada and thus permitted them to maintain the servicing of loans raised in London. At the same time the introduction of the tariff helped to safeguard the balance of payments and hence the value of the exchange rate so that sterling could remain an internationally attractive currency. The measures of 1931–2, therefore, embodied a modification of the liberal project rather than its abandonment. Interventionist recovery strategies based on the expansion of the home market via increases in public expenditure were rejected on account of their perceived implications for inflation, the balance of trade, and taxation. Throughout the pre-war decade British governments worked for the opening up of an international economy characterized by barriers to the movement of goods and capital imposed by countries grappling with the loss of export markets and foreign exchange as a result of the slump. The liberal-capitalist British state required an export-led recovery guaranteed by a world economy which would be open but not driven by market forces; their inherent destructiveness was to be surmounted by cartelization. There was no other path to prosperity which could be squared with the interests both of the electorate which supported all inter-war governments after the collapse of reconstruction and of the British ruling élite.

The policy of appeasement followed naturally from the politico-economic priorities, outlined above, of inter-war British governments. Nazi Germany, with a foreign economic policy based on exchange controls and on barter agreements, was constructing an increasingly autarkic system of trade and payments in central Europe. From 1933 onward British banks and manufacturers were threatened with the loss of access to markets they had been able to penetrate after the German collapse in 1918. At the same time the City, which had provided a significant amount of reconstruction and above all short-term credits to the Weimar Republic, became anxious lest the deterioration of Germany's foreign exchange position led to the repudiation of all debts and in so doing undermined the stability of some leading financial houses such as Schroder's and Kleinwort's.

Meanwhile Britain's strategy for international economic recovery was also jeopardized by the aggressive nationalism of Nazi foreign policy. A confrontational response based on rearmament and on the forging of anti-German alliances would damage business confidence. But this was not all. Chamberlain in particular was sensitive to the Nazi threat to national security and presided as chancellor of the exchequer and prime minister over a significant increase in defence spending. But the demands for greater investment in the services, particularly the army, emanating from those who possessed no hope of accommodation with Germany, were resisted out of a conviction that if implemented they would turn back the clock to the immediate post-1918 period and bring about all the undesirable consequences likely to follow from the unorthodox remedies for the slump preached by Keynes and his fellow heretics.

It might have been possible to square the confrontational path with economic orthodoxy had British administrations been prepared to ally against Germany with either or both of the Soviet Union and the United States. But throughout the inter-war period the Soviet Union was regarded with suspicion for ideological reasons. Meanwhile Washington's mistrust of imperial preference and London's suspicion of American expansionism limited the prospects for Anglo-American *rapprochement*, Chamberlain's support for this notwithstanding.

These circumstances left the National Government little choice but to strive for an accommodation with Germany if its domestic and international objectives were to be secured. Accordingly the administration of Neville Chamberlain offered wide-ranging territorial and economic concessions to Germany based on a revision of the Versailles Treaty and on access to hard currency and raw materials in return for conversion to the principles of liberal capitalism. Seen in this context the appeasement of Nazi Germany was not simply about responding to blackmail. It was an ambitious scheme to defuse international tension via an all-embracing Anglo-German settlement which would provide the basis for peaceful co-operation between Europe's leading capitalist powers. Commerce would expand and the resultant prosperity would guarantee the survival of the National Government and the *status quo* it was determined to preserve at home and abroad.

Given that appeasement was a strategy for the survival of a particular type of socio-economic order in Britain and the wider world it would be unrealistic to expect it to have terminated with the outbreak of war. For Chamberlain the onslaught on Poland was final proof that *Hitler and the Nazi regime* could never be trusted again. But the prime minister still hoped to achieve *détente* with a strong, albeit non-Nazi, Germany in the interests of returning stability and order to international relations. He therefore sanctioned covert discussions with the German resistance, or individuals purporting to belong to it, while war strategy aimed at strangling the enemy's economy via the blockade. The hope was that such an approach would foment a revolution against Hitler.

Even this limited strategy was too much for some. Following the invasion of Poland there were talks between British industrialists and emissaries of Goering as well as efforts, generally supported by the foreign secretary, Lord Halifax, to secure Hitler's consent to a peace settlement leaving a Greater Germany (the absorption of Austria and the Sudetenland having been accepted) with Danzig and the Polish corridor. Throughout the period of the 'phoney war' Halifax, with the support of that part of the Conservative Party most closely linked to the City, large-scale industry, and the land-owning aristocracy, repeatedly tried to come to an agreement with Germany, Hitler or no. After Chamberlain's resignation this same group worked behind the back of his successor Churchill to bring about a negotiated settlement, the terms of which were similar to and followed naturally from pre-war attempts at accommodation, except that after the Battle of Britain they generally also involved the removal both of the Führer and of the prime minister.

The year 1941 brought disaster to the appeasers. The movement of Britain on to a total war footing and the entry of the Soviet Union and then the United States into the conflict set in motion forces which would shape the new world whose creation the Chamberlainite agenda had been designed to prevent. The ability of any British government to negotiate a separate arrangement with Germany disappeared. The fiasco of the Hess mission in effect represented the last throw of appeasement before the pre-war world was overtaken by the welfare state and decolonization.

Prelude

The roots of the pre-war *status quo* can be traced back at least to the mid-Victorian order, when it became axiomatic for British politics and economics to centre on the defence of free trade, the convertibility of sterling into gold at a fixed rate of exchange, and the balanced budget. The state was to act as a 'nightwatchman', committed to *laissez-faire* in economic and social matters, concerning itself merely with defence, the protection of private property, and the maintenance of law and order. Indeed, the advantages of this agenda were believed by politicians, financiers, and civil servants to be self-evident to the extent that it became invested with all the trappings of a set of values.[5] The task of converting these values from moral precepts into active measures of policy was conducted by the Treasury, the Bank of England, and the City of London. By 1914 the City consisted of a network composed of the Stock Exchange, brokers, merchant banks, insurers, companies arranging for the shipment of

---

[5] Geoffrey Ingham, *Capitalism Divided: The City and Industry in British Social Development* (Cambridge, 1984).

goods as well as of people, and the joint stock banks. Whilst it cannot be denied that these activities were in some degree competitive, there was by this time, as Boyce has argued, a strong 'corporate spirit'. The complexity of financial enterprises in London, involving, for example, the flotation of new companies on the Stock Exchange, the raising of capital for foreign governments, and the arrangement of short-term credits to finance trade between third countries created a web of 'informal ties, often strengthened by interlocking directorships. And since much of their business as well as the commercial intelligence on which it depended was passed on through personal contacts, a club-like atmosphere prevailed, with the subtle threat of ostracism providing further assurance of a large measure of conformity.'[6] In terms of status the most prestigious form of activity was merchant banking. Deposit banking was, by the end of the First World War, the province of the joint stock banks, concentrated by now into the 'big five' with their head offices in London. These organizations were recent members of the financial community; their lack of pedigree and their willingness to lend to domestic industry delayed their acceptance into a City establishment distinguished by its closer ties to the international than to the home economy. It was not until 1934 that they were granted representation on the Bank of England's Court, six years after the election of the first industrialist, Sir Josiah Stamp, chairman of the London, Midland, and Scottish Railway.[7]

The City's external orientation was not new by 1914 and reflected its role in generating the invisible surpluses which had maintained a positive balance of trade since the end of the Napoleonic wars. Industrialization had stimulated a vast expansion of British exports, notably over the period between 1831 and 1870. At the same time, however, the demand for raw materials and for food to sustain a fast-growing population, acknowledged by the repeal of the Corn Laws in the 1840s, attracted an increasing volume of imports, so that even at the height of its supremacy as a manufacturing power Britain ran a commodity trade deficit. This was counterbalanced by the income earned by the City from banking, insurance, shipping, and overseas investments, building on the expertise gained in providing these services for British governments and chartered companies (such as the East India Company) during the mercantilist wars with France of the preceding century (Table 0.1).[8]

[6] Robert D. W. Boyce, *British Capitalism at the Crossroads 1919–1932: A Study in Politics, Economics and International Relations* (Cambridge, 1987), 22.   [7] Ibid. 22.

[8] P. J. Cain and A. G. Hopkins, 'The Political Economy of British Expansion Overseas, 1750–1914', *Economic History Review*, 2nd ser., 33/4 (1980), 463–90.

TABLE 0.1. *UK balance of payments, 1831–1875* (quinquennial averages, £ million at current prices)

	Balance of commodity trade	Income from services	Income from dividends and interest	Balance on current account
1831–5	−13.1	14.1	5.4	6.4
1836–40	−24.0	18.6	8.0	2.6
1841–5	−17.0	15.4	7.5	5.9
1846–50	−26.8	22.0	9.5	4.7
1851–5	−27.5	23.7	11.7	8.0
1856–60	−33.8	43.5	16.5	26.2
1861–5	−56.8	57.1	21.8	22.0
1866–70	−58.2	67.9	30.8	40.5

Source: P. Mathias, *The First Industrial Nation* (1983), Table IX, p. 279.

As industrial development spread through Europe and America during the period after 1870 Britain gradually lost its domination of world trade in manufactured goods. Between 1880 and 1913 Britain's share of total world manufacturing output slipped from 22.9 per cent to 13.6 per cent while the shares of the United States and Germany grew from 14.7 per cent to 32.0 per cent and from 8.5 per cent to 14.8 per cent respectively.[9] Yet the growth of rival industrial powers gave an expansionary twist to international trade.[10] Muffled calls on the part of Midlands industrialists for protection against cheap German and American imports in the 1880s and 1890s were therefore greeted unfavourably in the City because, as the world's largest and most sophisticated financial centre, it was able to increase its revenue from servicing the increasing volume of world commerce. The maintenance of free trade guaranteed multiplying opportunities for foreign investment, the domination of the world's carrying trade by British ships, and accumulating profits for banks and insurance companies, from, respectively, the short-term financing of international trade and from mounting premiums derived from overseas. The profits accruing to City bankers were used for new credits and for reinvestment abroad, where returns were generally higher than could be found at home, particularly after 1870, when the recurrence of speculative booms associated with the earlier 'railway mania' was becoming rare. In consequence Britain's accumulating balance of capital overseas rose from an annual average of £1,065 million in 1871–5 to £3,990 million in 1911–13. The experience of relative decline was therefore not paralleled

[9] See Paul Kennedy, *The Rise and Fall of the Great Powers: Economic Change and Military Conflict from 1500 to 2000* (1988), Table 18, p. 259.
[10] François Crouzet, *The Victorian Economy* (1982), 359–70.

in the City: visible export earnings grew from £187.8 million in 1865–70 to £488.9 million in 1911–13, a factor of 2.6, while over the same period invisible income expanded from £98.7 million to £340 million, a factor of 3.4. The ratio of invisible to visible income narrowed during these years from .53 : 1 to .70 : 1.[11]

It followed that there was no necessary compatibility between the interests of British manufacturers and those of the financial sector, a disjunction which became increasingly clear with the expansion of overseas investment. It is of course true that the export of capital to finance, for example, the construction of transportation infrastructures in developing countries stimulated demand for railway locomotives, rails, and other capital goods.[12] Nevertheless, the level of investment abroad during the late nineteenth and early twentieth centuries (consistently larger than gross domestic capital formation) was a clear indication that the City took a closer interest in overseas economic developments than in those at home. Even the liberal *Economist* was driven to note that 'London is often more concerned with the course of events in Mexico than what happens in the Midlands and is more upset by a strike on the Canadian Pacific than by one in the Cambrian Collieries'.[13] City institutions did indeed keep their distance from British manufacturers during this period, and in 1905–6 no more than 600 of the 5,000 securities quoted on the London Stock Exchange were 'home industrials'. At the end of the Victorian era all but five of the City's leading wealth-holders owed their fortunes to commercial rather than to industrial activity.[14] For their part, domestic industrialists did not look to the City for finance but to the reinvestment of their own profits and to short-term personal loans.

The two worlds of an increasingly sophisticated financial system and an industrial base in relative decline in the period after 1870 were reproduced in the sociological and geographical map of Britain. This did not escape perceptive contemporary commentators. The radical economist J. A. Hobson argued that voting behaviour in the 1910 general elections derived from the existence of two Englands, one dominated by the consumer and the other by the producer. Producer's England dominated the north, the Midlands, and south Wales. It was characterized by Nonconformist culture, the chapel, and the political hegemony of new

---

[11] Derived from Peter Mathias, *The First Industrial Nation* (1983), Table 9, p. 279.

[12] Scott Newton and Dilwyn Porter, *Modernization Frustrated: The Politics of Industrial Decline in Twentieth Century Britain Since 1900* (1988), 8.   [13] Quoted in ibid. 8.

[14] See W. D. Rubinstein, 'The Victorian Upper Classes: Wealth, Occupation and Geography', *Economic History Review*, 2nd ser., 30 (1977), 602–3.

liberalism and organized labour. Consumer's England was centred on southern England and above all the Home Counties, the seaside resorts, and on the cathedral and university towns. It was mainly Anglican and Conservative in its politics. At its apex was a network of families whose fortunes, once derived from high farming, were now built upon high finance. Ties between landed property and commercial wealth had in fact been common since at least the aftermath of the Glorious Revolution; both had been regarded as possessing high social status. During the second half of the nineteenth century these had been reinforced by shrewd investment policies or commercially smart marriages into banking dynasties on the part of landowners facing declining rents and falling agricultural prices as a result of foreign competition. The experience of the Devonshires, who moved their assets out of land and industry so extensively that by the 1920s two-thirds of their income came from overseas investments, is perhaps extreme if not untypical.[15] This, then, was an England 'full of well-to-do and leisured families, whose incomes, dissociated from any present exertion of their recipients, are derived from industries conducted in the North or in some over-sea country. A very large share, probably the major part, of the income spent by these well-to-do residential classes in the South, is drawn from investments of this nature . . .'[16] The income accruing to this subclass of *rentiers* stimulated the expansion of the tertiary sector, supplying domestic labour, legal, educational, and financial services, and businesses concerned with property, distribution, and leisure.

Hobson's dissection of pre-war Britain has received significant backing from contemporary economic historians. C. H. Lee has pointed out that the expansion of the service sector fuelled the growth of the south-east economy to the extent that by 1911 25 per cent of the population lived there. Lee estimated that as early as 1914 no other region of the United Kingdom enjoyed so high a per capita income as the south-east, whose wealth and political influence was growing *pari passu* with the reliance of the economy on invisible exports.[17] The prosperity of the south-east and of the City were in fact mutually reinforcing: the savings generated by the

[15] John Scott, *The Upper Classes: Property and Privilege in Britain* (Cambridge, 1982), 44; P. J. Cain, 'J. A. Hobson, Financial Capitalism and Imperialism in Late Victorian and Edwardian England', in A. N. Porter and R. F. Holland (eds.), *Money, Finance and Empire 1790–1960* (1985), 15.

[16] J. A. Hobson, 'The General Election: A Sociological Interpretation', *Sociological Review*, 3 (1910), 112–13.

[17] C. H. Lee, 'Regional Growth and Structural Change in Victorian Britain', *Economic History Review*, 2nd ser., 34 (1981), 438–52.

service sector were ploughed into what Cain has called 'rentier home and foreign stocks'.[18] British export earnings grew, enhancing the profitability of the staple industries in the pre-war decade. By 1914 a formidable overseas lobby had been created. At its heart was the City, whose activities developed a common interest in the pursuit of free trade on the part of the *rentier*, the service sector, the export industries, and shipbuilding.

The City's international financial role was underpinned by its alliance with the Bank of England and the Treasury. The Court of Directors of the Bank of England was made up mainly of members of the Accepting Houses Committee such as 'Barings, Rothschilds, Hambros, Morgan Grenfell and Lazard Brothers'.[19] The Bank's duty was to act as lender of last resort and to maintain international confidence in the convertibility of sterling into gold at a fixed rate, otherwise known as the gold standard. To this end the Bank had manipulated the rate of interest to enhance its own liquidity and attract foreign capital to London. Britain's reliance on invisibles after 1870 made currency stability essential, since neither bankers and small investors nor insurance companies would have felt inclined to transact so much business with a financial centre incapable of guaranteeing that the assets with which it had been entrusted would hold their worth. This commitment to 'sound money' was finally assured by the Treasury, whose historic duty as guardian of the public purse had given it institutional power over all the other departments of state. Since the 1850s the pursuit of 'Gladstonian finance' had meant the balancing of government income and expenditure at levels commensurate with low taxes and a minimal national debt. This generous fiscal regime combined with a scarcity of government stock to encourage investors to maintain the flow of capital abroad.[20]

The pursuit of common economic objectives by the City, the Bank, and the Treasury was facilitated by well-established familial and social links and by an educational system based on the public schools and Oxbridge, designed to produce successive generations of bankers and administrators along with the lawyers, doctors, teachers, military officers, and Conservative MPs needed to service and protect them. Down to 1914, for example, more than twice as many pupils from Winchester went into commerce as into manufacturing.[21] The proportion of permanent

---

[18] Cain, 'J. A. Hobson, Financial Capitalism and Imperialism', 13.

[19] Boyce, *British Capitalism at the Crossroads*, 22.

[20] Cain, 'J. A. Hobson, Financial Capitalism and Imperialism', 13.

[21] Scott Newton, 'Operation ROBOT and the Political Economy of Sterling Convertibility 1951–52', *European University Institute Working Paper* 86/256 (Florence, 1986).

secretaries from public schools reached two-thirds between 1900 and 1919.[22] It was therefore perfectly natural for governments to turn in troubled times, such as that of the Baring crisis of 1890, to the City and the Bank for advice. More than this, the years of co-operation had by 1914 at the latest generated a world-view at the heart of the British establishment which identified the prosperity of the City with the national economic interest. The highly interventionist rescue of the Acceptance Houses and the Stock Exchange mounted in 1914 by the Asquith government, when the outbreak of war led to the stand-still of the international trading system and thus precipitated a liquidity crisis in the City, was testimony to this fact.

It might of course, be argued that there was no choice but to abandon free market principles in response to the emergency of war. But such dramatic sacrifices of economic principle had never been made for manufacturers, as the fates of the campaigns for 'Fair Trade' and then Tariff Reform make clear. Furthermore, the management of the 1914 crisis, with a three-month moratorium for City institutions facing claims and unable to raise money from overseas, was characterized by only perfunctory consultations with domestic traders and producers, who were not exempted from the obligation to pay wages as well as taxes and other duties owed to the state.[23]

In fact, at the start of the First World War the government anticipated a relatively short and limited conflict. Britain's military commitment would be low-level, the bulk of its efforts centring on the use of maritime power to blockade the enemy and keep the seas open for British and allied trade. The shopkeeper's slogan 'business as usual', which was quickly taken up by the government, therefore reflected a confidence that the essentials of the pre-war order could be preserved: strict Treasury control of public expenditure, an open trading system, and the gold standard would all be supported so that the City could continue to function, even if its role for the time being was to finance Britain's allies. Such confidence was not, however, to be justified, and by 1918 the politico-economic agenda of the City–Bank–Treasury nexus was being challenged by Producer's England, with its own manifesto of managed trade, industrial corporatism, and an interventionist state.

[22] Scott, *The Upper Classes*, 158–9.
[23] See John Peters, 'The British Government and the City–Industry Divide: The Case of the 1914 Financial Crisis', *Journal of Twentieth Century British History*, 4 (1993), 126–48.

PART 1

The Liberal–Conservative Consensus

1

The Failure of Reconstruction and the Political Economy of Normalcy, 1914–1931

Corporatism and the Liberal Reaction, 1914–1925

The First World War was marked by growing reliance on economic interventionism by the British state. At first arrangements were largely *ad hoc*.[1] But all pretence at 'business as usual' disappeared during 1915. It was clear that there was no foreseeable end to the conflict and that Britain would have to organize a modern, well-equipped mass army if the Germans were going to be permanently stopped. Such a task was beyond the market economy, a fact made apparent by the shell scandal of May 1915, by rising inflation, and by shortages of labour at home. In consequence the government was driven to adopt conscription, rationing, and rent and price controls as well as centralized allocation of resources. It took over responsibility for the management of mines and shipping as well as railways. The need to preserve shipping space and reserves of gold and foreign exchange forced the state to assume responsibility for foreign trade, and by November 1918 government purchasing accounted for 90 per cent of British imports. At the same time the Treasury lost its grip over Whitehall and was superseded in importance by the Ministry of Munitions. The Ministry became the chief instrument of wartime intervention, largely as a result of its responsibility for war production, and imposed direct industrial controls on iron and steel, engineering, aircraft production, chemicals, and explosives.[2]

The national emergency of war and the need to mobilize the full resources of the community therefore drove the British state down a path which led it to break every rule of pre-war political economy. The gold standard was suspended on the outbreak of war and in consequence the Bank of England lost control of the money supply in an economy fuelled

---

[1] See Scott Newton and Dilwyn Porter, *Modernization Frustrated: The Politics of Industrial Decline in Britain Since 1900* (1988), 34. [2] Ibid. 37.

by the widespread circulation of Treasury bills. No wartime budget was balanced, the government's deficit growing from £333.8 million in 1914–15 to a high of £1,989.0 million in 1917–18, the gap being bridged by large-scale borrowing which left the Treasury grappling with a swollen national debt between the wars.[3] Free trade was abandoned in 1915, and in 1916–17 representatives of the government, having met with opposite numbers from the Allied powers in Paris, began to draw up plans for a post-war international economic order inspired by the mercantilist notions that trade is the continuation of war by other means, and that national power and prosperity stand at the apex of a government's list of priorities. At Paris the Allies agreed on a common reconstruction policy characterized by state support for private industry via subsidies and tariffs, the withholding of most-favoured-nation status from Germany and Austria, and a programme of retaliatory measures in the event of German post-war dumping. Such a manifesto could not of course be reconciled with the restoration of the balanced budget and a return to a non-interventionist economic policy in peacetime: indeed, it formed the external counterpart to an ambitious programme of social and industrial reconstruction, recognized in Lloyd George's commitment to the creation of a 'land fit for heroes to live in'.

Given the centrality of industrial production to the wartime economy it is not surprising that for the first time the ranks of government were swelled by industrialists and trade unionists, groups unable to break the gentlemanly grip on the levers of power prior to 1914. Lloyd George's Coalition was populated by businessmen such as Lord Weir of the Federation of British Industries (FBI), Allan Smith of the Engineering Employers' Federation (EEF), Lord Cowdray, a civil engineering contractor who served as air minister, and Lord Rhondda, a coal-owner appointed by the prime minister to the post of food controller. At the same time the government contained Labour leaders such as Arthur Henderson, George Barnes, and John Hodge.

The agenda which emerged from this extension of the state's role in the economy was corporatist rather than socialist. The objective was a partnership between the state and private industry. But Lloyd George and his industrialist allies recognized that to be successful this partnership would necessitate the integration of the labour movement into decision-making; industry could only work more effectively if capital and labour worked together. Thus the Commissions on Industrial Unrest of

---

[3] Sidney Pollard, *The Development of the British Economy, 1914–1990* (1992), 24.

1917 encouraged the conciliation of labour and isolated profiteering, poor housing, and bad conditions at work as the roots of working-class discontent. The Whitley Councils, with joint representation for employers and employees, seemed to many to be precisely the initiative to be adopted to build on the wartime mood of unity whilst avoiding the perils of socialism. The vision was one of class collaboration in pursuit both of national security and of national efficiency.

Yet the vision faded once the war was over. The apparatus of wartime collectivism was rapidly dismantled. Food rationing and most price controls ended in 1920. Factories owned by the Ministry of Munitions were sold off and the Ministry itself, along with the Ministries of Shipping and Food, was wound up at the end of March 1921. Control of the railways and the mines was abandoned in 1921 and parliament vetoed plans for the public management and reorganization of electricity generation and distribution. In 1925 Britain's return to the gold standard at the pre-war point signalled the triumph of old-fashioned liberal economic orthodoxy.

The rise of corporatism notwithstanding, Britain's pre-war policy-making élite had undergone no intellectual conversion.[4] Within the Square Mile as within the Treasury the liberal optimism which regarded war as a deviation from normality continued to prevail. It was therefore accepted, first, that abnormal circumstances justified abnormal measures, and secondly, that once the emergency ended there was every reason to return to the *laissez-faire* policies which were seen to be responsible for pre-war prosperity. The crisis which might have precipitated a questioning of orthodoxy was avoided by the flow of dollars across the Atlantic resulting from the liquidation of British investments throughout the American continent (about 10 per cent of the total) and from private loans organized by syndicates in the United States. Both the Treasury and the Bank remained committed to cosmopolitanism, and in 1918 the Cunliffe Committee, appointed to consider currency and financial policy after the war, recommended that Britain should make the return to gold at pre-war parity the central objective of economic policy.

Domestic institutional pressures were always going to make it difficult for the realization of a reconstruction programme based on corporatism and planned trade. But after 1917 these were reinforced by external pressure from the United States, which was committed to the pursuit of

[4] R. H. Tawney, 'The Abolition of Economic Controls', *Economic History Review*, 13 (1943), 1–7.

the 'open door'—equal access for all nations to the world's markets and
raw-material resources. Ideology and pragmatism worked hand in hand
to shape Washington's international objectives. In Washington the Paris
resolutions of 1916 were regarded with a great deal of suspicion, on the
grounds that they not only contained within them the seeds of future
conflict with Germany but in addition would have an adverse effect on
American trade. The war had accelerated the development of a powerful
cluster of manufacturing and financial interests in the United States
whose welfare was bound up with the continuing openness of the international economy. The American share of world exports grew from 13.5
per cent in 1913 to over 25 per cent in 1920, and over the same period
the United States had become the world's creditor. London had lost its
place to New York; British war debts with American syndicates totalled
$3.7 billion by the end of 1918.[5] It is therefore unsurprising that free
trade was seen by President Wilson and his advisers as the best guarantee of international co-operation after the war and as an insurance
that American producers would be able to find overseas markets so that
domestic demand and employment could be sustained. In consequence
the financial dependence of Britain and the Allies on the United States
by the end of the war guaranteed the abandonment of schemes to plan
foreign trade.[6]

The American challenge was regarded with ambivalence in the City.
On the one hand it stimulated a fierce determination to recapture international financial leadership from New York. Yet simultaneously transat-
lantic economic internationalism evoked a sympathetic response in London
and formed part of an agenda shared by bankers and politicians on both
sides of the Atlantic, namely, the encouragement of Anglo-Saxon leadership of the world into an era of peace, prosperity, and liberal consti-
tutionalism. Prior to the outbreak of war lobbying to this end had
been conducted by the Round Table, which had well-placed members
on both sides of the Atlantic. After its conclusion these efforts were
placed on a more formal footing, with the foundation in 1919 of the
Royal Institute for International Affairs (RIIA) and what was intended
to be its parallel organization in the United States, the Council on Foreign Relations (CFR) in 1919. Bankers were prominent in the Round
Table–RIIA–CFR network; their number included representatives of

---

[5] Cain and Hopkins, *Innovation and Expansion*, 59–60.
[6] See *Final Report of the Committee on Commercial and Industrial Policy After the War*,
Cmd. 9035 (1918), para. 318. This condemned the idea of a general tariff and called for a
return to 'normal industrial conditions within the shortest possible time'.

Baring Brothers, Rothschilds, Lazards, and J. P. Morgan, who had taken a leading role in organizing the war credits for Britain.[7]

Despite the existence of these internal and external pressures on the government, an immediate return to 'normalcy' after the war was politically impossible. After November 1918 the Lloyd George Coalition was confronted by the problem of demobilization, by a self-confident labour movement, some of whose more radical representatives were inspired by recent events in Russia, as well as by growing concern on the part of employers about government intervention and trade-union power. In particular, there was mounting evidence that the doctrinaire owners of the mines and the railways wanted de-control and an assertion of the 'right to manage' via the introduction of wage cuts and a confrontation with labour over jobs, hours, and pay rates.[8] It was against this background of political instability and contemporary fears of 'Bolshevism' that Lloyd George attempted to corral enlightened employers into a corporatist political programme based on the avoidance of undisguised class politics, the appeasement of labour, and state-led reconstruction. Since this experiment would have been wrecked by deflationary policies, the government formally abandoned the gold standard, Cunliffe notwithstanding, and maintained a high level of expenditure. Old-age pensions were increased, unemployment insurance was made universal, and the state supported a major programme of school and local authority housebuilding. Concessions to labour were accompanied by compulsion and the employment of black propaganda. The shop stewards' Clydeside revolt of 1919 was terminated by the military occupation of Glasgow, and the government covertly encouraged press scare stories about the association between Bolshevism and 'irresponsible' trade union activity.[9]

Although the Coalition had seen its survival in terms of neutralizing the political and industrial Left, it was in the end brought down from the Right. The complicated story of how and why the Conservative Party finally overthrew Lloyd George has been well enough documented.[10]

---

[7] Laurence H. Shoup and William Minter, *Imperial Brain Trust: The Council on Foreign Relations and United States Foreign Policy* (New York and London, 1971), 11–17. The Round Table-RIIA–CFR network has been analysed in Carroll Quigley, *The Anglo-American Establishment from Rhodes to Cliveden* (New York, 1981).

[8] See W. R. Garside, 'Management and Men: Aspects of British Industrial Relations in the Inter-War Period', in Barry Supple (ed.), *Essays in Business History* (Oxford, 1977).

[9] Keith Middlemas, *Politics in Industrial Society: The British Experience Since 1911* (1979), 131.

[10] E.g. Lord Beaverbrook, *The Decline and Fall of Lloyd George* (1963), and K. O. Morgan, *Consensus and Disunity* (Oxford, 1979), chs. 12–14.

What is perhaps less familiar is that key sectors of the ruling élite—
the Treasury, the Bank, and the City—mobilized their own coalition
to undermine reconstruction.

The era of reconstruction lasted from the end of the war until April
1920. High state spending, the existence of cheap credit, and a floating pound stimulated a spectacular boom. By December 1919 there was
virtually full employment and by 1920 industrial production had reached
its 1913 level—not attained again until 1924. But by dismantling price
controls and rationing the government deprived itself of the weapons to
control the inflationary side-effects of the boom. The period was characterized not only by industrial growth but by speculation and inflation.
Wholesale prices stood at 226 in January 1919 (1914 = 100)[11] and rose
to a peak of 323 in March 1920. Wages increased as well but could not
keep pace: by July 1920 they stood at 260 (1914 = 100). The rising cost
of living, together with labour outrage at the government's plans to
intervene against the Soviets in the Russian civil war, destroyed lingering
hopes of industrial harmony. If inflation and union militancy antagonized
employers, small savers, and middle-class consumers, the downward float
of the pound, to £1 = $3.40 by February 1920, seriously concerned the
Bank and policy-makers in the Treasury. The anxiety was that continued
inflation, fuelled by unbalanced budgets and cheap credit, would destroy
social cohesion and lead to a collapse of confidence in sterling which
would undermine the City's traditional financial role.[12]

The crisis provided the ideal opportunity for those wanting to return
to pre-1914 orthodoxy. In the context of 1919–20, of course, orthodoxy meant a return to gold at the pre-war parity and its essential accom-
paniment, balanced budgets. The only effective route back to gold lay
through deflation, involving an increase in the bank rate and government
retrenchment. This course of action was successfully pressed on the
Coalition despite opposition from Lloyd George himself. In December
1919 Chancellor Austen Chamberlain accepted the recommendations of
the Cunliffe Committee and by April 1920 the bank rate stood at the
high level of 7 per cent. Quite abruptly the government changed its
commitments to employment and reconstruction for determination to
control inflation above all else. The sharp deflation was a major influence behind the rise of unemployment to 15 per cent of the insured
work-force by March 1921. At the same time the index of industrial

---

[11] C. L. Mowat, *Britain Between the Wars, 1918–1940* (1955), 27.
[12] Newton and Porter, *Modernization Frustrated*, 43.

activity slipped in just one year from 117.9 to 90.0 (1913 = 100). Tough budgets and pressure to reduce government expenditure, symbolized officially by the 'Geddes axe' and at a more popular level by the *Daily Mail*'s 'Anti-Waste' campaign, ensured a rapid fall in prices, from 310–40 in mid-1920 to 160–70 in February 1922. In this deflationary climate the pound moved back up to $4.40 by 1924.[13]

Moving back to gold implied the acceptance of an external discipline on the economy which would bring British costs and prices down into line with her most significant rival, the United States. It meant reverting to the pre-war international order of free trade and convertible currencies desired by Washington. This return to 'normalcy' was, furthermore, essential if British invisible earnings were to be maximized. In 1911–13 income from services, interest, and dividends had been sizeable enough to outweigh a commodity trade deficit of £134.4 million and leave Britain with a favourable current account balance of £206.1 million.[14] But the war weakened London's ability to play its international role. The sale of overseas assets, the war debt with the United States, the failure of the European Allies to meet their obligations to Britain (worth $7 billion), and the downward float of sterling after November 1918 combined with international economic disorder to reduce the value of income from overseas investments. Invisible income had been worth 44 per cent of all imports in 1913: by the early 1920s its value had declined to 29 per cent.[15] Before 1914 invisible income had not only generated a continuing expansion in overseas lending: it had sustained living standards by protecting Britain from the consequences of its declining share of the world's commodity trade. After 1918, however, the decline in invisibles both reduced London's international financial clout and threatened to leave Britain dependent on its ailing industrial structure to pay its way in the world. It was only within the context of an open world economy run according to the pre-1914 rules of the game that London could hope to strengthen the invisible prop to the balance of payments.

By the lights of contemporary orthodoxy, therefore, there was a reputable case to be made for the adoption of dear money. It was one way of addressing real economic problems, centring on inflation, uncompetitive export industries, and an exposed balance of payments. But the strategy represented the conventional wisdom of Treasury and Bank officials who were themselves part of a ruling élite dependent for its wealth and power

---

[13] Pollard, *Development of the British Economy, 1914–1990*, 106–7.

[14] M. W. Kirby, *The Decline of British Economic Power Since 1870* (1980), 138.

[15] Cain and Hopkins, *Crisis and Deconstruction*, 36–41.

on the continuation of Britain's commitment to liberalism in external and internal economic relations.[16] The post-war crisis might have been countered by the programme of public investment, protection, and a floating exchange rate outlined by the prime minister at Criccieth in 1919.[17] But the adoption of such measures would have threatened the survival of the liberal state. Sterling would have lost much of its international attractiveness and Britain would have started along a path which might have led to isolation from the world economy. This was why the issue of inflation was so sensitive for officials from the Treasury and the Bank, why they condemned the Coalition's immediate post-war financial policy as 'extravagant' and 'unsound'. In 1919–20 Britain's ruling élite considered itself to be acting 'in the public interest'[18] when it defended the liberal system it had been trained to administer. Sound money and sterling–gold convertibility were not merely policy options: they were the domestic and international economic expressions of British liberal society.

It was because the appeal of normalcy spread far wider than Whitehall and the Square Mile that it would be wrong to suggest that the era of reconstruction was brought to a close by a conspiracy of bankers and civil servants. Lloyd George himself did not fall from power until 1922. But well before his political demise the establishment was mobilizing the liberal consensus which dominated the British political economy up to 1940. It was the creation of this consensus which helped to preserve social stability at a time when the deflationary policies preparing the way for a return to gold, finally achieved in 1925, helped to keep unemployment above the 1 million mark.

To start with, the pursuit of sound money and a stable exchange rate benefited savers and the owners of property abroad. These groups were not composed merely of the idle rich and gentlemen of leisure. In particular, the first decade of the twentieth century saw a rise in the proportion of national savings owned by small and institutional investors. This socio-economic trend was reflected by both building societies and life-insurance companies. Membership of building societies rose from 617,423 in 1913 to 2,082,652 in 1937, while deposits expanded from £82 million in 1920 (1.5 per cent of GNP) to £717 million in 1938 (14 per cent of GNP). Life-insurance premiums more than doubled between 1913 and

---

[16] Cain and Hopkins, in *Innovation and Expansion*, chs. 3 and 4, provide an extended analysis of this theme. It is also discussed at some length by Geoffrey Ingham, *Capitalism Divided?* esp. 175–8.   [17] Middlemas, *Politics in Industrial Society*, 134.

[18] See Susan Howson, 'The Origins of Dear Money, 1919–20', *Economic History Review*, 2nd ser., 37 (1974), 88–107.

1925, rising from £28.1 million to £57.9 million. Thereafter they continued to mount steadily, reaching £80.5 million by 1937.[19]

These figures reflected the increase in numbers of the lower middle class and of white-collar workers generated by the vitality of the service sector, particularly around London and the Home Counties. The rise of the service sector had proceeded hand in hand with the development of the world's 'first large-scale consumer society' in south-east England before 1914.[20] After the war this trend continued. Employment in occupations such as retail distribution, entertainment, and local government grew by 873,000 between 1921 and 1931. But over the same period employment in primary and secondary industries fell by 957,000.[21]

The growth in small savings was one reflection of the expansion of the tertiary sector. Another expression of this development came in the field of housing. Between 1919 and 1930 more than 1.5 million houses were built in Britain, a gross increase of 20 per cent in the country's housing stock.[22] The encouragement given to municipal house-building by the Addison and Wheatley Acts of 1919 and 1924 is well documented. Less apparent, perhaps, is the concurrent growth of private house-building, a trend which was to become more noticeable in the 1930s. Two-thirds of the houses constructed between 1919 and 1930 were constructed by private enterprise, and the suburbs of London, Birmingham, and Manchester were increasingly characterized by the proliferation of semi-detached dwellings inhabited by the new 'salariat'.

This slow and unspectacular movement toward property-ownership on the part of the middle class did not mean that post-war Britain was characterized by a major redistribution of wealth. But there was a small movement away from the concentration of wealth in the hands of the top 1 per cent. Between 1911 and 1913, for example, the top 1 per cent had owned 69 per cent of the nation's wealth: by 1924–30 this proportion had fallen to 60 per cent.[23] Supertax payers, who had received 8 per cent of the national income in 1911, took 5.5 per cent in 1924.[24] Indeed, the

[19] Scott Newton, 'The "Anglo-German Connection" and the Political Economy of Appeasement', *Diplomacy and Statecraft*, 2 (1991), 180; *Statistical Abstracts of the United Kingdom 1913 and 1924–37* (1939), Table 173; John Stevenson, *British Society, 1914–45* (1984), 126; C. H. Feinstein, *National Income, Expenditure and Output of the United Kingdom, 1855–1965* (Cambridge, 1972), Table 1, T4.

[20] See C. H. Lee, 'Regional Growth and Structural Change in Victorian Britain', *Economic History Review*, 2nd ser., 34 (1981), 438–52.

[21] Pollard, *Development of the British Economy, 1914–1990*, Table 4.7, 148.

[22] A. J. Youngson, *The British Economy, 1920–57* (Oxford, 1960), 64.

[23] Stevenson, *British Society, 1914–45*, 330.

[24] Mowat, *Britain Between the Wars*, 205.

taxation system in general was weighted in favour of the middle class. After reaching a high point of 6s. (30p.) in the pound in 1923, income tax rates fell to an average of 4s. 6d. (22.5p.), leaving a generous sum of disposable income for saving and for the purchase of consumer durables such as private cars and radio sets. In general, those earning between £250 and £1,000 a year lost a lower proportion of their income to direct or indirect taxation than either the very rich or the very poor.[25]

The political effect of these social changes could be felt at the level both of party and of policy. First of all, the growth of an affluent, property-owning middle class favoured the Conservative Party in general elections. Perhaps the greatest sufferers from this trend were the Liberals, who before 1914 had relied heavily on the provincial middle class and entrepreneurial citizen making a virtue out of his independence, thrift, hard work, and impatience with an aristocratic, Anglican establishment dominated by landowners. The 1918 election, however, revealed a shift of this provincial, propertied interest into Conservatism: nearly half of the new recruits to the Conservative dominated Coalition were businessmen.[26] It has, however, also been suggested that the growth of salaried groups damaged Labour's chances after 1918. Professional families tended to have a relatively low birth-rate and the need to recruit from below led to an absorption of ambitious working-class children who might have been tempted by radical and socialist ideas.[27] Not even at the high point of its inter-war fortunes in 1929 was the Labour Party able to win enough seats to command a parliamentary majority, while the Liberal presence in the House of Commons slumped from 158 in 1923 to 42 in 1924, recovering slightly to 59 in 1929.

The Conservative Party welcomed the opportunity to accommodate the service-based meritocracy. During the inter-war years it steadily lost its old identification with the landed aristocracy and became associated with the defence of propertied interests in general. The development of an ideological style which appealed to the upwardly mobile was a natural reflection of this change.[28]

In 1925, during the second reading of the Pensions Act, Neville

[25] Stevenson, *British Society, 1914–45*, 131.

[26] Cain and Hopkins, *Crisis and Deconstruction*, 29.

[27] Pollard, *Development of the British Economy, 1914–1990*, 149.

[28] Cain and Hopkins, in *Crisis and Deconstruction*, 30, point out that by 1939 181 Conservative MPs held directorships in a variety of transport, distribution, and manufacturing enterprises. Although 60% of Conservatives in parliament were still products of the public-school system and the same proportion retained some connection with the land, the impact of this change in composition did cause Tory traditionalists some concern.

Chamberlain stated that: 'Our policy is to use the great resources of the State, not for the distribution of indiscriminate largesse, but to help those who have the will and desire to raise themselves to higher and better things.'[29] This was not, as C. L. Mowat has argued, 'Tory socialism' but a secularized version of old-fashioned Nonconformist liberalism: it was no longer God but the state which helped those who helped themselves. Since those who helped themselves tended to be home-owners and small savers, it followed that they would support a policy which emphasized sound money, the repayment of the National Debt (which absorbed 7 per cent of the national product in 1930), and the defence of private property. The international liberalism of the Treasury and the Bank therefore found domestic support in a middle class which favoured financial and social stability.

Corporatist-minded industrialists such as Sir Dudley Docker of Birmingham Small Arms and Sir Allan Smith's 'Industrial Group' of MPs, who had lined up behind reconstruction, were unable to organize much resistance to orthodoxy. Their influence had waned in the face of both renewed class conflict and divisions between employers. Within the Federation of British Industries (FBI) there had been growing evidence of disharmony between the protectionists, who derived most of their support from iron and steel and from the new industries of motor-car and cycle manufacturing, and the free traders, located especially in traditional export industries of coal, textiles, and shipbuilding.[30] Meanwhile the rapidly growing light, consumer-product industries based in southern England had never been closely associated with the Federation. Such disunity, exacerbated as early as 1919 by the foundation of the National Confederation of Employers' Associations, made the dismissal of anxieties about the return to gold relatively straightforward for the Bank and the Treasury.[31]

The Return to Gold, 1925

The government was, all the same, aware that the return to gold was likely to be painful: in view of Britain's meagre reserves and a massive American gold surplus it seemed as if sharp and sustained deflation would be necessary to bring about an external financial position healthy enough to assure the operation's success. The government's anxiety about

---

[29] Quoted in Mowat, *Britain Between the Wars*, 338.
[30] Cain and Hopkins, *Crisis and Deconstruction*, 54.
[31] Newton and Porter, *Modernization Frustrated*, 42–3.

the likely implications for social stability and industrial recovery led it to promote at the Genoa Conference of 1922 an ambitious scheme whereby sterling rather than gold should form the bulk of continental governments' foreign-exchange reserves.[32]

Although the Bank of England succeeded in stabilizing the Austrian and Hungarian currencies on sterling, the Genoa initiative failed. It ran into American enthusiasm for the straightforward use of gold as a reserve by members of the international monetary system. There was little the British could do to counter this. The success or failure of their efforts to put Europe onto a sterling-dominated standard would be decided by the outcome of German reconstruction. Here the Americans were in the driving seat. Inevitably, most of the German stabilization loan was taken up by American investors and it followed that New York and Washington would dictate the terms. These involved the stipulation that 75 per cent of German reserves be held in gold—a requirement which effectively placed the Weimar Republic on the gold standard.[33]

The rejection of the Genoa initiative left the Treasury and the Bank feeling that Britain had no alternative but to return to the gold standard at the pre-war parity as soon as possible. It was a clear sign that the world was returning to fixed rates of exchange even though sterling was still a floating currency. Officials worried that London might become isolated and so lose all claim to global financial leadership, a fear intensified by signs that the white Dominions were preparing to stabilize their currencies on the dollar.[34]

The return to gold at the pre-war level of £1 = \$4.86 meant a 10 per cent revaluation for sterling, which had stood at £1 = \$4.40 in 1924. The result was pressure on the old staple industries above all to cut costs so that they would remain internationally competitive. The strains of adjustment were heaviest in the coalfields, resulting in the industrial dispute which provoked the General Strike, the first serious challenge to the emerging liberal consensus.

There is no need to repeat here the history of the nine-day strike.[35] But

---

[32] For a discussion of the Genoa proposals, see Cain and Hopkins, *Crisis and Deconstruction*, 63–5, and Frank Costigliola, 'Anglo-American Financial Rivalry in the 1920s', *Journal of Economic History*, 37 (1977).

[33] Cain and Hopkins, *Crisis and Deconstruction*, 67.

[34] L. S. Presnell, '1925: The Burden of Sterling', *Economic History Review*, 2nd ser., 31 (1978), 67–87.

[35] See e.g. Julian Symons, *The General Strike* (1957); Ralph Miliband, *Parliamentary Socialism* (1972 edn.); Middlemas, *Politics in Industrial Society*; Margaret Morris, *The General Strike* (1976).

we should note that it confirmed the political dominance over British society of the liberal consensus, in two distinct ways. First, Baldwin made no concessions to the TUC. This was not because the government was struck by the merits of the coal-owners' case. The major reason for its unyielding stance lay in its appreciation that compromise would admit the TUC back into the policy-making circles from which it had been ejected after the war. Selling that pass implied a movement back toward the Lloyd George corporatism deemed incompatible with the international orientation of the state. The defeat of the strike ensured that the pass was not sold.

Secondly, Baldwin's handling of the crisis undermined the position of the hard Right in the Cabinet and the Conservative Party. During the dispute the prime minister had informally assured the General Council of the TUC that he had no sympathy with bellicose anti-trade unionism.[36] TUC leaders were not arrested and the strike was not put down by force. After the dispute the 'capitalist offensive' on wages which had preceded it was not maintained[37] and the privileges granted to the trade union movement in 1906 were left untouched. Retribution was confined to individual strikers and to the 1927 Trade Disputes Act, outlawing sympathy strikes and forcing those wishing to pay the political levy to 'contract in' rather than leave dissenters to 'contract out' as they had under the old dispensation.

This avoidance of outright reaction followed from Baldwin's appreciation that it would be likely to destabilize the liberal consensus which underpinned 'normalcy'. Throughout the 1920s public expenditure ran far ahead of its pre-war levels, even after the wielding of the 'Geddes axe'. In 1913–14 total expenditure stood at £197,492,969; in 1924–5 the figure was £795,776,711; the following year spending passed the £800 million mark and did not fall below it for the rest of the decade.[38] In part this growth reflected the heavy demands of the National Debt; but it was also an expression of the government's determination to maintain a level of social provision, which would have been hard to defend before the war, on education, health, labour, and insurance. This social expenditure fulfilled a dual purpose. First, it softened the extreme hardships of unemployment and, along with the impact of the General Strike, effectively killed post-war working-class militancy. Secondly, the investment,

---

[36] Miliband, *Parliamentary Socialism*, 137.
[37] W. A. Lewis, *Economic Survey, 1919–39* (1949), 43–4; Pollard, *Development of the British Economy, 1914–1990*, 107.
[38] *Statistical Abstract for the United Kingdom*, Table 148.

particularly in housing and education, squared with the Conservatives' determination to provide a safety net for the 'deserving' poor and a ladder offering limited social mobility for those with the financial resources to help themselves.

Keeping up spending on social benefits meant cutting elsewhere if the canons of orthodoxy were to be obeyed. Post-war governments, Conservative and Labour, therefore embarked on a policy of defence cuts. After 1920–1 Britain worked for global disarmament, the rehabilition of Germany, and the settlement of international disputes by the League of Nations. Under American pressure Britain abandoned its naval hegemony in the Pacific at the Washington Conference of 1921–2.[39] The old liberal principles of inexpensive military establishments and world peace reinforced the construction of a liberal world economy where trade expanded and pulled Britain back to high employment and growth. But it was not only by providing a framework for the expansion of British commerce that liberalism abroad was intended to guarantee stability at home. The reductions in military spending, from a defence budget of £766 million in 1919–20 to £116.5 million in 1928–30, facilitated the social spending which secured organized labour's acquiescence in the post-war order.[40]

The pursuit of military retrenchment while spending on social services was maintained allowed governments to keep down the tax burden. The policy also ensured that the governments of the day kept in step with the revulsion against militarism which seems to have cut across all classes during the 1920s. Before and during the war the Conservative Party had become identified with aggressive imperialism: throughout its years of power after 1918 it accommodated the Cobdenite views of pre-1914 liberalism which also inspired Labour foreign policy in the era of MacDonald and Snowden. In domestic and external affairs, therefore, governments identified normalcy with the isolation both of the radical Left and of the far Right. Although the Labour Party's first brief spell in power had shown it to be impeccably orthodox, middle-class fears for property and the association of socialism with Bolshevism, intensified by the smear of the Zinoviev letter, created a climate in which voters who might have been drawn to the Liberal Party before 1914 chose the Conservatives in 1924. The service-based meritocracy, small shopkeepers, bankers, and export-oriented industrialists all came together behind a party which

---

[39] J. A. Gallagher, *The Decline, Rise and Fall of the British Empire* (Oxford, 1982); for the Washington Conference see Paul Kennedy, *The Realities behind Diplomacy* (1981), 260.

[40] *Statistical Abstract for the United Kingdom*, Table 148.

offered them sound finance, tax reductions, disarmament, piecemeal social reform, and free trade.

Normalcy: Economic Failure, Political Success?

The period 1925–9 was one of economic failure. Hopes that a return to gold would stimulate an export-led revival were disappointed. Although 1929 represented the height of post-war recovery, export volume languished at 86 per cent of the 1913 level[41] while manufactured imports continued to expand: between 1924 and 1928 exports and re-exports financed only 77 per cent of imports compared with 85 per cent over 1919–23. Invisible earnings failed to increase significantly as a result of the sterling revaluation; the wartime loss of overseas assets, American debts, and a fall in shipping income as a result of foreign competition all took a toll. Between 1911 and 1913 the invisible surplus had been worth 43.8 per cent of gross imports; between 1924 and 1928 the proportion fell to 28.6 per cent.[42] It followed that the balance of payments surplus, at an average of just over 2 per cent of GDP in 1921–9, failed to approach the 5 per cent mark it had held for a generation prior to 1914.[43] A steady outflow of gold, from a comparatively small reserve of £150 million,[44] developed, and was checked by the imposition of a high bank rate to attract foreign credit, much of it short-term. Given its fragile external financial position Britain was therefore pushed into the hazardous policy of 'borrowing short and lending long' in the attempt to resume its role as the world's leading international lender. At the same time the deflationary policies needed to sustain this unhappy return to normalcy kept unemployment at over 10 per cent of the insured work-force and strengthened growing criticisms of the banking and industrial system as well as of trade policy.[45]

The overall tone of these protests was critical of the economic orthodoxy which had been reimposed, apparently conclusively, with the return to gold. In 1927 the TUC called for Empire Free Trade. The following year talks between a delegation of trade unionists led by Ben Turner and employers drawn by Sir Alfred Mond of ICI from the more dynamic sectors of industry, known as the Mond–Turner talks, revived the wartime vision of a corporatist producers' alliance. Although consensus between the two sides of industry was limited it did extend to a critique of

[41] Cain and Hopkins, *Crisis and Deconstruction*, 32.   [42] Ibid. 36.
[43] Ibid. 44.   [44] Pollard, *Development of the British Economy, 1914–1990*, 109.
[45] See ibid. 107–10.

Bank and Treasury monetary policy, joining to this the call for modification of the financial system so that it might in future stimulate industrial
expansion. By mid-1929 protests about the gold standard and its implications for industry could be heard from a widening coalition embracing
traditionally protectionist iron and steel producers, the newer industries
represented at the Mond–Turner discussions such as chemicals, motor-
vehicle manufacturing, and electrical goods, and even Lancashire textile
interests.[46]

At the 1929 general election the level of dissatisfaction provoked on
both sides of industry by normalcy, not to mention the popular disillusion-
ment with the Conservatives caused by unemployment, was enough to
bring to power a minority Labour government. But a change in the government did not mean a shift in the strategy. During and after the
election MacDonald and Snowden showed themselves as scornful as the
Conservatives of unorthodox schemes to stimulate growth through public
investment. The Bank–Treasury view prevailed against enlightened industrialists, against Lloyd George and what was left of the Liberals, and
against independent-minded radicals in the Labour movement such as
Oswald Mosley or Ernest Bevin.

The alternative strategies of Bevin and Mosley presented a particularly serious threat to the *status quo*. Both envisaged a recovery through
departure from the gold standard, reflation of the domestic market, and
reorganization of industry within a protected, self-sufficient imperial economic bloc. It was not merely the positions occupied within the Labour
movement by their proponents—Bevin was general secretary of the Transport and General Workers' Union and Mosley was a Cabinet minister—
that made these heretical critiques of orthodoxy more powerful than at
any time in the past decade. Timing was also essential. International trade
went into decline as a result of the slump during 1930, and governments
throughout the world embraced economic nationalism in response to
bankruptcies and factory closures. In Britain the coming of the Depression intensified the pre-existing deflationary pressures and the FBI swung
round to a pro-tariff position with the backing of the Beaverbrook newspapers and Tory imperialists such as Leo Amery.[47]

The Labour government of 1929–31 did not achieve much but it did
stave off the radical challenge to economic orthodoxy. MacDonald and

---

[46] Boyce, *Capitalism at the Crossroads*, 153 f., 214–16.

[47] The radical alternative is explored in Newton and Porter, *Modernization Frustrated*,
68–71. The TUC published Bevin's strategy, co-authored with G. D. H. Cole, as a
pamphlet called *The Crisis*, in 1930.

Snowden stood by the gold standard and free trade, their commitment to normalcy condemning to unemployment many of the working-class voters who had seen in Labour the instrument of their release from enforced idleness. Thus, although Snowden, in a gesture towards the Mond–Turner initiative, established the Macmillan Committee to investigate all aspects of banking, financial, and credit policy, he took care to exclude from membership any representatives of the FBI and other producer organizations.[48] The fact that despite this the Committee did display some very limited sympathy for critics of the Bank and the City, concerning the inadequacy of the London money markets as providers of funds for medium and small businesses, was, however, immaterial. The work of the Committee was never discussed in Cabinet and the Bank of England refused point blank to countenance its suggestions for credit expansion via a reduction in the minimum reserve requirement.[49] Rejecting all calls for reflation, with or without protection, and using the trade union block votes to marginalize Mosley at the 1930 Labour Conference, the government chose to shore up the *status quo*.[50] MacDonald argued that recovery could only be guaranteed with the reversal of the international trend to protectionism and identified himself with Bank and Treasury enthusiasm for the balanced budget: the world would understand that with experimental financial policies out of the question sterling's parity was safe.[51]

The Labour Party's economic liberalism reflected both its own origins and electoral politics. In its early days the bedrock of its support was to be found within trade unions representing workers in the coal, textile, and shipbuilding industries whose welfare was linked to buoyant exports and an open international economy. This material interest in cosmopolitanism reinforced its ideological appeal to workers and intellectuals for whom the most practical manifestation of the brotherhood of man was a system of free trade which undermined the imperial rivalry likely to breed war. On a more mundane level the protectionist cause had long been associated with dear food by large sections of the working class, as the 1923 general election result had shown.

By 1930, as the career of Ernest Bevin had made clear, working-class faith in free trade was evaporating. Yet the Cabinet was left behind, and even had it opted for protectionism it would not have been easy to have combined this with the proto-Keynesian reflation supported by Bevin and Mosley. Labour could not escape the electoral logic of the post-war

[48] Boyce, *Capitalism at the Crossroads*, 281.   [49] Ibid. 301–3.
[50] Newton and Porter, *Modernization Frustrated*, 70.
[51] Boyce, *Capitalism at the Crossroads*, 301–3.

era. The arrival of universal suffrage notwithstanding, Labour could not
ride to power purely on the votes of trade unionists. It needed to compete
with the Conservatives and Liberals for the support of both of the small
business community and of the growing salariat, where attitudes to public
expenditure were still predominantly Gladstonian. The deficit financing advocated by Lloyd George as well as by Bevin and Mosley was distrusted; it was associated with high taxes and inflation.[52] Such was the
strength of the liberal consensus created by post-reconstruction governments that it was both politically straightforward and ideologically attractive for a Labour government to respond to the crisis of 1931 by turning
to retrenchment.

[52] See Cain and Hopkins, *Crisis and Deconstruction*, 73–4.

2

Crisis and Restabilization, 1931–1937

Sterling, Protectionism, and the Balanced Budget

The struggle to keep Britain on the gold standard was abandoned in
September 1931. During the summer London had been caught in the
European-wide scramble for liquidity which had followed the failure of
the Austrian Credit Anstalt Bank in May. The crisis had exposed the
vulnerability of London's position, short-term claims on the Continent,
many of them frozen by a panic-stricken German government, amount-
ing to £153 million while sterling balances held in London amounted to
£407 million.[1]

This revelation, disclosed by the Macmillan Committee, was followed
by the May Committee's gloomy prognostications concerning the public
finances. A crisis of confidence in London, and in the Bank's ability to
keep Britain on gold, resulted and was intensified by a steady drain on the
reserves. In August the Labour administration committed itself to a programme of spending cuts to reassure financial opinion at home and abroad.
But the Cabinet broke up on the issue of cuts in the dole and a National
Government was formed, composed of representatives from all three
main parties, to drive through the austerity package.

For a very brief time the strategy worked. Credits from the New York
Federal Reserve Bank and from the Bank of France, were negotiated. However, the drain resumed and turned into a panic when a naval mutiny,
provoked by economies in pay, was reported to have occurred at Inver-
gordon on 15 September. Over the next three days London lost more
than £43 million, taking the total of withdrawals since early July past
the £200 million figure. On 21 September the National Government
capitulated.[2] Legislation went through parliament ending the Bank's
obligation to sell gold, and sterling became a floating currency.

The departure from gold facilitated a number of initiatives in economic policy which, given their similarity to some of the prescriptions
offered by the heretics, would have been unthinkable at any time between

---

[1] A. G. Kenwood and A. L. Lougheed, *The Growth of the International Economy, 1820–
1980* (1983), 206. [2] Ibid. 207.

May 1925 and September 1931. Thus, sterling became a managed currency, its operations controlled by the Exchange Equalisation Account, established in 1932. Overseas lending was severely restricted, and Britain turned protectionist for the first time in peace since the repeal of the Corn Laws. This decisive step away from free trade, manifested in an import tariff on manufactured goods, was reinforced by the move to regionalism: Britain put itself at the head of a bloc, known as the sterling area, and at Ottawa in 1932 agreed with the representatives of Dominions' governments to embrace Imperial Preference. Finally, the decoupling of sterling from gold permitted the pursuit of a 'cheap money' policy based on a low bank rate.

The new set of policies did not, however, reflect the rejection of liberal orthodoxy; rather, its modification. It is true that protectionism and Imperial Preference were welcomed both by the pressure groups which had advocated them in the 1920s, such as the Iron and Steel Trades' Confederation and the Empire Industries Association (formed in 1924), as well as by the FBI.[3] But although the end of free trade and economic internationalism marked a compromise between the financial and industrial wings of British capitalism, it was one whose terms suited the former more than the latter.

This should not be surprising. The National Government had been formed to keep Britain on the gold standard; the fact that it had proved impossible to achieve this in the face of international speculation did not mean abandoning the commitments to the defence of sterling and its corollary, sound money, which had governed macroeconomic policy since 1921. Thus, civil servants, bankers, and politicians may have joined industrialists in agreeing that the fall in sterling, to £1 = $3.40 early in 1932, would provide exporters with a competitive edge, but there was no support in the Cabinet, the Treasury, or the Bank for further depreciation.[4] A steadily falling exchange not only facilitated the abandonment of financial prudence by the government itself, but was associated with the wage–price spiral experienced in central European countries during the aftermath of the war. At the trough of the Depression therefore, as unemployment mounted towards the 3 million mark and industrial production slumped (Table 2.1), the government was preoccupied by the 'threat' of inflation.[5] It recoiled from unbalanced budgets and uncontrolled exchange rates:

---

[3] Newton and Porter, *Modernization Frustrated*, 74.
[4] Cain and Hopkins, *Crisis and Deconstruction*, 77–8.
[5] Newton and Porter, *Modernization Frustrated*, 74.

TABLE 2.1. *Gross Domestic Product and industrial production* 1929–1932 (1933 = 100)

	GDP at constant factor cost	Industrial production
1929	107.8	125.5
1930	107.0	120.1
1931	101.5	112.3
1932	102.3	111.9

Source: S. Newton and D. Porter, *Modernization Frustrated* (1988), 68.

both were engines of an inflation ruinous to small savers, *rentiers*, and sterling-holders alike.

It followed that budgetary orthodoxy was as central to economic policy after the departure from gold as it had been before. Deficit finance was shunned until forced on an unwilling Treasury by the demands of rearmament in 1937 and beyond. Alternative strategies based on the regeneration of the economy via loan-financed public works were all dismissed with the scepticism which had greeted the proposals of the Liberals, of Bevin, and of Mosley in 1929–30. Public investment schemes took too long; they required the establishment of an elaborate bureaucracy; they merely diverted savings from the private sector to public. The government put its faith in market forces, believing that low taxes and a balanced budget provided the keys to recovery. Its initiatives were therefore generally modest. They were limited to aid for slum clearance and to help for depressed areas. Both were constrained by the Treasury, only £10 million being spent on regional policy between its inception under the Special Areas (Development and Improvement) Act of 1934 and the start of 1939.[6] Overall, the impact of budgetary policy during the Depression was initially deflationary and then broadly neutral, the strict attitude to public spending being matched by a loosening of the fiscal regime and an expansionary monetary policy which together may have encouraged some expansion of business activity after 1933.[7]

Even the two fundamental departures from the macroeconomic framework of the 1920s, cheap money and protectionism, were provoked in the first place by the financial crisis; the impact on industrial recovery was

[6] Ibid. 85–6. In addition the modest programme of road-building and improvement pursued by the 1929–31 Labour government in the cause of relieving unemployment was repeatedly trimmed. Schemes supported by the Unemployment Grants Committee had provided 150,000 jobs in the late 1920s. After 1932 this figure never exceeded 60,000 and by 1937 it had shrunk to a few hundred. See Pollard, *Development of the British Economy, 1914–1990*, 129.

[7] See Roger Middleton, *Toward the Managed Economy: Keynes, the Treasury and the Fiscal Policy Debate of the 1930s* (1985).

only a secondary consideration. First, the bank rate tumbled from 6 per cent at the climax of the National Government's efforts to keep sterling on gold, to 2 per cent in April 1932, and did not deviate far from this level for the rest of the decade. While there is no doubt the Treasury understood that the move would stimulate economic activity, it seems clear that the real point of the operation was to bring down government spending in a painless manner by reducing the charge of the national debt on the public finances.

Secondly, the decision to introduce a tariff was in large part the function of Treasury concern over the consequences of an uncontrolled downward drift of the exchange rate. The benefit of a tariff was that it would raise revenue and so help to balance the budget, and at the same time discourage imports, reducing the visible trade gap in the process.[8] The measure was therefore aimed at minimizing inflationary pressures stemming from a falling pound and disorderly public finances so that foreign holders of sterling could rest secure in the knowledge that they held a stable asset.[9] As Neville Chamberlain, who succeeded Snowden at the Exchequer, pointed out, 'the essential point [of the tariff] is the value of sterling'.[10]

In external economic policy the National Governments never questioned the value to the country and to the world economy of maintaining sterling's international role—a commitment which underlined the importance of measures designed to prevent its depreciation from going too far.[11] Thus, the efforts of the EEA to keep sterling depressed against industrial competitors, especially France and the United States, ran in tandem with the encouragement of traditional parities between Britain and its main suppliers of food and raw materials. This policy led to the emergence of the sterling bloc, comprising most of the British Empire (apart from Canada and British Honduras, both preferring to stabilize on the dollar), as well as a number of independent countries, including the Baltic States and Argentina, which had historically relied on the British market.[12]

The creation of the sterling area marked an appreciation on the part of the Bank, the Treasury, and the City that sterling's departure from gold

[8] This the point convincingly made by B. J. Eichengreen, 'Sterling and the Tariff, 1929–1932', *Princeton Studies in International Finance*, 48 (Princeton, NJ, 1981).

[9] Cain and Hopkins, *Crisis and Deconstruction*, 78.

[10] Quoted in Newton and Porter, *Modernization Frustrated*, 75.

[11] John Redmond, 'An Indicator of the Effective Exchange Rate of the Pound in the 1930s', *Economic History Review*, 2nd ser., 33/1 (1980), 83–91.

[12] See Cain and Hopkins, *Crisis and Deconstruction*, 79.

had signalled the impossibility of aspiring to the retention of world currency status. But it could still perform as an international currency, albeit on a regional scale, to be used by countries whose commercial connections dictated a need for sterling as a trading and reserve currency. The existence of the area militated against the expansion of trade via a low exchange rate, given, first Australian and New Zealand devaluations against sterling in 1930, and secondly the accumulation of sterling as a reserve currency by members throughout the decade. The net effect of this was to increase international demand for sterling, putting upward pressure on the pound and therefore improving terms of trade which had already turned in Britain's favour as a result of the collapse in commodity prices. In consequence the British market became a lucrative source of foreign exchange for overseas producers while British exports lagged.[13]

The restrictive effect of the sterling area on British exports was compounded by the system of Imperial Preference which emerged from the Ottawa Conference, held in 1932. Initially the agreements were welcomed by the industrial groups which had lobbied for protectionism and the apparent security of the imperial market throughout the period 1927–31. Yet the results proved a disappointment. During the 1930s the annual average level of exports from Britain to the Dominions fell from £143 million (1924–9) to £111 million (1934–8). At the same time the annual average level of imports into Britain from the Dominions rose from £183 million (1925–9) to £189 million (1934–8)—while overall imports fell by 29 per cent over the same period. The pattern was repeated in trade with India and the colonies, with exports falling by 44 per cent between 1925–9 and 1934–8 as the level of imports from this source dropped by only 15 per cent.[14]

It is possible to cite the effects of low prices on world markets for primary produce, and the buoyant level of British national income produced by the favourable terms of trade as partial explanations for what happened after Ottawa. But the most significant reason for the poor performance of British exporters is that the agreements were intended to bolster sterling and the City. There was real danger that the purposive pursuit of a British surplus with Commonwealth and Empire countries, most of which were primary producers suffering from the fall in primary product prices, would weaken sterling.[15]

[13] Ibid. 83.   [14] Ibid. 85.
[15] See Hubert Henderson's paper, 'Sterling and the Balance of Trade', in H. D. Henderson, *The Inter-war Years and Other Papers* (Oxford, 1955). Henderson was a member of the government's Economic Advisory Committee.

Many Commonwealth and Empire countries had suffered from the fall in primary product prices; the result was mounting external deficits. Australia, which had taken 40 per cent of all overseas flotations in the City between 1925 and 1928, was perhaps the most exposed of these states. There was anxiety in the City and the Bank about a series of defaults, started perhaps by the Australians (where the option had been canvassed). The immediate effect on London banks, not to mention the wider sterling system, would have been highly disruptive. Such an alarming prospect now receded because, in guaranteeing access to the British market, the Ottawa system provided Colonial and Dominion producers with the means to service their debts.[16]

The floating pound, cheap money, and the tariff therefore reflected an adjustment of the traditional relationship between production and commerce but not its reversal. There was still no place for state-led growth and the full employment of capital and labour on the agenda, which continued to be dominated by the balanced budget, sound money, and the international role of sterling. After 1931 it was still the Treasury, the City, and the Bank which called the macroeconomic tune. Nevertheless, the level of unemployment and disused capacity was such that the National Governments had to commit themselves to industrial 'recovery'. In the circumstances the resort to protectionism was the easiest option: it was an accommodation of Producers' England which was simultaneously a tactical necessity for the financial wing of British capitalism.[17]

The State and the Corporate Economy

Protectionism hardly amounted to an industrial strategy, but along with low taxes and cheap money it was enough to reconcile the FBI and most of British industry to the National Government's cautious economic policy. It signalled a breach with the economic liberalism which had characterized state policy during the 1920s, an acknowledgement that while recovery could only be market-led, industrial reconstruction needed some guidance from the state after all.

The shift away from a *laissez-faire* attitude towards industry had started in 1930, when Ramsay MacDonald's Labour government opted for a modest experiment in the encouragement of rationalization as an alternative to

---

[16] See Cain and Hopkins, *Crisis and Deconstruction*, 84 and 116–22, for an extended discussion of this point.

[17] See ibid. 85; Ingham, *Capitalism Divided*, ch. 5; Newton and Porter, *Modernization Frustrated*, 76–89.

the *dirigiste* schemes of Mosley. Thus, the BIDC (Bankers Industrial Development Corporation) was established in 1930 and made responsible for the policy. A quarter of the BIDC's capital was subcribed by the Bank of England, the rest by a variety of banks and City institutions. Its most successful work was located in textiles and shipbuilding, where it was responsible for, respectively, the Lancashire Cotton Corporation, designed to limit competition in cotton spindles, and National Shipbuilders' Security, set up to purchase and dispose of redundant shipyards. The efforts of the BIDC were then supported by the Coal Mines' Act (1930), passed to encourage the amalgamation of pits into larger units of production than had hitherto characterized the industry.[18] In 1932 the government turned its attention to the iron and steel industry, whose dependence on capital goods industries had made it particularly vulnerable to the world Depression. Between 1929 and 1932 production of pig iron and of steel fell, respectively, by 53 per cent and by 45 per cent.[19] At this point the government granted an import tariff, first of 33.3 per cent then (in 1935) of 50 per cent, on condition that the industry undertake its own rationalization exercise. This was to be conducted under the direction of the British Iron and Steel Federation (BISF), itself created largely at the state's behest. The new policy facilitated a spectacular recovery. Output in 1934 was back at the level achieved in 1929 and still growing, an expansion which allowed Britain's share of world output in steel to rise from 7.6 per cent in 1932 to 9.7 per cent in 1937.[20]

The National Government's willingness to encourage rationalization was well received. Industrialists might have developed a paranoia about 'socialism' after 1918 but they were not enthusiasts for unfettered free enterprise. During the 1920s there was a growing interest in rationalization to remove surplus capacity in favour of 'huge industrial consolidations, with ample resources, specialised production, collective agencies for sale and distribution, and with full equipment for scientific research'[21] on the German and American example of, for example, I. G. Farben and General Motors. It became commonplace to argue that British industry was too individualistic and competitive: but the necessary reorganization could be achieved by private industrialists acting together. Thus, Imperial Chemical Industries (ICI) was formed in 1926 from a fusion of companies in

[18] G. C. Allen, *The Structure of Industry in Britain: A Study in Economic Change* (2nd edn., 1968), 52–9.

[19] Pollard, *Development of the British Economy, 1914–1990*, 52.

[20] Newton and Porter, *Modernization Frustrated*, 87.

[21] Leslie Hannah, *The Rise of the Corporate Economy* (2nd edn., 1983), 37.

the mining, explosives, and electrical industries. Associated Electrical Industries (AEI) was created in 1928 by the consolidation of British Thomson-Houston, Ferguson Pailin, Edison Swan, and Metropolitan Vickers. The establishment in 1929 of Cable and Wireless followed the merger of almost all telegraph and telecommunications' systems in the British Empire. Other products of the same wave of amalgamations included Tube Investments, Hawker Siddeley, Unilever, and Cadbury-Fry. By 1930 the British industrial economy was dominated by a handful of large companies such as ICI, Unilever, Distillers', AEI, and Cable and Wireless (the largest of them all, with a market capitalization of $2.5 billion in 1937). The process was reflected in the share of net manufacturing output taken by the top 100 firms, which rose from 15 per cent in 1907 to 26 per cent in 1930.[22]

In general the rationalization movement of the 1920s had embraced industries in the more advanced industrial sectors, food processing, and retailing. The growth of a mass market throughout the industrialized world had stimulated demand for a range of goods, including vehicles, aircraft, electrical equipment, and a wide range of domestic consumables, whose manufacture required the application of advanced scientific techniques to industrial processes. Expensive outlays on investment, research and development, and on skilled personnel had become necessary. It followed that it was in these sectors that the arguments for economies of scale and the creation of large firms capable of controlling all the different stages of production and distribution were most powerful. Of course, with a few exceptions such as ICI the newly formed large companies did not embrace a centralized managerial and divisional company structure. They operated as confederations of subsidiaries under a holding company. British Thomson-Houston, Edison Swan, and Metropolitan Vickers, for example, all continued to function autonomously after their absorption into AEI.[23] This pattern was followed by Marconi Wireless Telegraph and EMI-Marconi Television, although both were part of Cable and Wireless.[24] Yet even in the absence of what Hannah calls 'the organizational economics of rationalization' companies had access to 'pooled overheads, risk spreading, the interchange of commercial and industrial

[22] Hannah, *Rise of the Corporate Economy*, 180. For Cable and Wireless, see Christopher Schmitz, *The Growth of Big Business in the United States and Western Europe, 1880–1939* (Basingstoke, 1993), 24.

[23] Geoffrey Channon, 'Felix Pole', in David Jeremy and Christine Shaw (eds.), *A Dictionary of Business Biography*, vol. 4 (London, 1986), 748–51.

[24] Public Records Office, London (hereafter PRO), BT 64/431, 'Electrical Machinery and Apparatus Cartels'.

methods and some degree of co-ordination of new investment'.[25] This all constituted a major advance towards a managed market, a privatized version of the wartime interest in industrial reconstruction. It is no accident that the businessman most responsible for the establishment of AEI, Felix Pole, was described by his biographer as a believer in a planned form of capitalism, based on co-operation between large firms.[26]

The onset of the slump however derailed the commitment to rationalization *as a means to greater efficiency*. The enthusiasm for market management did not fade, but increasingly the objective became the creation of a cartel. Thus, the steel industry retained its fragmented structure, the BISF being capable only of uniting around the importance of maintaining the tariff, keeping up prices, and developing an influential 'national voice to lobby for those aims'.[27] Orthodox economists such as Cannan, Hayek, or Robbins might preach the virtues of market-clearance via price-cutting and free competition.[28] But given the combination of glutted markets with stagnant demand and high overheads, it is easy to see why a liberal strategy which many felt outmoded anyway should have been repudiated in favour of 'organized marketing'.[29] With the encouragement of the FBI, trade associations took advantage of the protection afforded the domestic economy by the tariff to co-operate in fixing prices and restricting output throughout most of the economy.[30] The upshot by the second half of the 1930s was a strengthening of monopolistic tendencies not just in the newer industries but in the staples and agriculture, hitherto competitive.[31]

This experience of 'organized marketing' was matched in the United States and industrial Europe, where some governments, notably the German, gave it particular encouragement. But the trend to cartelization did not stop at national boundaries. Given the prevalence all over the capitalist

[25] Hannah, *Rise of the Corporate Economy*, 87.   [26] Channon, 'Felix Pole', 750.

[27] Steven Tolliday, 'Steel and Rationalization Policies, 1918–1950', in Bernard Elbaum and William Lazonick (eds.) *The Decline of the British Economy* (Oxford, 1985), 102.

[28] For a discussion of the intellectual disputes concerning economic policy in the inter-war years see Peter Clarke, *The Keynesian Revolution in the Making* (Oxford, 1988); Michael Stewart, *Keynes and After* (2nd edn., 1975); and Donald Winch, *Economics and Policy* (London, 1971).

[29] See Allen, *The Structure of Industry in Britain*, 57. 'Organized marketing' was no novelty. Producers had taken collective action through their trade associations in the past, but such combines had generally collapsed because of the free-trade policy.

[30] See Stephen Blank, *Industry and Government in Britain: The Federation of British Industries and the International Economy* (Farnborough, 1973), 28–30; R. F. Holland, 'The Federation of British Industries and the International Economy', *Economic History Review*, 2nd ser., 34 (1981), 287–301.   [31] Allen, *The Structure of Industry in Britain*, 60.

world of unemployed resources and low prices, its extension to international trade was predictable. During the 1930s British companies became increasingly involved in agreements with foreign producers limiting competition in the manufacturing, sale, and distribution of, for example, electric lamps, gramophones, telecommunications equipment, radios, explosives, steel, wire rods, tubes, rails, and rolling stock.

Where companies were based in one country alone the international cartels would generally be negotiated by the respective trade associations. The result would be a set of rules fixing prices and allocating markets and quotas, the agreement being policed by an international body such as the Entente Internationale d'Acier (International Steel Cartel), the International Lamp Cartel, the International Glass Convention, or the International Rolling Stock Cartel. Large multinational enterprises, however, tended to deal with each other directly. Thus ICI, I. G. Farben, and Du Pont divided between each other the world market for explosives and chemicals; a handful of large corporations, in which Anglo-Iranian and Anglo-Dutch Shell featured significantly, controlled the marketing and distribution of oil; telecommunications throughout most of the British Empire and the western hemisphere were shared between Cable and Wireless, the Radio Corporation of America, International Telephone and Telegraph, and Telefunken.[32]

By 1937 the extent of cartelization was such that one American academic was able to argue that 'free competition has nearly disappeared . . . self-government in industry is rapidly becoming a reality'.[33] International markets were increasingly parcelled into spheres of influence where selling rights were reserved to nationals from particular countries. Where such agreements obtained British firms had a recognized claim to imperial markets; central and eastern Europe tended to be allocated to German firms; American companies dominated north America; while Latin American markets were generally partitioned between the advanced industrial powers, concerns rooted in Britain, Germany, and the United States taking the lion's share.

The National Government took a generally benign attitude to this process of 'industrial self-government', although it did not abandon its hostility to any measure which smacked of *dirigisme*. Thus in 1935, when a number of corporatist-minded Tory MPs and peers attempted to secure the backing of the state for the extension of rationalization to fifteen major

---

[32] See Ervin Hexner, *International Cartels* (1946).

[33] A. F. Lucas, *Industrial Reconstruction and the Control of Competition* (1937), 65.

industries, the government cited the interests of consumers and small producers, offering instead its support for 'voluntary reorganization'.[34]

This was enough to satisfy most industrialists. No more than the Treasury or the City did they support a proto-Keynesian route out of the Depression. Quite apart from anxiety about the fiscal implications of expansion led by public investment, they and their representatives in the FBI relished the independence involved in 'industrial self-government'. It was a strategy which opened the door to a world made by and for the cartel, and in so doing transformed producers who had once been critics into supporters of the post-reconstruction political economy.[35]

Recovery, 1932–1937

The economic record of Britain under protection shows a modest recovery. Between 1932 and 1937 Gross Domestic Product rose from 102.3 to 126.1 (1913 = 100),[36] while industrial production rose from 111.9 to 163.1 (1913 = 100).[37] Over the same period unemployment fell from a peak of 22.1 per cent of the insured work-force to 10.8 per cent in 1937.[38] The most spectacular increases in output were shown by the public utilities, but the recovery was led by a building boom. Even during 1930–3 200,000 dwellings a year were being constructed; in 1934 the figure jumped to 293,000 and thereafter exceeded 350,000 every year up to and including 1938.[39] After 1934 an expansion of commercial and industrial building delivered a new stimulus to the construction industry. Between 1932 and 1935 building accounted for 30 per cent of the increase in employment and 40 per cent of the rise in investment. The result was an increase in demand for concrete, steel, glass, furniture, and household goods.[40]

The housing boom occurred for the most part in the private sector. Local authority programmes were responsible for 79,013 new homes in 1932 but numbers fell back subsequently before recovering (see Table 2.2). The expansion could be attributed to three fundamental causes. First, the cheap money policy made investment in housing construction attractive at a time when rents remained high. Secondly, the price of property fell: a house costing £350 in 1931 was worth only £300 two

---

[34] PRO, CAB 24/251, CP 66 (35), 18 Mar. 1935.

[35] Hannah, *The Rise of the Corporate Economy*, 46–7.

[36] Feinstein, *National Income, Expenditure and Output*, Table 6, T19.

[37] Ibid., Table 51, T112.   [38] Ibid., Table 58, T128.

[39] *Statistical Abstracts for the United Kingdom, 1913 and 1924 to 1937* (London, 1939), Table 33, p. 49.   [40] Pollard, *Development of the British Economy, 1914–1990*, 120.

TABLE 2.2. *Private and local-authority house-building, 1931–1938*

	Private	Local authority	% Local authority
1931	132,944	63,996	48.1
1932	135,517	79,013	58.3
1933	151,101	68,156	45.1
1934	213,174	72,343	33.9
1935	293,609	57,326	19.5
1936	279,829	70,486	24.0
1937	282,480	87,423	30.9
1938	265,032	92,053	34.7

Source: Derived from *Statistical Abstract for the United Kingdom 1939 and 1924 to 1937* (1939), Table 33, p. 49.

years later.[41] Thirdly, 75 per cent of the additional private houses were financed by the building societies, whose growth was so notable a feature of inter-war Britain. Between 1930 and 1939 building society balances out on mortgage rose from £316 million to £706 million.[42]

Many of the new housing estates tended to be located in the Midlands and the Home Counties, reflecting the comparative prosperity of regions whose welfare depended on the newer industries such as motor cars, electrical goods, and household appliances, as well as on the rise of the service sector, where employment grew by 2.08 million during the inter-war years.[43] In addition, the relatively high proportion of private to local authority housing built in 1934 and after can be seen as a function of the continuing expansion of the salariat within both industry and public administration. The recovery from the slump tended to reinforce the socio-economic trends of the 1920s. It has been estimated that between 1911 and 1931 salaried personnel in both the private and the public sectors (including teaching) grew by 1.4 million persons.[44] Wage statistics bear out the increasing significance of the white-collar worker at this time: managers and administrators saw their incomes rise from 247 to 272 between 1913/14 and 1935/6 (incomes of all groups = 100), while skilled and semi-skilled wages fell back, respectively, from 131 to 121 and from 85 to 83.[45]

The growth of both the tertiary sector and the salariat, a process common to all advanced economies, was an important factor in keeping the British economy of the 1930s relatively buoyant. Demand was also sustained by the favourable shift in the terms of trade and the cheap

[41] Pollard, *Development of the British Economy, 1914–1990*, 121.   [42] Ibid. 120.
[43] Ibid. 148.   [44] Ibid.   [45] The wage statistics are to be found in ibid. 151.

TABLE 2.3. *Exports of goods and services as a proportion of GNP, 1929–1939* (£ million, market prices; 1913 = 100)

Year	Exports	GNP	Exports : GNP
1929	1,096	4,970	73
1930	884	4,900	60
1931	632	4,552	46
1932	578	4,403	44
1933	573	4,413	43
1934	608	4,680	43
1935	690	4,902	47
1936	697	5,100	46
1937	843	5,494	51
1938	757	5,764	44
1939	700	6,118	38

Source: C. H. Feinstein, *National Income, Expenditure and Output of the United Kingdom, 1855–1965* (Cambridge, 1972), Table 3, T11.

money policy. But it is arguable that a greater contribution was made by the tariff. Britain's inter-war trade performance was weak: income from exports of goods and services as a proportion of Gross National Product dropped from 73 to 46 (1913 = 100) and only recovered to 51 in 1938 before slipping back to 38 in 1939 as an increasing volume of production was devoted to rearmament (Table 2.3). The slump therefore intensified the difficulties already created for the export sector by the spread of international competition. After 1930 the balance of payments on current account lurched into the red as invisibles failed to offset the visible trade deficit (Table 2.4). With protection it was possible to reduce the level of imports without a commensurate fall in income and divert purchasing power into the home market, stimulating the newer industries which were clustered around the needs of the domestic consumer and private householder.

The liberal–conservative coalition which had supported the return to normalcy reaped the rewards of 'safety first' and re-elected the National Government in 1935. Opposition was weak, the Labour Party having been destroyed at parliamentary level by the fiasco of 1931, while by this time the Liberal Party had been reduced to Lloyd George and a handful of MPs. The political vacuum ensured that no alternative strategy would be tried; throughout the period 1931–7 successive National Governments presided over an increase in prosperity which by-passed the historic centres of British industry (Table 2.5).[46]

[46] Newton and Porter, *Modernization Frustrated*, 82; Pollard, *The Development of the British Economy, 1914–1990*, 49–57.

TABLE 2.4. *Balance of payments, current account, 1920–1939 (£ million)*

Year	Visible (deficit)	Invisible surplus (deficit)	Balance
1920	(148)	485	337
1921	(148)	341	193
1922	(63)	264	201
1923	(97)	280	183
1924	(214)	292	78
1925	(265)	317	52
1926	(346)	328	(18)
1927	(270)	368	98
1928	(237)	361	124
1929	(263)	359	96
1930	(283)	319	36
1931	(322)	219	(103)
1932	(216)	165	(51)
1933	(192)	184	(8)
1934	(220)	198	(22)
1935	(183)	206	23
1936	(261)	234	(27)
1937	(336)	289	(47)
1938	(285)	230	(55)
1939	(300)	50	(250)

Derived from C. H. Feinstein, *National Income, Expenditure and Output of the United Kingdom, 1855–1965* (Cambridge, 1972), Tables 3 and 15, T11 and T38.

The persistence of the slump in the old industrial sectors led to the appearance of what was called at the time 'poverty amidst plenty'. Large areas of South Wales, Scotland, and northern England were disfigured by mass unemployment and mass poverty.[47] The spectacle provoked growing disenchantment with the market mechanism. Although this was expressed by organizations lacking a political base, such as Political and Economic Planning, a proto-Keynesian pressure group established in 1931, the government was disturbed enough to seek ways of encouraging a revival of the export sector which were compatible with economic orthodoxy, albeit in the modified form of the 1930s. It worked with a handful of multinational corporations and Far Eastern conglomerates to open up China with privately financed development projects, hoping that investment in railway construction would stimulate the capital goods industries at home.[48] From 1933 it tried to persuade the French and the Americans, both possessing healthy balance of payments surpluses, to reflate and lower

[47] 67.8% of the insured work-force and 61.8% in Merthyr were on the dole. See Newton and Porter, *Modernization Frustrated*, 76.

[48] Stephen L. Endicott, *Diplomacy and Enterprise: British China Policy, 1933–1937* (Manchester, 1975).

TABLE 2.5. *Index of industrial production, selected industries, 1929–1937* (1913 = 100)

Year	Shipbuilding	Electrical engineering	Vehicles	Textiles
1930	61.2	188.2	291.4	68.8
1931	23.1	181.0	249.1	72.5
1932	7.2	195.2	242.5	78.5
1933	8.9	196.6	270.8	85.3
1934	30.8	241.3	318.7	88.0
1935	37.8	280.2	379.8	91.5
1936	58.1	314.1	454.5	99.8
1937	75.3	339.0	504.3	100.5

Source: C. H. Feinstein, *National Income, Expenditure and Output of the United Kingdom, 1855–1965* (Cambridge, 1972), Table 52, T115.

tariffs in order to stimulate world trade. Not much progress was made in this direction, but in 1936 the administrations in London, Paris, and Washington did come together in the Tripartite Monetary Agreement, whereby the British and the Americans agreed to refrain from competitive devaluations in response to the franc's departure from gold. It was a modest arrangement but did constitute a small step towards a system of international economic co-operation in which exchange rates were managed to prevent disruptions to trade and capital flows.[49]

In the course of 1937 the uneven British recovery began to stall. The catalyst was an inventory recession in the United States which was then exacerbated by a short-lived experiment with financial orthodoxy.[50] Deflationary pressures spread to the sterling bloc as American imports of Empire commodities fell back, putting the pound under strain on the exchange markets. During the second half of 1937 unemployment began to mount in response to the squeeze in overseas markets, rising from 10.1 per cent of the insured work-force in July to 13.2 per cent in December.[51] Although trade figures for 1937 were respectable, showing an increase in exports from £693 million to £843 million,[52] the warning signs were present by the end of the year. The current account deficit rose from £27 million to £47 million over 1936–7.[53] By the conclusion of 1938 the figure

[49] PRO T 160/840/13427/6, telegram to British missions in Stockholm, Oslo, and Copenhagen, 26 Sept., 1936. The Treasury was at pains to reassure sterling-holders that signing the Tripartite Monetary Agreement implied no shift in foreign-exchange policy, merely a commitment to avoid competitive depreciation. See also Charles P. Kindleberger, *The World in Depression, 1929–1939* (1987), 255–60.   [50] Ibid. 270–3.

[51] *Statistical Abstracts for the United Kingdom*, Table 127, p. 143.

[52] Feinstein, *National Income, Expenditure and Output*, Table 3, T11.

[53] Ibid., Table 37, T82.

was £55 million, or 0.95 of the Gross National Product, as exports slipped back to £757 million.[54]

The recession compounded the longer-term threat overhanging the National Government's efforts to lead Britain out of the slump. This was presented by the Nazi German state. It was bad enough that Berlin's commitment to planned trade put obstacles in the way of British exports. Even more serious were the implications of the expansionist foreign policy which went hand in hand with Nazi economics. Unless this could be accommodated the British government would be obliged to formulate a strategic response whose financial consequences would undermine the politico–economic foundations of the post 1921 *status quo*.

[54] Calculations made on the basis of statistics presented in Feinstein, *National Income, Expenditure and Output*, Tables 3 and 37, T11 and T82.

PART 2

The German Challenge and the Search
for a Settlement, 1933–1940

3

The Genesis of Appeasement,
1933–1938

The Challenge of the New Order

The capture of Europe's most powerful economy by National Socialism was a profoundly disturbing event for Germany's neighbours and for all those who were committed to the complex of Enlightenment values which had sustained the growth and development of western society since the Industrial Revolution. It also posed a specific challenge, initially economic but in time also strategic, to British interests.

This challenge arose from the political and economic philosophy which lay at the heart of Nazism. The extent to which National Socialism could be identified with Fascism is a subject which can be discussed at length. However, German National Socialists and Italian Fascists rejected capitalism and socialism alike. Capitalism was divisive, encouraging greed and responsible for social insecurity; socialism flew in the face of nature, offering liberty, equality, and fraternity in a world where both human and natural history were determined by the struggle for survival. Nazism elevated instinct above reason; the attempt to guide human development along rationalist principles had resulted in a profound trauma for European society which could only be healed through warfare. War was merely an extension of the Darwinian conflict to society, organized into competing nations: in accordance with natural law the victory went to the strongest. In expounding the principles of Fascism Mussolini had argued 'the more it considers and observes the future and development of humanity, quite apart from the political considerations of the moment, [Fascism] believes neither in the possibility nor the utility of perpetual peace . . . War alone brings up to its highest tension all human energy and puts the stamp of nobility upon the peoples who have the courage to meet it.'[1] Hitler took the same view, seeing war as the instrument by which Germany could be purged of the sectionalism, selfishness, and decadence of the post-Versailles era.[2]

[1] Quoted in Alan S. Milward, *War, Economy and Society, 1939–1945* (1977), 5–6.
[2] Ibid. 6.

There was nothing new about the idea that war put humankind in touch with its basic instincts and in so doing drew it closer to nature, away from the materialism and individualism of the modern era. However, these repugnant commonplaces of the radical Right were given an even more insidious twist by Nazi racist ideas. In *Mein Kampf* Hitler had maintained that the regeneration of European society could only be achieved by a racially pure élite drawn from the Aryan people, responsible throughout history for the triumphs of European civilization and identifiable above all with the Germans.[3] The survival of the Aryans could not, however, be guaranteed within Germany's existing frontiers. The nation was vulnerable to blockade in time of war, as in 1914–18, but in any case the development of air power had left all states strategically vulnerable unless they possessed vast geographical depth. From this followed the doctrine of *Lebensraum*, which involved the eastwards expansion of Germany until it possessed the Ukraine.[4] The inhabitants of these conquered territories were then to be exterminated or enslaved and the area would be settled by Germans. Germany, therefore, was destined to comprise all of central and eastern Europe as well as much of the European Soviet Union. In consequence, the new Reich would achieve strategic invulnerability, based on territorial size and control of the food and raw material resources of the east.[5]

What determined whether conquered populations were to be exterminated or enslaved was race. Given the biological interpretation of history, no compassion could be shown to the losing races. Slavs were therefore to be turned into chattels serving the Aryan master race while Jews were to be wiped from the face of the earth. Hitler identified the Jews with all the false notions of progress, internationalism, capitalism, and socialism which had scarred European society over the previous century-and-a-half and which above all had reduced Germany to the humiliations of Versailles and Weimar. The Jews, plotting world domination from their two centres of power, one at the heart of world capitalism (New York) and the other at the focal point of international socialism (Moscow), had to be destroyed before they undermined civilization.[6]

[3] Milward, *War, Economy and Society*, 6.

[4] William Carr, *Arms, Autarky and Aggression: A Study in German Foreign Policy, 1933–1939* (1972), 12.

[5] Avraham Barkei, *Nazi Economics: Ideology, Theory, and Policy* (Oxford, 1988), 22–3; Carr, *Arms, Autarky and Aggression*, 12.

[6] Carr, *Arms, Autarky and Aggression*, 14; Milward, *War, Economy and Society*, 16–17.

Lebensraum was therefore a programme for conflict with the Jews and the Soviet Union. Yet Hitler's determination to secure the Ukraine was not merely a function of strategic planning for war. It also followed from Nazi economic policy, whose objective was the material and spiritual reconstruction of German society.[7] The creation of this Nazi 'New Order' in Germany required a major investment in social overhead capital, of which the *Autobahnen* were the most famous example, agricultural protection and price support, and finally rearmament. Government spending on goods and services rose from RM 9,472 million in 1932 to RM 21,909 million in 1936, or from 16 per cent to 26 per cent of the GNP (in Britain the figure remained close to 20 per cent over the same period). The annual average rate of growth in GNP over these years was 9.5 per cent, and by 1936 unemployment had practically disappeared.[8]

The pursuit of state-led reflation marked Germany out from most other European states, where cautious economic policies were the general rule. Given the depressed international context, such a strategy could not be successful in the absence of extensive trade and exchange controls to retain demand inside the home market. The National Socialist experiment therefore took a trajectory which led it steadily away from participation in the international economy; it continued the reaction against liberal capitalism which had commenced in 1931. This was confirmed with the New Plan of 1934, whose purpose was the foundation of a German-dominated *Grossraumwirtschaft* (large trading area) comprising central and eastern Europe. There was nothing specifically new about this concept, which had informed attempts to establish *Mitteleuropa* a generation before.[9] But the large area was exceedingly useful to Hitler and the economic planners of the Third Reich searching for an alternative to the world market. Membership of a *Grossraum* would provide Germany with access to a regional market large enough to sustain demand and to satisfy it from internal industrial and agricultural production as well as from available raw material resources.[10]

Whilst it is true that before 1939 political factors militated against an expansion of trade between Germany and Poland and between Germany and the Soviet Union, foreign trade policy as revealed by the New Plan and the Four Year Plan (1936) was influenced by the concept of the *Grossraumwirtschaft*. Under the New Plan the state took powers to regulate imports according to political and economic desirability. This meant

---

[7] Milward, *War, Economy and Society*, 7.   [8] Barkei, *Nazi Economics*, 250–1.
[9] Alan S. Milward, 'Fascism and the Economy', in Walter Laqueur (ed.), *Fascism: A Reader's Guide* (1979), 440.   [10] Milward, *War, Economy and Society*, 9.

TABLE 3.1. *German trade with south-east Europe, 1928 and 1938, as a percentage of all German trade*

	Imports from south-east Europe	Exports to south-east Europe
1928	17	16
1938	35	34

Note: The figures refer to the aggregate trade of Bulgaria, Greece, Hungary, Romania, Turkey, and Yugoslavia.
Source: *Europe's Trade* (League of Nations, Geneva, 1941, Table 26).

TABLE 3.2. *German trade with Latin America, as a percentage of all Latin American trade, 1928 and 1938*

	% Total imports	% Total exports
1928	21.7	22.0
1938	32.4	25.7

Source: United Nations Department of Economic Affairs, *A Study of Trade between Latin America and Europe* (Geneva, 1953), app. Table V, pp. 30–1.

restricting imports of manufactured goods and encouraging the bilateral exchange of finished German manufactures at subsidized prices for food and raw material resources from the countries of south-eastern Europe and Latin America. By the start of 1938 there were bilateral clearing arrangements with twenty-five nations, as a result of which the substantial Reichsmark balances built up during the 1920s were now to be spent on German products. This process allowed Germany to assume economic hegemony in south-east Europe (Table 3.1) and to carve out a growing share of Latin America's trade with the wider world (Table 3.2).

In 1939 German goods accounted for 65 per cent of all Bulgaria's exports, the equivalent figure for Turkey reaching 51 per cent, for Hungary 48.4 per cent, for Yugoslavia 47.6 per cent, and for Romania 39.2 per cent.[11] Not surprisingly, even before the outbreak of war German business groups which had penetrated the economies of south-eastern Europe, notably I. G. Farben and Karl Zeiss, had presented the administration with plans for the furtherance of their interests in the region.[12]

The emergence of an ultimately autarkic Reichsmark bloc in central and eastern Europe was taken a stage further by the Four Year Plan. This came as a response to the foreign-exchange shortages created by rearmament: if targets for the expansion of the army and the air force

[11] Milward, 'Fascism and the Economy', 440.   [12] Ibid.

were to be met by early 1937, the forces needed in 1936 to double the amount of raw materials used in 1935. But the hard currency which would finance such essential imports did not exist. In the summer of 1936 inability to pay for raw materials set the rearmament programme back on its heels, and the munitions industry was obliged to work at only 70 per cent of full capacity.[13] Clearly the ultimate objectives of the Nazi state could not be achieved without significant steps towards self-sufficiency, and to this end the Plan unveiled the priorities for public investment—synthetic fuel, synthetic rubber, explosives, basic chemicals, aluminium, steel, and non-ferrous metals.[14] The political imperative behind this decision was powerful enough to place the regime at loggerheads with the steelmasters who had been prominent in supporting its rise to power. Protests from Thyssen, for example, about the abandonment of dependence on Swedish ore in favour of low-grade German ore were overridden and the vast Herman Goering Works were constructed at Salzgitter.[15]

The Four Year Plan demonstrated the subordination of macroeconomic policy to the National Socialist political agenda. Based on the assumption that Germany would be ready for war in four years, it was accompanied by increases in spending under military and related headings, so that before the year's end they surpassed 50 per cent of all government disbursements.[16] By the start of 1937, its original mass electoral support in agriculture and small business notwithstanding, the regime was allied with a handful of large firms such as I. G. Farben and Vereinigte Aluminiumwerke in pursuit of a strategy designed to bring victory in a continental conflict.[17] Two parallel sets of developments followed. First, prospects that Nazi Germany would at some stage be integrated into the international economy became increasingly remote, given the need for a battery of exchange, wage, and price controls to preserve foreign currency and suppress inflation; the Third Reich had by 1937 developed a cost and price structure largely divorced from those applying outside it.[18] Secondly, under the pretext of putting right the injustices of Versailles Nazi foreign policy became preoccupied with gaining the strategic concessions which would facilitate eastwards expansion.[19] The first sign of this policy came in 1936 with the unopposed reoccupation of the Rhineland. This

[13] Carr, *Arms, Autarky and Aggression*, 54.
[14] Milward, 'Fascism and the Economy', 431.   [15] Ibid. 434.
[16] Barkei, *Fascist Economics*, 220.   [17] Milward, 'Fascism and the Economy', 431.
[18] Milward, *War, Economy and Society*, 7.
[19] Carr, *Arms, Autarky and Aggression*, 7–9; Milward, *War, Economy and Society*, 26–7.

was the prelude to an aggressive diplomatic campaign which would continue through the *Anschluss*, the Munich Agreement, and the invasion of Czechoslovakia to the Polish crisis and the outbreak of war.

Standstill, the City, and Economic *Détente*

The British National Governments could not afford to ignore the Nazi challenge, in both the economic and the strategic spheres. Inevitably the response had to reconcile national security with the critical importance, accepted by all administrations since 1920, of preserving London's international financial position. Since some of the most important commercial interests at the heart of the City were dependent on *détente* with Germany, and given the dangers presented by rearmament to the maintenance of 'sound money' and a stable pound, the path of confrontation was unattractive: there was an institutional bias against it.

The financial connections between the City and Germany had grown considerably in the years after 1919. Merchant and joint stock banks had raised money for the reconstruction of German cities and had provided a considerable volume of finance, often in the form of short-term credits, for German foreign transactions. The acceptance business had proved lucrative for firms such as Hambro's, Baring's, Guiness Mahon, S. Japhet, Huth's, Lazards, Goschen & Cunliffe, and the Midland Bank, but above all for Kleinwort's and Schroder's in the prosperous years of the middle and late 1920s, helping Germany to maintain extensive trading connections not just with the United Kingdom but with the Dominions and with the rest of the world. For Kleinwort's, commissions from the German business rose from £15,000 (5.2 per cent of the total) in 1921 to £117,000 (28.9 per cent) in 1928.[20]

The penetration of Germany by British capital had been encouraged by Montagu Norman, governor of the Bank of England. For Norman this process was central to the construction of an Anglo–German financial partnership which would thwart French and American aspirations to continental hegemony. But Norman's vision went further: the governor's objective was a working European economy whose prosperity would be guaranteed by co-operation between its two leading members. At the same time the rebuilding of Germany as a flourishing capitalist state

---

[20] Stephanie Diaper, 'Merchant Banking in the Interwar Period: The Case of Kleinwort Benson and Sons, Ltd.', *Business History*, 28 (1986), 64; Scott Newton, 'The "Anglo-German Connection"', 182.

would provide a guarantee that Bolshevism would fail to spread beyond the borders of the Soviet Union.[21]

The level of Britain's financial commitment was such that the outflow of capital from Germany in the summer of 1931 naturally caused great anxiety in the City. Many of the banks which had provided short-term credit to Germany had already been caught out by the collapse of the Credit Anstalt. The introduction of exchange controls in Germany resulted in a severe embarrassment for Lazard's, which needed Bank of England assistance, and Kleinwort's, whose collection of frozen debts was so large that they were forced to negotiate a £1 million overdraft facility with the Westminster Bank.[22] Pressure to call in the loans was successfully resisted only after the intervention of Norman himself. The Bank of England co-ordinated a response from domestic and foreign bankers as well as from the Swedish, Swiss, and Dutch central banks, which guaranteed the Reichsbank 'that acceptance lines [are] to be kept at current levels, new bills being accepted unless their presentation involves an increase in acceptance lines; time deposits, advances and loans to be maintained at amounts now outstanding.'[23] To Norman it was axiomatic that a flood of panic withdrawals would simply result in moratoria all over central Europe, provoking a liquidity crisis for London, New York, and the whole international banking system. Enough time was bought to allow for the renewal of a $100 million central bank credit to Germany, a move which had the desired result of keeping the German banks afloat. The next step in managing the crisis came with the international Standstill Agreement of 19 September 1931, whereby it was accepted that existing credits would be frozen, while interest payments were to be continued.

The Standstill Agreement covered £62 million of the £100 million of acceptances held by the London acceptance houses.[24] It was meant to be temporary. But it was in fact renewed in early 1932 and every year thereafter until 1939 despite the unhappiness of many who were involved in the provision of credit to Germany. The fundamental difficulty was Nazi economic policy, which flew in the face of the liberal principles held by the City. London banks became increasingly uncomfortable, and in 1934 negotiations of the renewal of the Standstill Agreement came close to collapse. The British considered the possibility of a unilateral clearing,

[21] John Hargrave, *Professor Skinner, alias Montagu Norman* (1940), 219.

[22] Diaper, 'Merchant Banking', 69–73; Newton, ' "The Anglo-German Connection" ', 185.   [23] Bank of England file, OV34/128, 18 July 1931.

[24] Newton, 'The "Anglo-German Connection" ', 183.

which would have involved the sequestration of German balances to settle accounts, while German bankers protested about the rate of interest on the debts. But Norman and the Committee of Short-Term Creditors, chaired by F. C. Tiarks (significantly a partner in Schroder's and a director of the Bank of England), drew back from the consequences of such action. The Committee feared a German moratorium and the implications of this for the acceptance houses. The disruptive impact of a clearing on Anglo-German trade also rang alarm bells in large firms with significant central and south-east European interests, notably ICI and the Anglo-Dutch combine Unilever.[25] Negotiations involving Norman and Hjalmar Schacht, his opposite number at the Reichsbank, as well as representatives of the Treasury and the Joint Committee, were reinforced by the despatch to Berlin of a high-powered commercial delegation. This was led by E. W. Tennant, a City commodity broker. It included Francis D'Arcy Cooper, chairman of Unilever, and spent time meeting high-level National Socialists, notably William Keppler, 'Hitler's private economic adviser', the Führer himself, and senior officials such as Schacht.[26] Not surprisingly after all this intensive lobbying and networking, the Standstill Agreement was saved and in fact financial relations were formalized through the signature of a Payments Agreement allowing the Germans to spend 55 per cent of the sterling earned through trade with Britain on purchases therefrom, with 10 per cent reserved for debt service.

Clearly the Anglo-German Payments Agreement had an objective in common with the Imperial Preference system: to facilitate the payment of debts.[27] It was in addition seen by the Bank of England and the Treasury as a lever to keep at least a portion of German foreign trade within the international economy, and in so doing to encourage a revival of international trade and a continuing recovery in Britain.[28] German sterling receipts not used to service debts or to finance imports from Britain could be spent on commodities produced within the Commonwealth and Empire, an exchange which would in turn stimulate demand for British exports.

---

[25] PRO PREM 1/335, report by Tennant for Sir Horace Wilson, 22 July 1939. See also A. Teichova, *An Economic Background to Munich* (Cambridge, 1974), 57–8 and 360–4, for a discussion of Unilever's interests.

[26] PRO PREM 1/335, report by Tennant, 22 July, 1939.

[27] Cain and Hopkins, *Crisis and Deconstruction*, 80, 97; Henry J. Tasca, *World Trading Systems: A Study of American and British Commercial Policies* (Paris, 1939), 83–9.

[28] C. A. MacDonald, 'Economic Appeasement and the German "Moderates" 1937–1939. An Introductory Essay', *Past and Present*, 56 (1972), 115–17; Newton, ' "The Anglo-German Connection" ', 195.

The Payments Agreement worked reasonably well. By the end of 1936 acceptance credits provided to German banks and industry had fallen by 30 per cent: the credit line available to German bank debtors was £33.9 million and to industrial debtors it was £11.8 million.[29] At this stage, however, serious disagreement arose among the British creditors and the non-renewal of the Standstill became a genuine possibility. The result would be a German default, the denunciation of the Payments Agreement, and a clearing to settle as many debts as possible.

The dispute stemmed from a difference between the clearing banks and the acceptance houses. In January the Treasury was informed that the clearing banks would refuse to accept Standstill bills unless the renewed Agreement contained provisions for capital repayments. It was acknowledged that such a confrontational policy could provoke a German default and a clearing. Certain accepting houses would suffer 'grave difficulties', but this would only reveal the 'real facts', whose damaging impact would be cushioned by the 'present climate of comparative prosperity'.

The impatience of the clearing banks had been provoked by the announcement of the Four Year Plan and the growing evidence of the remilitarization of German society. It may also have had something to do with the fact that their fortunes were less bound up with the future of short-term credits to Germany than were those of the acceptance houses. In any event, the clearing bankers explained that they did not understand why the acceptance houses should have refrained from pressing for capital repayments ever since the Payments Agreement had been signed. Their inaction had assisted German rearmament.[30] Nevertheless, there was little sympathy for these protests, which appeared to have been instigated by Reginald McKenna, chairman of the Midland Bank. The reception only demonstrated that the claims of the acceptance houses generally took priority over those of the clearing banks in the City, and that this order of priority was supported by the Bank of England and the Treasury.[31]

Unity amongst creditors was preserved by agreement that their representatives at the forthcoming talks should ask for repayment of 10 per cent to be written into the new agreement. But Schacht turned this

[29] Papers of R. H. Brand, New Bodleian Library, Oxford, file 193A/21, 'German Credit Agreement: Acceptances(Availments) as on 31/12/36'; PRO T 160/818/12681/05/4, Report from HM Embassy, Berlin, 18 Jan. 1937.

[30] PRO T 160/818/12681/05/4, report by David Waley on the attitude of clearing bankers, 14 Jan. 1937.

[31] See PRO T 160/818/12681/05/4, note by Waley, 17 Feb. 1937.

proposal down flat. All he offered was a formula whereby credits not availed for three years could be cancelled. Robert Brand (Lazard's) and Charles Lidbury (the Westminster Bank), who had gone to Berlin on behalf of the Joint Committee of Short-Term Creditors, returned to London empty-handed.[32] A crisis was, however, averted because the full weight of pressure from Norman and the Treasury was brought to bear on the clearing banks and the agreement was renewed on Schacht's terms, which also satisfied the acceptance houses.

Norman persuaded the clearing bankers to accept this deal largely because he believed it to be the only one available and because he believed that any deal was better than none at all. The governor had invested considerable time and trouble in shoring up the Anglo-German financial relationship since 1931. In part, of course, this reflected his perception of his official responsibilities to the banking system: these did not include supporting measures likely to precipitate liquidity crises in leading merchant banks. But in addition Norman had not abandoned his earlier vision of collaboration between Europe's two largest capitalist economies. To this end he had built up an unusually close working and personal relationship with Schacht,[33] whose presence at the Reichsbank was taken as a sign that the Nazi regime had not abandoned financial respectability and could be steered back to orthodoxy.[34] In 1936 Schacht had stood out against the introduction of the Four Year Plan, making the case for a move away from autarky. But the prospects of such a change in policy would almost certainly disappear if Schacht's position were to be undermined by Germany's creditors in a dramatic coup whose effect would be to take money out of the Nazi economy and reduce its access to foreign exchange.

Norman's view of the Standstill issue was shared by the Treasury. Chamberlain made it clear that he believed it would be impossible to achieve Berlin's agreement to alteration of the Anglo-German payments arrangements so that Germany would apply 'substantial sums' to the reduction of Standstill obligations even if the Treasury itself became involved in the talks.[35] But this pragmatic argument merely reinforced Treasury determination to avert a rupture with Germany over the Standstill

---

[32] PRO T 160/818/12681/05/4, note by Waley, 17 Feb. 1937.

[33] Norman was godfather to Schacht's son; see also Bank of England file G1/417–19.

[34] See PRO T 160/818/12681/05/4, minute by Jerry Pinsent, 18 Jan. 1937, in which collapse of the Agreement was viewed with disfavour on the grounds that 'it would probably shake confidence on both sides and also weaken Schacht's position . . .'.

[35] PRO T 160/818/12681/05/4: Chamberlain's view was communicated to Norman on 15 Jan. 1937.

question. There was no enthusiasm for any measure likely to wreck the Payments Agreement, which, it was argued, had performed well both in assisting British trade and in facilitating debt service. The importance of sustaining Schacht's position was cited: as long as he was at the Reichsbank there was still hope that the credits would be repaid or made liquid again.[36] All this added up to a formidable case for the *status quo*: it should come as no surprise that the clearing bankers were told after the German rejection of the Joint Committee's initial negotiating position that the government was unlikely to denounce the Payments Agreement in order to obtain capital for the debtors. It was this piece of arm-twisting which revealed beyond any doubt the Treasury's priorities and forced the clearing bankers to accept the official line as developed by Norman, Tiarks, and the Treasury.

A new crisis arose in 1938 when the Anglo-German Payments Agreement came up for renewal following the *Anschluss*. Much to the dismay of the Treasury and many British creditors the Nazi Government threatened to repudiate Austrian debts.[37] On this occasion the Treasury took a more robust line than Tiarks and the Joint Committee. The government's chief economic adviser, Sir Frederick Leith-Ross, was alerted by Schacht to the real problem in Berlin: party ideologues argued that Austrian liabilities had been incurred for 'political' reasons, to draw the country into an international network of trade and payments dominated by Anglo-American finance.[38] Schacht suggested that the threat of a clearing might help him fend off the Nazi 'extremists' and achieve a settlement which honoured the Austrian obligations. The Treasury, anxious to reach an agreement which would boost exports by increasing the proportion of German sterling receipts to be spent on British goods, began to institute a clearing. Tiarks complained to Norman that 'it [was] most unfortunate that HMG should arrive at a decision which was tantamount to economic war', but the governor, privy to the same information as Leith-Ross, argued that it would be 'difficult' to avoid drastic action if no headway could be made with the Germans.[39] This time acceptance that confrontation might be necessary followed from the need to bolster Schacht's struggle against economic isolationism. The tactic worked, and a revised Payments Agreement was concluded by which Germany assumed responsibility for the Austrian debts and agreed to

[36] PRO T 160/818/12681/05/4, minute by Pinsent of 18 Jan. 1937.
[37] See Bank of England file OV6/291/335/2, 'Revision of Anglo-German Payments Agreement'.   [38] MacDonald, 'Economic Appeasement', 116.
[39] Bank of England file OV34/139, note by the Deputy-Governor, 31 May 1938.

spend up to 60 per cent of the foreign exchange generated by trade with Britain on British products.

Before the agreement was reached the Treasury was prepared to soften the blow of a clearing to the accepting houses by removing the Standstill creditors from the clearing order, in acknowledgement of the Joint Committee's case that such flexibility might facilitate the continued servicing of the debts even after the collapse of the Payments Agreement. If the Germans did denounce the Standstill arrangements, however, the Treasury accepted that the first call on the clearing would be the claims of the short-term creditors.[40] Thus, the differences between the Treasury and the Bank on the one hand and the short-term creditors on the other should not be exaggerated. It was fundamentally a tactical affair: the Joint Committee took the view that debt service should be maintained at practically all costs,[41] while the Treasury and the Bank believed that the dynamics of repudiating Austrian debts would inevitably lead to the denunciation of all foreign financial entanglements, including Standstill and the post-1919 reconstruction credits.[42]

The tenderness shown by the Treasury to the accepting houses over the Standstill followed from its historic identification of the national interest with the external orientation of British capitalism. In general terms this meant the pursuit of macro- and microeconomic policies which resulted in the widest possible use of sterling as a trading and reserve currency. Specifically it meant, in the context of the 1920s, the return to gold, and in that of the 1930s, the creation of the sterling area. During the 1920s the Treasury and the Bank had pursued policies designed to enhance London's position as a source of international credit; during the 1930s it became necessary to establish machinery for the collection of debts in order to prevent the defaults which would have threatened sterling and undermined City institutions involved in the financing of international trade. Imperial Preference was one example of such machinery. The Standstill arrangements and the Anglo-German Payments Agreements formed the two halves of another.

Even allowing for these helpful facilities the collapse of the German banking system and the subsequent imposition of trade and currency restriction left its mark on the City as the 1930s developed. After the

---

[40] Brand Papers, 193A, file 20, Waley to Vickers (of Slaughter and May, one of the Short-Term Creditors), 28 June 1938.

[41] See Brand Papers, 193A, file 19, letter from the Joint Committee of Short-Term Creditors to B. G. Catterns, Deputy-Governor of the Bank of England, 15 June 1938.

[42] Bank of England file OV34/139, 'Revision of Anglo-German Payments Agreement'.

rescue of Kleinwort's and Lazard's in 1931, Huth's were forced into a merger with the British Overseas Bank in 1936. In April 1939 Kleinwort's ran into fresh liquidity problems and had to renew their £1 million overdraft with the Westminster Bank, while Goschen & Cunliffe went into liquidation shortly after the outbreak of war.[43] What would have been the consequences of taking the line advocated by the clearing banks in 1936–7? Leith-Ross spoke for the acceptance houses as well as for the Treasury and the Bank when he pointed out early in 1939 that a financial rupture with Germany would mean 'some £40 million of short-term bills could no longer be carried by the London market and at least a proportion of these would have to be supported by the Government, while a further £80 or £90 million of long-term debts would come into default. The net effect would be seriously to disorganise the London market and to weaken our balance of payments, without any advantage to us.'[44]

It was not, however, simply a question of Hobson's choice for the City. The existence of powerful financial ties between the two countries provided a rationale for economic *détente* which was not motivated by fear. British and German banking institutions had collaborated for decades, to considerable mutual advantage. Germany was one of Britain's leading customers outside the Empire (Table 3.3) and over the years had brought a good deal of business the City's way. The Standstill negotiations had been fraught with difficulties but they had nevertheless generated an unusually close relationship between the banking representatives of each nation, symbolized in the co-operation of Norman with Schacht. In Norman's words, an 'Anglo-German connection' had been created.[45]

Clearly the material interests of the most powerful and prestigious part of the City were wrapped up with the maintenance of the 'Anglo-German connection'. But there was more at stake than the fate of the Standstill credits and the banks which were dependent upon them. Were the connection to be broken everything Norman had been working for since 1919 would be undermined. The institutional links which, it was hoped, would guarantee European peace and its corollary, profitable commerce, would suffer disruption. Only domestic socialists and their friends in the Soviet Union, the avowed enemy of capitalism, would benefit from a worsening of relations between London and Berlin. In these circumstances it was hardly surprising that important banks and their directors figured prominently

[43] Diaper, 'Merchant Banking', 69–73.
[44] PRO FO 371/22950, C2581/8/18, minute by Leith-Ross, 24 Jan. 1939.
[45] PRO FO 371/23000, C469/3218, note of conversation with Norman by Frank Ashton-Gwatkin, 15 Jan. 1939.

TABLE 3.3. *Britain's twelve leading customers in 1938 (£ million)*

Destination of exports	Value	% of all exports
India, Burma, Ceylon	39.9	8.5
South Africa	39.5	8.4
Australia	38.2	8.1
Canada	22.5	4.8
Germany	20.6	4.4
USA	20.5	4.4
Eire	20.3	4.3
Argentina	19.3	4.1
New Zealand	19.2	4.1
Denmark	15.8	3.3
France	15.1	3.2
Netherlands	13.1	2.8

Source: *Statistical Abstract for the United Kingdom* (1939), Table 281, p. 384; *The Economist* (21 Jan. 1939), 113–14.

on the membership list of the Anglo-German Fellowship, formed in the wake of D'Arcy Cooper's successful mission with the objective of exploiting the opportunity provided by the Payments Agreement to promote continuing good relations. Guiness Mahon, Lazard's, and Schroder's were corporate members. At the same time Tiarks, notwithstanding his work for Schroder's and for the Bank of England, joined in an individual capacity, as did Lord Stamp and Sir Robert Kindersley, both governors of the Bank of England, and Lord Magowan, who was a director of the British Overseas Bank and the Midland Bank (as well as chairman of ICI). The Fellowship was a powerful lobby, providing the City with networking facilities in favour of Anglo-German *détente* additional to those created by its historic but more informal ties to the Treasury.[46]

Finance and Strategy

The lobbyists of the Anglo-German Fellowship found that the government was prepared to listen sympathetically to calls for *détente* with the Nazi regime. In particular, from the time that Neville Chamberlain became prime minister at the start of 1937 the National Government made a series of attempts to reach an understanding with Germany which would embrace outstanding economic and territorial issues.

Although the chiefs of staff were left to work out the military details of this policy, known then and now as one of 'appeasement', they were

[46] Simon Haxey, *Tory M.P.* (1939), 230–2.

operating within a strategic framework which was dictated by Treasury rules. As early as 1934 the Defence Requirement Committee (DRC) had identified Germany as Britain's main long-term enemy,[47] while it was recognized that Japan and Italy were also potential foes.[48] But plans to counter this combination of threats were consistently held up in the Whitehall machine. In November 1935 the Committee proposed the 'Ideal Scheme', which recommended the expansion of air force reserves, a 2 Power standard (maintenance of parity in capital ships with the US Navy), which would have left the Navy large enough to meet the Japanese challenge in the Far East and deal with the threat to home waters, and the creation of a partially mechanized army 'Field Force' which could be sent to the Continent in an emergency.[49] The projected cost of this programme between its commencement in 1936 and its completion in 1940 amounted to an increase of 67 per cent in defence expenditure over the period (maintaining the budget at current levels meant spending an estimated £620 million by 1940; under the Ideal Scheme this total reached £1,037.5 million).[50] Acknowledging that implementation of the Scheme would involve a substantial rise in government outlays, the DRC argued for a defence loan in order to minimize the cost to the taxpayer. This suggestion raised Treasury hackles, although it had originally been supported by Sir Warren Fisher, the permanent under-secretary. The chancellor, however, disapproved and the second secretary, Sir Richard Hopkins, dismissed the defence loan as a 'comfortable Lloyd George device'.[51]

Association with the unorthodox ideas of Lloyd George, who at the time was campaigning for a British 'New Deal' based on loan-financed public expenditure, was enough to condemn the Ideal Scheme in Treasury eyes. Hopkins attempted to make the programme square with the principles of sound finance by initiating a costing exercise. The outcome suggested that projected spending levels could be revised downwards to figures of £170 million in 1936 rising to £215 million by 1941, which could be met wholly from tax increases.[52] Chamberlain and Fisher, however, took the view that such an increase in the fiscal burden would damage the recovery. The chancellor argued that the Scheme would have to be drastically pared and reorganized in a way which would make the

---

[47] Brian Bond, *British Military Policy Between the Two World Wars* (Oxford, 1980), 194 ff. [48] Ibid. 218.
[49] R. P. Shay Jr., *British Rearmament in the Thirties: Politics and Profits* (Princeton, NJ, 1977), 56. [50] Ibid. 56.
[51] Ibid. 75. [52] Ibid. 77.

most of existing resources if the government was to avoid the evils of either deficit financing or crippling taxation. In the circumstances of 1936 this meant reliance on the RAF, whose expansion had been agreed the previous year, as a strike force, and on the navy, both to defend home waters and Imperial interests in the Far East, and to protect the lines of communication along which food and raw materials would be imported into Britain. Investment in bombers would deter any possible German aggression and a naval blockade would starve the Third Reich into submission. Chamberlain believed that the claims of the army came last: he was prepared to accept the need for a Field Force of five divisions (one of which should be mobile) but opposed the provison 'of a land army of indefinite size for continental warfare'.[53] In the event of a conflict most of the fighting on land would be done by the French, who had built up the largest army in Europe and who would, it was believed, be invulnerable behind the Maginot Line.[54]

This strategy of defence formed the basis of British military policy at least up to 1939, although it was of course subject to significant modifications. One example was the switch of Treasury support away from the creation of a large bomber force in favour of investment in fighters and a chain of radar stations in order to protect Britain from air attack.[55] The shift in tactics was accompanied by a downgrading of the Field Force: by the end of 1937 there was practically no support for its European role and it was seen principally as an instrument for the defence of Imperial possessions, particularly against Italian expansionism in the Middle East.[56] The Treasury's synthesis of finance and strategy led to the pursuit of 'imperial isolationism' by a Britain which was to be transformed into an island fortress.

Chamberlain was not blind to the Nazi threat. In June 1936 he admitted to a suspicion 'that there is no real bona fides in Germany'.[57] Confronted by spiralling defence estimates (£211 million had been allocated to the 1937 budget, but the projections submitted to the Treasury from the services came to £286 million), he authorized a defence loan of £400 million, repayable over five years at 3 per cent, rather than pin the forces back to their original financial targets.[58] As a result of these preparations

[53] Neville Chamberlain Papers, Manuscripts and Rare Books Reading Room, Main Library, University of Birmingham, NC 2/24A, diary entry for Dec. 1936; Shay, *British Rearmament in the Thirties*, 77–9.   [54] Bond, *British Military Policy*, 257.
[55] Ibid. 250.   [56] Ibid. 257.
[57] Neville Chamberlain Papers, NC 7/7/4, letter to Lord Lothian, 10 June 1936.
[58] Bond, *British Military Policy*, 247.

TABLE 3.4. *Percentage of GNP devoted to military expenditure: Britain and Germany, 1935–1940*

Financial year	Great Britain	Germany
1935	3.3	7.4
1936	4.2	12.4
1937	5.6	11.8
1938	8.1	16.6
1939	21.4	23.0
1940	51.7	38.0

Source: G. C. Peden, 'A Matter of Timing: The Economic Background to British Foreign Policy, 1937–1939', *History*, 69 (1984), 25.

Britain was able to defeat the Luftwaffe in 1940, and in so doing put paid to any serious hopes Hitler may have entertained of invasion. Overall, as chancellor and prime minister, Chamberlain presided over an increase in the share of defence spending unprecedented in peacetime and which by 1939 compared well with the efforts of Nazi Germany (Table 3.4).

The problem was the pattern of rearmament. Its neglect of investment in the army had by the spring of 1938 reduced it to a position from which it was powerless to achieve anything, whether at home, on the Continent, or in the Middle East.[59] When Anglo-French staff talks were held following the *Anschluss* and throughout the Sudeten crisis of summer 1938, the British could offer only two divisions, a gesture which did nothing to stiffen French resolve in the face of Hitler's aggressive diplomacy (perhaps this was intentional: Foreign Secretary Lord Halifax had advised the Germans 'not to take an exaggerated view' of the talks' significance).[60]

Could more have been achieved if the canons of sound finance had been abandoned? In some ways this is an unfair question. First, the Treasury took the view that finance was 'the fourth arm of defence'.[61] Both the Treasury and the chiefs of staff believed that the Nazis, once thwarted in their attempt to deliver an early knock-out blow, would gradually run out of raw materials and foreign exchange. However, this might take three years.[62] During that time Britain would be dependent on imports of food and raw materials from the sterling area and the western hemisphere. Members of the sterling area would be expected to accept sterling or to supply goods on credit if Britain were unable immediately to pay for them in exports or in currency. Additionally, supplies from the

[59] Ibid. 270.   [60] Ibid. 275–6.
[61] G. C. Peden, 'A Matter of Timing: The Economic Background to British Foreign Policy, 1937–1939', *History*, 69 (1984), 16.   [62] Ibid. 17.

Americas would have to be financed by exports, gold, or the liquidating of overseas assets held by British subjects. In consequence, Britain needed to retain a sound external financial position, healthy gold reserves, and international creditworthiness. None of this would be achieved if the government expanded the rearmament programme to a point at which the diversion of productive resources from exports, coupled with the generation of excess demand, destabilized the balance of payments and led to a run on the pound.[63] How would Britain be able to pay for essential imports without the wherewithal in gold and foreign currencies, if not by exports? The alternative of issuing sterling IOUs to creditors depended on their willingness to hold the currency, and this would not be enhanced if it became a depreciating asset. At the same time sterling's decline against other currencies, but especially the dollar, would put more pressure on the import bill, setting up a vicious circle in the process.[64]

Secondly, the Treasury had a public duty to perform in ensuring that private defence companies receiving defence contracts did not manipulate costs in order to make windfall profits. The government quarrelled with Austin's overpayment for the manufacturing of aircraft engines, suggesting a price of £152,000 for 900 against the company's estimate of £435,000 for the same number. In the end both sides agreed to a compromise figure of £250,000.[65] Another case of government campaigning against what public opinion, expressed through the newspapers, Conservative backbenchers, and the Opposition, considered to be profiteering, occurred in a show-down with the Society of British Aircraft Constructors (SBAC). The Treasury did not believe there was any justification for a 10 per cent profit margin on contracts, notwithstanding agreement on this figure between the Air Ministry and the SBAC. After negotiations lasting throughout the best part of 1937 the SBAC came down to a figure of 7.5 per cent, a reduction considered fair by the Treasury in view of the elimination of commercial risk.[66]

Thirdly, it has been argued by George Peden that the Treasury was by the late 1930s a good deal more sympathetic to Keynesian ideas than has hitherto been appreciated—and that these 'alternative' approaches to economic management were themselves often close to prevailing wisdom in the citadel of economic orthodoxy.[67] For example, in 1937–8

[63] G. C. Peden, *British Rearmament and the Treasury, 1932–9* (Edinburgh, 1979), 64–92.

[64] R. A. C. Parker, 'Economics, Rearmament and Foreign Policy: the United Kingdom before 1939. A Preliminary Study', *Journal of Contemporary History*, 10 (1975), 637–9.

[65] Shay, *British Rearmament in the Thirties*, 111–12.   [66] Ibid. 121–5.

[67] See G. C. Peden, 'Keynes, the Economics of Rearmament and Appeasement', in Wolfgang Mommsen and Lothar Kettenacker (eds.), *The Fascist Challenge and the Policy of Appeasement* (London, 1983), 142–55.

both Keynes and the Treasury were anxious to contain public spending in order to hold down inflationary pressure arising from the rearmament programme. In 1938, however, both became concerned at the downturn in economic activity and agreed that in the circumstances there was no inflationary risk in the acceleration of the rearmament programme that year. Putting these principles into action, the Treasury approved the expenditure of £400 million on defence, not only considerably more than the £265 million spent in 1937 but also well beyond what the global figure of £1,500 million for 1937–42 implied for 1938.[68] In addition, Keynes shared Treasury anxieties about the impact of rearmament on the balance of payments and sterling's international position. Finally, in 1939–40 both were driven to suggest the extension of public authority over the Stock Exchange, including compulsory dividend restraint and controls over share issues, building society loans, and bank advances, in order to prevent an increase in interest rates on government stock arising from the need to guarantee its precedence over the demands of the private sector in the financial markets.[69]

None the less, the government's engagement with economic heterodoxy was limited. Much to the relief of the FBI a return to the controls over wages, prices, profits, and production which had accompanied military mobilization during the First World War was ruled out.[70] The creation of a Ministry of Supply was postponed until May 1939.[71] The government refused to initiate discussions with the TUC about the dilution of skilled labour until the spring of 1938, even though in its absence shortages might threaten the expansion of the rearmament programme and lead to inflationary wage settlements liable to undermine the competitiveness of British exports. Any policy which smacked of wartime corporatism was regarded with suspicion, even if it meant taking risks with the pace of rearmament. The Chamberlain administration, therefore, tried to avoid dislocation of the labour market via the establishment of labour exchanges and the placing of contracts in a way designed to ensure that no area had more work than could be fulfilled by existing labour resources, over a period which left contractors with time to hire and train workers rather than buy them away from other firms.[72]

It is true that in 1937 Keynes expressed his opposition to '(quasi) wartime controls, rationing and the like'.[73] In 1938 and after, however, he began to move away from this liberal position. Contemplating the balance of payments deficit and the possibility of a run on sterling, he urged

---

[68] Ibid. 151.   [69] Ibid. 150.   [70] Shay, *British Rearmament in the Thirties*, 94 ff.
[71] Ibid. 128 ff.   [72] Ibid. 125–8.
[73] Peden, 'Keynes, the Economics of Rearmament, and Appeasement', 151.

consideration of exchange controls and limits on overseas lending in the City. The Dominions and India should be encouraged to raise money in the United States. These proposals, which involved subordinating external financial commitments to the needs of domestic production, were predictably opposed by the Bank and the Treasury, which argued that such radical steps might be taken as a sign of weakness, so reducing international confidence in sterling. The whole point of the exercise would then have been frustrated.[74]

Ultimately, the most that could be said about the Treasury is that it was prepared to modify its traditional caution in the face of mounting international danger. Its recommendations were not merely pragmatic; they stemmed from a commitment to economic liberalism too deep-rooted for the principles of orthodox finance to be finally jettisoned until the eleventh hour had almost come and gone, in 1940–1. In April 1939 Keynes argued that an increase in loan-financed expenditure on rearmament would wipe out abnormal unemployment and lead to an increase of 8 per cent in the national income, large enough to generate the extra savings which would be necessitated by the increase in borrowing. This was too much for the Treasury, which fell back on the conventional wisdom that 'there was no action which the Government could take which would increase the total volume of savings of the country as a whole'.[75] This repudiation of Keynesian principles was reinforced by the anxiety expressed by Chamberlain's successor at the Exchequer, Sir John Simon, when he told the Cabinet in April 1938 that a higher level of defence expenditure than had already been agreed would not be possible 'unless we turned ourselves into a different kind of nation'.[76] The Treasury stood by its determination not to borrow more than private citizens were willing to lend: refusal to follow such an injunction would mean printing money to cover commitments, leading to inflation, injustice 'to the owners of fixed incomes', and to the spread of socialistic ideas and practices.[77]

Rearmament was about more than technical financial issues. The criticisms made by Keynes and, increasingly, by a coalition of centre-Left forces grouped around Winston Churchill's Focus group, embracing progressive Conservatives, Liberals, the TUC, and much of the parliamentary Labour Party, went to the heart of the British political economy. Chamberlain had always understood this point; it was why he

[74] Peden, *Keynes, the Economics of Rearmament, and Appeasement*, 147–8.
[75] Ibid. 148–9.　　　[76] Peden, 'A Matter of Timing', 22.
[77] Shay, *British Rearmament in the Thirties*, 160–1.

was opposed to the creation of a large Continental army. By attempting to side-step investment in the army the government believed, throughout the period from 1937 until the outbreak of war and even beyond, that it could avoid the scale of economic intervention which had been necessitated after 1914. With a relatively small land force there would be no need to organize and co-ordinate an elaborate regime of economic controls.[78] Rearmament based on a strategy of deterrence was designed to reconcile national security with the interests of the liberal–conservative coalition which had sustained most governments since the demise of reconstruction.

Colonial Appeasement, 1937–1938

This attempt to preserve the *status quo* lay behind Chamberlain's search for a settlement with Germany. The prime minister hoped to avoid an open-ended commitment to higher levels of defence expenditure through the pursuit of a rearmament programme which would deter the Nazis from an adventurist foreign policy and bring them to the conference table. From the moment Chamberlain became prime minister, therefore, the National Government single-mindedly pursued a twin-track policy of deterrence and *détente*.[79] But if rearmament was the basis of deterrence what was to be the foundation of *détente*? In fact there already was an agenda, which had been developed by the liberal imperialists and bankers whose influence on British foreign and financial policy had been in the ascendant since the abandonment of social-imperialist dreams at the close of the First World War. As early as the aftermath of Versailles it was conventional wisdom in the Foreign Office, the Treasury, the Bank, and the City as well as in the well-connected Round Table–RIIA network which fed advice to the government, that Germany had been harshly treated. Hitler's arrival in power made little if any difference to the conviction that Germany had legitimate grievances which could only be put right by a revision of the Versailles Treaty.[80] Such thinking lay

[78] Newton and Porter, *Modernization Frustrated*, 91.

[79] Bond, *British Military Policy*, 243; W. Medlicott, *Contemporary England, 1914–64* (1967), 74; A. J. P. Taylor, *English History, 1914–1945* (2nd edn., 1975), 501–29.

[80] See A. Crozier, *Appeasement and Germany's Last Bid for Colonies* (1988), 164 ff; W. Medlicott, 'Britain and Germany: the Search for Agreement, 1930–37', in D. Dilks (ed.), *Retreat from Power: Studies in British Foreign Policy in the Twentieth Century*, vol. 1 (1981). At least until the mid-1930s mainstream Labour and Liberal policy reflected the consensus that Germany had a case. This congenial political climate certainly made the government's work easier but the point is that it had its own reasons for appeasement. And these did not include the need to keep or to seek the approval of the Left.

behind the Anglo-German Naval Agreement (1935) as well as British policy during and after the reoccupation of the Rhineland in 1936. Under the terms of the Naval Agreement Britain recognized the legitimacy of German maritime power in defiance of Versailles, albeit in a restricted form. The German navy was to be limited to 35 per cent of the British, although flexibility was to be applied to submarines where the Nazis were permitted parity with the United Kingdom in the event of danger from the Soviet Union.[81] When the reoccupation of the Rhineland occurred Britain took no action to prevent it and argued against the Soviet proposal that the League of Nations implement sanctions against Germany since it had broken the Locarno Treaty.[82]

The liberal imperialists were well placed in the Conservative Party as well as in Whitehall and the City. Lord Halifax supported their ideas, as did Samuel Hoare and Sir John Simon. Lord Londonderry, a more Right-wing imperialist, consistently supported pan-Germanism. All four were in the Cabinet after 1931, Hoare holding the foreign secretaryship in 1935 and Halifax taking it in 1938. Simon had served as foreign secretary under Ramsay MacDonald and was Chamberlain's chancellor. Outside government, belief that the German menace would fade if the Versailles Treaty were revised was shared by members of the Anglo-German Fellowship, some of whom were connected to the political establishment via membership of the RIIA. One such was Robert Brand, a colleague of Frank Tiarks on the Joint Committee of Short-Term Creditors by virtue of his role as chairman of Lazard's, itself a corporate member of the Fellowship. Another was Lord Lothian, a governor of the National Bank of Scotland and a member of the Council of the RIIA. In the press the leading advocate of Anglo-German *rapprochement* was *The Times*, whose editor, Geoffrey Dawson, was himself a frequent participant in Round Table meetings held at Cliveden, home of Lord Waldorf Astor, chairman of the Council of the RIIA and proprietor of the newspaper, and his wife Nancy, a Conservative MP.[83]

A full-blown statement of the pro-German lobby's approach to the Nazi problem was made by Lothian to Chamberlain in June 1936. Lothian argued that Britain should support the *Anschluss* with Austria rather than

---

[81] Taylor, *English History*, 465.   [82] Ibid. 475–8.

[83] See Haxey, *Tory M.P.*, 230–2; Carroll Quigley, *The Anglo-American Establishment from Rhodes to Cliveden* (New York, 1981), ch. 10, for details of RIIA membership; Robin Ramsay, 'Clinton and Quigley: A Strange Tale From the US elite', *Lobster*, 25 (1993), 14–15. W. W. Astor, son of Waldorf and Nancy, was a member of the Anglo-German Fellowship.

join with France and the Soviet Union in an alliance of 'encirclement' which would only drive Hitler into the arms of Mussolini. This should be followed by a settlement of the Danzig and Memel issues on Germany's terms, a revision of the Hungarian boundary, and a frank discussion of 'the colonial economic and raw material problem'. Chamberlain's suspicions of Nazi Germany led him to demur at the Lothian package, but one aspect of it interested him and proved to be at the centre of his first attempt to reach an understanding with Hitler.[84]

After becoming prime minister Chamberlain spent a year attempting to address what Lothian called 'the colonial economic and raw material problem'. This 'problem' derived from Nazi complaints, echoed in discussions held during February 1937 between Schacht and Leith-Ross, that quite apart from humiliating German prestige, the removal of colonies and their transfer to rival powers under the terms of Versailles had cut off the Reich from important sources of foodstuffs such as the oils and fats which were in plentiful supply throughout west Africa. Autarky and exchange controls were, therefore, in part at least a function of the vindictiveness of the Versailles settlement. Schacht suggested that colonial concessions to Germany, apparently seen by Hitler as a question of honour as well as 'of vital necessity for the German economy in the first place', might provide a critical part 'of a general settlement which would secure the peace and economic progress not only of Germany but of the whole world'.[85]

What interested Chamberlain, the Foreign Office, the Treasury, and the Bank, as well as significant pro-German lobbyists such as Lothian, was Schacht's suggestion that Germany's reintegration into the world economy as well as into international political organizations such as the League of Nations might follow from a 'general settlement'. Schacht explained that he wished for the re-establishment of 'normal trading relationships', based on resolution of the Standstill issue, the abolition of exchange controls (initially on current transactions only), and the removal of import quotas on industrial goods. He argued that there was no need to take the Four Year Plan 'too seriously'. Germany's willingness to manufacture its own petrol, rubber, and sugar was dependent on finance and upon the possibilities of obtaining 'normal supplies'.[86] Such arguments were attractive to the government, given its commitment to

[84] Neville Chamberlain Papers, NC 7/7/74, memorandum from Lothian to Chamberlain, 3 June 1936, 'Crisis in British Foreign Policy'.

[85] PRO T 188/288, note by Leith-Ross of a conversation with Schacht, 2 Feb. 1937.

[86] Ibid.

recovery based on the expansion of trade and its suspicions that the Four Year Plan was a harbinger of German political ambitions in eastern Europe. It is therefore not surprising that Chamberlain and his advisers jumped at what looked like an opportunity to resolve political and economic tensions and to start laying the foundations of a reconstructed world economy in so doing.

The question was, how to facilitate such a process. Chamberlain was not prepared to sacrifice the British colonial mandates in east Africa, and for a time played with the idea of offering Belgian and Portuguese possessions to Germany apparently over the heads of the governments in Brussels and Lisbon, let alone the inhabitants of the territories in question.[87] However, this radical scheme receded into the background following the publication of the Van Zeeland Report. The Report, drawn up by the Belgian prime minister Paul Van Zeeland and published in January 1938, set out how the commitments to international trade liberalization and currency stability made in the Tripartite Monetary Agreement might be implemented. Van Zeeland recommended tariff and quota reductions, together with the creation of a currency stabilization fund run by the Bank of International Settlements to help governments maintain stable exchange rates without resorting to controls. As far as access to raw materials was concerned, Van Zeeland suggested internationalizing colonial mandates, with the extension of the 'Open Door' principle to 'colonies proper'.[88]

The Van Zeeland Report was welcomed by London. Its recommendations on trade and currency policy squared almost exactly with what the Treasury and the Foreign Office had been advocating at least since the Tripartite Agreement.[89] London now hoped that the Germans would move away from autarky and agree to come within the framework of the Tripartite Agreement in return for participation within an international consortium, established to develop not simply mandated territories but 'the whole of tropical Africa'.[90] This would then prove to be the prelude to a general settlement of the kind outlined by Schacht in February 1937.

The hopes of a settlement based on colonial appeasement were dashed. Indeed, they never really existed outside the minds of British ministers and civil servants and, perhaps, Hjalmar Schacht. The fundamental difficulty was Hitler. Although the Führer had mentioned Germany's lost

[87] Cain and Hopkins, *Crisis and Deconstruction*, 228.
[88] Crozier, *Appeasement and Germany's Last Bid for Colonies*, 253.
[89] See PRO T 160/840/F13427/8, minute by Phillips of 31 May 1937.
[90] Crozier, *Appeasement and Germany's Last Bid for Colonies*, 255–6.

colonies as a grievance arising from Versailles, there is no reason to believe he ever believed their restoration, in whatever form, would be acceptable as part of a general settlement. This was because he had no particular interest in extra-European expansion, at least not at so early a stage in the history of the Third Reich. As Hitler wrote in *Mein Kampf*: 'We National Socialists consequently draw a line beneath the foreign policy tendency of our pre-war period. We take up where we broke off six hundred years ago. We stop the endless German movement to the south and west, and turn our gaze toward the land in the east. At long last we break off the colonial and commercial policy of the pre-war period and shift to the soil policy of the future.'[91] There was no possibility of exchanging the ambition of formal control over eastern Europe and the Ukraine for colonial concessions, which was ultimately what London was hoping for. Hitler's purpose in raising the issue had been merely tactical: he had hoped that the British would acknowledge the Nazi *Drang nach Osten* (drive to the east) in return for the surrender of colonial ambitions which had never existed anyway.[92] The futility of attempting to found a settlement which would bring Germany back into a liberal international political and economic community solely on an agreement about colonies became apparent during the spring of 1938. At this juncture the intensification of controls over the Nazi economy was accompanied by the *Anschluss* with Austria just when the British were trying to persuade Hitler to go with the Van Zeeland Report.[93]

By the summer of 1938 the Cabinet had had to accept the failure of the colonial initiative. This should not have occasioned any surprise. As far back as the autumn of 1937 Halifax had been sent to Berlin by Chamberlain in order to test the response to a general settlement founded on colonial appeasement.[94] Very little headway had been made. So why did the National Government persist in following such a will o' the wisp? Probably out of a belief that Hitler's concern about Germany's lost colonies was genuine and because Schacht was thought to possess more influence over the Nazi regime than he had in reality. Even so, in the autumn of 1938 Goering himself was reported to have become impressed with the difficulties of autarky and to be 'feeling his way to a freer policy'. There is no reason to suppose that the British deliberately deceived themselves about the true nature of the Nazi regime. It is undeniable that as long as Schacht with his 'liberal' and 'moderate' friends inside the

---

[91] Quoted by Carr, *Arms, Autarky and Aggression*, 9–10.
[92] Crozier, *Appeasement and Germany's Last Bid for Colonies*, 272–3.
[93] Ibid. 258–63.   [94] Ibid. 228–30.

Foreign Ministry, the Economics Ministry, and the army such as Neurath, Funk, and Blomberg, not to mention Goering, were thought to be capable of influencing Hitler away from autarky and expansion, there would be no need to reconsider the financial and strategic synthesis behind the twin-track policy of deterrence and *détente*.[95] The failure of colonial appeasement provoked no review of policy towards Germany; it merely formed the prelude to Munich.

[95] For Goering and the 'moderates' see MacDonald, 'Appeasement and the German Moderates', esp. 119. See also PRO T 188/288, retrospective note of 3 Dec. 1945 by Leith-Ross.

4

The Climax of Appeasement, 1938–1939

Munich

The high tide of British attempts to reach a lasting settlement with Germany ran from the summer of 1938 until March 1939. It was a period which started with the Sudeten crisis, peaked at Munich, and came to an end with the German invasion of Czechoslovakia. During this time the British government stepped up its efforts to reach *détente* with Nazi Germany on the basis of political and economic agreements intended to redress the perceived injustices of Versailles and simultaneously to draw the Third Reich away from autarky.

In 1938 it began to appear that resolution of the crisis concerning the status of the Sudeten Germans in Czechoslovakia could provide the foundation-stone for what Chamberlain liked to call 'the appeasement of Europe'. The problem was one of the legacies of Versailles: over 3 million German speakers who had previously occupied a dominant position in the old Austro-Hungarian Empire discovered in 1919 that they were now a minority in the 12-million strong republic of Czechoslovakia.[1] Modest demands for cultural autonomy were transformed by the impact of the Depression and the rise of Nazism in Germany into calls for outright secession and unity with the Reich. By the spring of 1938 the vehicle for the Sudeteners' aspirations, the Sudeten German Party, was making demands for political autonomy which were obviously incompatible with the integrity of the new Czechoslovak state.[2]

Hitler had no affection for the multinational democratic republic. Its existence was a living contradiction of the pan-Germanism which was at the heart of Nazi philosophy. It stood in the way of eastwards expansion and, through its alliances with France and the Soviet Union, threatened the security of the Nazi state. By November 1937 the Führer had decided

---

[1] One of the most useful recent books on Munich, Robert Kee, *Munich: The Eleventh Hour* (1988), ch. 6, provides a concise history of the tensions which had dogged relations between Czechs and German-speakers during the time of the Austro-Hungarian empire and after its collapse.   [2] Ibid. 124–33.

that the moment for the destruction of Czechoslovakia would arrive either when it was obvious that internal divisions in France rendered that country unable to fulfil its commitments or in the event of a Franco-British conflict with Italy in the Mediterranean.[3] All the same, Hitler did not take a close interest in the Sudeten issue until after the *Anschluss*, whose strategic effect had been to weaken Czechoslovakia by turning its frontier. Thereafter he effectively took control of the Sudeten German Party and turned it into an instrument of Nazi foreign policy. Relations between the Sudeteners and the Czech government deteriorated rapidly throughout the spring as Nazi *agents provocateurs* invented 'atrocities' and provoked violent clashes with the police. Hitler now had a pretext for interference in the affairs of Czechoslovakia, and during the summer of 1938 Nazi diplomacy made much of the supposedly miserable plight of the Sudeteners while at the same time Berlin secretly prepared for invasion.[4]

The situation in Czechoslovakia was a cause of deep concern to the French and British governments because it contained the seeds of another European war. The French were directly in the firing-line as a result of the 1924 treaty by which they were committed to war with Germany in the event of it invading Czechoslovakia. In addition, the Czechs had in 1935 signed a treaty of mutual assistance with the Soviet Union, although this could only be invoked if the French stood by their 1924 agreement. The British had no obligations to Czechoslovakia but they were pledged under the Locarno Pact to guarantee the French frontier against unprovoked aggression. It followed that the British could be dragged into war as a result of the chain of events likely to unfold following conflict between the Germans and the Czechs.[5]

London was determined to avoid such an eventuality. The British government did not believe it had the means to prevent Germany taking the Sudetenland by force. In March 1938 the chiefs of staff told Chamberlain that:

No pressure that we and our possible Allies can bring to bear, either by sea, or land or in the air, could prevent Germany from invading and overrunning Bohemia and from inflicting a decisive defeat on the Czechoslovak Army. We should then be faced with the necessity of undertaking a war against Germany for the purpose of restoring Czechoslovakia's lost integrity and this object would only be achieved by the defeat of Germany and as the outcome of a prolonged struggle.[6]

---

[3] Kee, *Munich*, 104–5.   [4] Ibid. 138; 148–50.
[5] Ibid. 109–110; Taylor, *English History*, 520.
[6] Quoted in Bond, *British Military Policy*, 277.

As if this scenario was not grim enough, the chiefs of staff went on to warn that a European conflict might well be globalized, given the likelihood of Japanese and Italian intervention on the side of Germany.[7]

In fact there was no hard evidence to suggest that a war over Czechoslovakia might turn world-wide. Whatever the Japanese might have done, the Italians were keen to avoid a European conflagration. It is true that Anglo-Italian relations had deteriorated after 1936 as a result of British unease about the aggression against Abyssinia and the intervention of Italian 'volunteers' in Spain. Earlier in 1938, however, Chamberlain and Halifax had gone to considerable trouble to mend fences. On 16 April an Anglo-Italian agreement was signed. This committed Mussolini to withdrawal from Spain in return for British recognition of the Italian conquest of Abyssinia. The resulting diplomatic thaw was to give Chamberlain the influence to call on Mussolini's services as a mediator when it seemed as if the Germans were intent on war over the Sudetenland: the result was the Four-Power Munich Conference.[8]

Yet there was a military case for avoiding conflict. First, it became clear at the height of the crisis in September that the Dominions would not go to war for Czechoslovakia and that, if Britain fought, the Imperial unity of 1914–18 would be absent. This would not be particularly significant in terms of manpower available for a war in Europe, but it did threaten to leave Britain strategically exposed in the event of hostilities occurring in the Middle East and in the Far East.[9]

Secondly, the British discovered that French strategic plans were extremely vague, a state of affairs which reflected the bitterness and division in French society. 'Better Hitler than Blum' was a popular slogan on the French Right, where the veteran leader of the Popular Front administration in power during 1936–7 was regarded with distaste. Blum's government had embarked upon an ambitious rearmament programme before collapsing as a result of a financial crisis, in part at least politically motivated and resolved by its successor in a strictly orthodox fashion. In consequence, the defence programme was cut back and full production of many new French weapons did not start until 1938 or, in the case of aircraft, 1939. There had to be a question-mark over the performance

---

[7] Ibid. 277–8.

[8] See Sidney Aster, 'Guilty Men: The Case of Neville Chamberlain', in Robert Boyce and Esmonde M. Robertson (eds.), *Paths to War: New Essays on the Origins of the Second World War* (Basingstoke, 1989), 247; Kee, *Munich*, 195.

[9] See Ritchie Ovendale, *Appeasement and the English-Speaking World: Britain, the United States, the Dominions and the Policy of Appeasement* (Cardiff, 1975); and 'Why the British Dominions Declared War', in Boyce and Robertson (eds.), *Paths to War*, 269–96.

of the French in a war with Germany, a function both of inadequate preparation and of the schism in French society.[10]

Thirdly, there was no reassurance to be gained from the prospect of
Soviet intervention. Neither the British nor the French governments had
ideological sympathy for the Soviet Union and were unclear about the
true aims of Soviet foreign policy. The French foreign minister, George
Bonnet, argued that the Soviet Union wanted 'to stir up a general war
in the troubled waters of which she will fish'.[11] The real difficulty for the
British and the French was, however, caused by Stalin. A series of dev-
astating purges had just swept through the Red Army, resulting in the
trial and execution on charges of espionage and treason of an estimated 65
per cent of all higher ranking officers.[12] Among the victims were three out
of five Soviet marshals, including the most senior, Marshal Tukachevsky.
So great an upheaval left western governments wondering what the Soviet forces would be capable of anyway—even if they managed to reach
Czechoslovakia, given the refusal of Polish and Romanian administrations
to allow them right of transit. Any help from the Soviet Union would
therefore have had to come from the air.[13] The result of all this was that
throughout the crisis the British and French ignored the repeated affir-
mations of Soviet Foreign Minister Litvinov that the Soviet Union would
honour its commitments to Czechoslovakia if the French did the same.[14]
These perceptions of Dominion intentions, French irresolution, and Soviet weakness reinforced the gloomy appraisal of British resources with
which Chamberlain had been furnished by his chiefs of staff. At the same
time the government was deriving from intelligence reports what was
in fact an exaggerated picture of German power on land and in the air.
On the basis of such evidence Chamberlain concluded that war could
not be risked nor even seriously threatened, notwithstanding the formidable Czech defences, because of the inadequacy of the forces ranged
against Hitler.[15] The policy of appeasement was not meant to be a one-
way street; it depended upon Britain possessing a military capacity large

---

[10] David E. Kaiser, *Economic Diplomacy and the Origins of the Second World War* (Princeton,
NJ, 1980), 204.   [11] Kee, *Munich*, 146.
[12] Ibid. 147; Taylor, *English History*, 510.   [13] Kee, *Munich*, 147.
[14] Ibid. 146. There is no reason to doubt the sincerity of the Soviets on this point.
Whether they ever believed that the French would fight in the first place is, however,
another question.
[15] This is the argument of W. K. Wark, *The Ultimate Enemy: British Intelligence and
Nazi Germany 1933–1939* (1985). See also Bond, *British Military Policy*, 277–8; and Kaiser,
Economic Diplomacy and the Origins of the Second World War, 227–9.

and threatening enough to deter Hitler from using force to settle German grievances. The trouble in 1938 was that the British did not believe they possessed a credible deterrent at this stage, and as a result could not afford to call Hitler's bluff.[16]

In consequence, when Hitler finally activated the crisis by demanding the Sudetenland and rejecting all Czech attempts to achieve a settlement based on autonomy within the Republic Chamberlain was determined to let the French and the Soviets know that Britain would not fight as long as the handover was peaceful. Prague came under tremendous pressure to cede the territory and finally cracked in September. But war loomed all the same, because it seemed as if Hitler was intent on aggression anyway. Apparently he knew that the British would never fight to preserve Czechoslovak integrity, having been so informed by his foreign minister, Ribbentrop. Ribbentrop had been the German ambassador in London in 1937 and during that time had made a number of influential high-level contacts, amongst them the Duke and Duchess of Kent, whose intelligence was now exceedingly useful.[17] Desperate to avoid being pushed over the brink, Chamberlain flew to meet the Führer and finally, at the Munich Conference, succeeded in persuading him that he could have all he wanted peacefully. The dismemberment of the Czechoslovak Republic followed swiftly.

Although there was a respectable strategic case against war in September 1938, there is some evidence to suggest that the British would have avoided confrontational diplomacy even if they had believed the balance of forces to have been more favourable. The Chamberlain government regarded the Sudeten issue as one of the anomalies created by Versailles whose removal could be part of a general European settlement. Halifax had pointed this out to Hitler as early as November 1937, and Chamberlain had told his sister shortly afterwards, 'I don't see why we shouldn't say to the Germans give us satisfactory assurances that you won't use force to deal with the Austrians and Czechoslovakians and we will give you similar assurances that we won't use force to prevent the

---

[16] This point is conceded by Aster in 'Guilty Men', 243 and 256, although the essay is hostile to Chamberlain. See also Simon Newman, *March 1939: The British Guarantee to Poland* (Oxford, 1976), 58–61.

[17] PRO FO 371/21665, C14252/62/18, letter from Horace Rumbold to Orme Sargent, 19 Nov. 1938, referring to a recent conversation with the former chancellor of Germany, Bruning. Bruning had gone on: 'the Nazis were very well informed, through their numerous spies in this country, about the political situation here as well as through indiscretions on the part of Englishmen in responsible positions.'

changes you want if you can get them by peaceful means'.[18] In fact Chamberlain did not expect Hitler's method of 'dealing with' the Austrians to include *Anschluss*. But this shock did not lead him or his colleagues to alter their attitude towards the Sudeten question. It is therefore hard to believe that Britain would ever have fought to defend a principle—the territorial integrity of the new Czechoslovak Republic—which it did not acknowledge.[19]

For the British government, not only were there no moral issues at stake in the Czech crisis: there were no strategic ones either. Despite some loose talk from Sir Alexander Cadogan,[20] permanent secretary to the Foreign Office, there was no support for the establishment of a German empire which would embrace all central and eastern Europe, including the Ukraine. Exclusive access to the raw materials and food resources available in so vast a politico-economic bloc, including above all grain and oil, would render the Reich invulnerable. It would then be in a position to dominate the European continent, immune both to diplomatic persuasion and to blockade in the event of a conflict. British security would be threatened by the collapse of a European balance of power, and it would not be possible to reconstruct this by a strategy of appeasement based on deterrence and *détente*.[21] On the other hand, the Chamberlain administration believed that there was no alternative to German political and economic hegemony over eastern and central Europe—on condition first, that it must not be established by force, and secondly, that it eschewed autarky and recognized the commercial interests of other states.[22] There was, therefore, no reason to assume that Hitler's ambitions concerning the Sudeteners represented a danger to British interests as long as their fulfilment took place within these parameters. Such views were not confined to Chamberlain and his advisers. They represented the

[18] Quoted in Kaiser, *Economic Diplomacy and the Origins of the Second World War*, 194.

[19] Kee, *Munich*, 122.

[20] Shortly after Munich Cadogan argued that Britain should 'let Germany, if she can, find her "Lebensraum" and establish herself, if she can, as a peaceful economic unit' (quoted in Wark, *The Ultimate Enemy*, 212). The juxtaposition of 'Lebensraum' with 'peaceful economic unit', however, indicates that Cadogan had as yet no real understanding of what was involved in the concept.

[21] This view is developed by Newman, *March 1939*. Newman, however, takes the argument too far, stating that the British Government wanted the maintenance of the *status quo* in eastern Europe. There is very little justification indeed for such an interpretation of British strategy at any point in the period from 1937 to 1939.

[22] See Kaiser, *Economic Diplomacy and the Origins of the Second World War*, 228; and D. N. Lammers, 'Fascism, Communism and the Foreign Office', *Journal of Contemporary History*, 6 (1971), 66–86.

accepted wisdom within the Foreign Office and were challenged by only a very small minority of officials, notably Sir Robert Vansittart and Laurence Collier, who did not believe that Hitler had any long-term interest in the maintenance of peace.[23]

Yet Munich represented something more than a recognition of the realities of power in modern Europe. It was also founded on the notion that Nazism, however unpleasant and imperialistic, was in the end no more than the expression of frustrated nationalism. Although Chamberlain was certainly suspicious of its ultimate objectives, he did not believe there was enough evidence to confirm the pessimistic view, expressed by Sir Robert Vansittart and by Churchill and his Focus group, that Nazism meant war. He took the view that reason would prevail in Berlin and that Hitler's signature to the Munich Agreement was proof of this. The government therefore saw Munich as the prelude to 'that final appeasement of Europe in the era after Versailles for which British foreign policy had striven so long'.[24] Chamberlain's policy was backed by *The Times* and the *Round Table*, the latter arguing in September 1938 that the *status quo* represented an 'injustice'.[25] It followed that the Munich Agreement embodied the application of justice to international relations, both in its recognition of the rights of the Sudeteners and the claims of Germany and in its method of solving international disputes through negotiation.

The establishment of international 'justice' was essential to peace, which in turn was the pre-condition of prosperity. Indeed, the settlement of the Sudeten question on terms acceptable to Hitler was regarded as a continuation of the attempt to build a world safe for liberal capitalism which had started with the rejection of social imperialism and corporatism in 1918–20. In a private conversation with Hitler on 27 September, Chamberlain's chief industrial adviser and confidant, Sir Horace Wilson, suggested that once the Sudetener issue had been peacefully resolved 'there were many things which ought to be discussed between England and Germany to the great advantage of both countries. He would not waste time by enumerating these matters, but they included arrangements for improving the economic position all-round. He himself and many other Englishmen would like to reach an Agreement with Germany on these lines.'[26] Munich represented the political half of a project whose inspiration was essentially Cobdenite. Anglo-German political and economic

---

[23] Kaiser, *Economic Diplomacy and the Origins of World War Two*, 260.
[24] Kee, *Munich*, 154.   [25] Quigley, *The Anglo-American Establishment*, 291.
[26] PRO FO 371/21741, C10822/1941/18, record of a conversation with Hitler on 27 Sept. 1938, by Sir Horace Wilson.

co-operation would generate the confidence essential to an expansion of global trade and investment. It was intended to be the first step in the creation of an international environment which would sustain continuing recovery from the Depression in a manner compatible with the mainten-ance of the *status quo* in British society. By contrast, the prime minister believed that a policy of confrontation would have precipitated a political crisis and the formation of 'a Left-Wing National Government' dedicated to a provocative foreign policy and 'far-reaching Socialist legislation at home'. It was not surprising that share prices in the City rose sharply when the Munich Agreement was announced, nor that Chamberlain received a congratulatory telegram from the Stock Exchange.[27]

None the less, it has been argued that the main purpose of the Munich Agreement was to provide Britain with more time to rearm, so that the country was in a better position to fight when war came in Septem-ber 1939 than it could possibly have been in October 1938.[28] Problems exist with this theory, quite apart from the fact that Nazi Germany had another year to build up its military capability, soon to be enhanced by the arms produced at the Czech Skoda Works, for a war to establish *Lebensraum* and the unchallenged domination of Europe.[29] Certainly, Chamberlain expressed a determination to press on with rearmament after Munich,[30] and to this end the programme of investment in the air force, above all in radar, fighters, and heavy bombers, was accelerated.

---

[27] For the behaviour of the Stock Exchange see the *Financial News*, 30 Sept. 1938. For Chamberlain's anxiety about the politico-economic implications of a failure at Munich see 'The Crisis in Retrospect: Industry and Foreign Policy', Box 3 Folder 7, Kenneth de Courcy papers, Hoover Institute of War, Revolution and Peace, University of Stanford, California. Kenneth de Courcy was at this time secretary to the Imperial Policy Group (IPG), an association of Conservative MPs and peers established to lobby for a policy of 'imperial isolationism'. But de Courcy was in addition an MI6 agent and one of Chamberlain's unofficial advisers, using his overseas trips for the IPG as exercises in the collection of covert information and gossip. The memorandum on 'The Crisis in Retrospect' was written for Chamberlain, and a covering note described it as 'his explanation' (personal information from de Courcy). For more on de Courcy see John Costello, *Ten Days that Saved the West*, app. 11.
[28] See R. A. Butler, *The Art of the Possible* (1972). Butler was parliamentary under-secretary of state to the Foreign Office at the time. He was a passionate advocate of appeasement. See Paul Stafford, 'R. A. Butler at the Foreign Office, 1938–1939: Political Autobiography and the Art of the Plausible', *Historical Journal*, 28 (1983), 901–22.
[29] See Richard Lamb, *The Drift to War, 1922–1939* (1989), 265–6; and Richard Overy, 'Hitler's War Plans and the German Economy', in Boyce and Robertson (eds.), *Paths to War*, 112–13.
[30] After Munich Chamberlain said British policy was to 'drive two horses abreast: con-ciliation and rearmament'. See Ovendale, 'Why the British Dominions Declared War', in Boyce and Robertson (eds.), *Paths to War*, 287.

The government, however, continued to resist demands for the establishment of a Ministry of Supply, and Chamberlain dismissed calls for the introduction of conscription. The prime minister argued that there was no parallel between 1938 and 1914, and as a result there was no need to contemplate 'the equipment of an army on a continental scale'.[31] In strategic terms, therefore, these measures represented no deviation from the well-established policy of deterrence. If the Agreement was intended to gain time, it was time to build up British defences and offensive bombing capacity to the point at which Hitler would be forced to concede that war was at best futile and at worst counter-productive. The point of the exercise was not to postpone war but to avoid it.[32]

Economic Appeasement (1): Trade and Payments

The British did follow the Munich Agreement with a series of initiatives designed to achieve Anglo-German economic *détente*. They believed that there was some urgency about this in view of disturbing reports emanating from the Embassy in Berlin. Ambassador Henderson said that the combined effects of the *Anschluss* and the mobilization during the Czech crisis had put a severe strain on the German economy. In addition, it appeared as if the Balkan states were prepared to resist German efforts at an expansion of trade unless the barter method was abandoned. But if German foreign-exchange difficulties were intensifying there was little prospect of a move to liberalization: it therefore appeared as if there was serious risk of another European diplomatic crisis unless steps were taken to inject hard currency into the Reich.[33]

Aware of the reports, Sir Frederick Leith-Ross put a proposal for European economic co-operation to a German trade delegation passing through London in October. He suggested that Germany's payments agreements, not just with Britain but also with France and Holland, should be revised. For example, after the amendments to the Anglo-German Agreement made earlier in the year, Germany was entitled to spend 60 per cent of her income from exports to Britain on British goods. The rest continued to be devoted to purchases on the world market and to debt service. Leith-Ross's idea was that Germany should be allocated an extra

---

[31] See Bond, 'British Military Policy', 287–9.

[32] Sir Horace Wilson explained, 'our policy was never designed just to postpone war, or enable us to enter war more united. The aim of appeasement was to avoid war altogether, for all time.' Quoted in Aster, 'Guilty Men', 250.

[33] See MacDonald, 'Economic Appeasement', 106.

25 per cent of the free foreign exchange, which could then be spent on imports from the Balkan states.[34] At a stroke the causes of tension between the Reich and the governments in south-eastern Europe would be removed. The scheme was designed, in addition, to stimulate British trade: Balkan states would use the currency to buy British and colonial imports which they needed but could not obtain under the prevailing system of bilateralism. It was an initiative which linked the wellbeing of the domestic economy to the establishment of a peaceful and more open international order.[35]

There has, however, been some disagreement about the true meaning of this policy. Newman has argued that the initiative was part of a policy designed not to recognize but to contain German expansion in eastern Europe. Back in June Halifax had supported the establishment of an Interdepartmental Committee on South-East Europe which was intended to co-ordinate economic aid to the region. The idea was not 'to create an anti-German bloc' but to provide what Halifax called an alternative '*point d'appui*' for the Balkan states.[36] Strategic issues were involved. As gateway to the Middle East, Turkey, for example, had to be protected from German hegemony. The same was true of Romania, where Nazi access to reserves of grain and oil would weaken the effect of an economic blockade. In fact, prior to Munich the only notable achievement had been the provision of a £16 million credit for Turkey, £6 million of which was earmarked for the purchase of warships. This had been approved in May, before the creation of the Interdepartmental Committee. After Munich, however, Chamberlain agreed to the purchase of 200,000 tons of wheat from Romania, having been warned that a forthcoming visit from the German economics minister Funk might lead to the elimination of British trade from that country.[37] The injection of convertible currency into the Balkan economies has therefore to be seen as a part of a conscious attempt to reduce their dependence on Germany and allow them to look further afield for imports—which was why Leith-Ross's idea failed to provoke a response from Berlin.[38]

[34] See Kaiser, *Economic Diplomacy and the Origins of the Second World War*, 287–8; MacDonald, 'Economic Appeasement', 106; Newman, *March 1939*, 37.

[35] Cain and Hopkins, *Crisis and Deconstruction*, 98 ff; MacDonald, 'Economic Appeasement', 106; B. J. Wendt, '"Economic Appeasement"—A Crisis Strategy', in Mommsen and Kettenacker (eds.), *The Fascist Challenge and the Policy of Appeasement* (1983), 163 f.

[36] PRO CAB 24/280, CP 257 (38), 'Central and South-East Europe: Implications of the Anschluss', 10 Nov. 1938; Newman, *March 1939*, 46–8.

[37] Kaiser, *Economic Diplomacy and the Origins of the Second World War*, 249–50, for Turkey; 290–3, for south-east Europe.   [38] Newman, *March 1939*, 57.

Newman's argument is based on a misunderstanding of British policy. There had never been any serious question of British acquiescence in a German monopoly of central and east European trade and payments. Quite apart from the strategic implications of such a development, it flew in the face of a macroeconomic economic policy in which recovery was dependent on the expansion of export markets. All the same, it had repeatedly been made clear that Britain recognized German economic predominance in the area. Chamberlain himself acknowledged it when speaking in the House of Commons at the start of November.[39] In January 1939 Montagu Norman stressed his belief that south-east Europe was 'a natural field for the development of German trade'.[40] The following month Leith-Ross stressed the importance of trying to 'get the Germans to understand what we are after, i.e. that we are not trying to oust them from that market but to keep a share in it and to help support their economic and financial structure. This must ultimately be in the German interest too, and the only question is how far we can go without competing with them.'[41] This point was repeated by Ashton-Gwatkin when he saw Wiehl, head of the Economic Department at the German Foreign Office, shortly afterwards.[42] Clearly, therefore, British policy was not aimed at the containment of German economic expansion. Rather, the objective was the same as it had been when colonial concessions were being discussed earlier in the year. The British government hoped to encourage the 'moderates' within the Nazi regime to take control of the economy and liberalize it. Ministers and civil servants continued to believe that Germany's difficulties were caused by a shortage of raw materials. If this could be remedied, by an injection of hard currency if not by a redistribution of colonies, it would be possible for the Reich 'to take her place among the countries with free and relatively stable currencies'[43] and complete the Cobdenite agenda whose implementation had started at Munich.

The attempt to strike an Anglo-German economic deal on the basis of Leith-Ross's proposal came to nothing. The German response was slow. It took the best part of three months for the Economics Ministry to deliver a rejection, apparently on the grounds that Germany's

[39] Kaiser, *Economic Diplomacy and the Origins of the Second World War*, 287.

[40] PRO FO 371/23000, C469/32/18, note by Ashton-Gwatkin of a conversation with Norman, 15 Jan. 1939.

[41] PRO FO 371/22950, C2105/8/18, minute by Leith-Ross on a proposed visit by Ashton-Gwatkin to Germany, 14 Feb. 1939.

[42] PRO FO 371/22950, C2345/8/18, Ashton-Gwatkin's record of talks with Ribbentrop, Max von Hohenlohe-Langenberg, and Wiehl, Feb. 1939.

[43] PRO FO 371/22950, C2345/8/18, report by Ashton-Gwatkin, Feb. 1939.

fundamental difficulty was the generation of enough foreign exchange from exports to service debts.[44] Convertible currency to pay for imports was, therefore, irrelevant. The only indication of the way the wind was blowing in Berlin came with the barbarities of *Kristallnacht* on 12 November, an event which provoked disgust in Britain and led to a hiatus in Anglo-German discussions. Even Chamberlain wondered whether Hitler could be controlled by the 'moderates'. Nevertheless, the prime minister did not abandon hope and at the end of November agreed to discussions between Montagu Norman and Hjalmar Schacht.[45]

The talks occurred in London and Berlin, either side of Christmas and the New Year. When in London Schacht met not only Norman but Leith-Ross and Ashton-Gwatkin. Discussions ranged across a broad area, covering Jewish emigration, trade negotiations, and events in the Far East. But Schacht stressed that the main issue he wanted to raise concerned the future direction of the German economy. Was Britain 'interested in the restoration of a free system of currency in Germany?' If the answer was positive London should be prepared to consider either a loan of between RM 500 million and RM 1,000 million (at a rate of RM $12 = £1$) to cushion the German economy from the impact of liberalization or a reduction in the rate of interest on foreign debts. Leith-Ross confirmed British support for decontrol, but argued that British creditors had already accepted lower interest rates and any further cuts would be bad for them and for German credit.[46]

The possibility of financial assistance was not, however, dismissed by London. When Norman went to Berlin he saw Schacht privately and in the company of other Reichsbank directors. Norman favoured a remodelling of the Payments Agreement 'on more liberal principles', and to this end proposed a scheme not unlike Leith-Ross's earlier suggestion, with Germany enjoying 'more freedom in buying in and through the UK, in which case a much greater amount of finance wd [*sic*] naturally become available for her in London'.[47] Norman made it clear that British willingness to take such an initiative would have to be dependent on German

[44] Kaiser, *Economic Diplomacy and the Origins of the Second World World War*, 289.

[45] MacDonald, 'Economic Appeasement', 120–1.

[46] There is an account of the December talks in London in PRO T 188/227, memorandum by Leith-Ross, 15 Dec. 1938. Norman's contact with Schacht on this occasion is the subject of Bank of England file G1/418, but the papers here are extremely uninformative. Norman told interested parties that Schacht's visit was private, involving no business, concerned only with general issues and the 'question of German refugees'.

[47] PRO FO 371/23000, C469/32/18, note by Ashton-Gwatkin following conversation with Norman, 15 Jan. 1939.

agreement to cut down expenditure on armaments.[48] Norman's visit was dressed up as a private one, but this was only for public consumption. The reality was that, by giving his approval to the mission, Chamberlain had made Norman's offer of a new Anglo-German financial deal central to the attempt to reduce international tension.[49]

The belief in German willingness to exchange economic controls for financial assistance was not universal. The commercial attaché in Berlin, Magowan, had argued in December that the Nazis were using the Payments Agreement to purchase raw materials essential to their rearmament programme. The Nazi regime was deeply hostile to Britain and there was no chance of lasting *détente*. In consequence, the Payments Agreement was positively harmful to British interests and should be denounced.[50] During the course of a debate which lasted for nearly three months Magowan had little support. He was backed by Mason-MacFarlane, the military attaché in Berlin, and by Roger Makins in the Central Department of the Foreign Office.[51] But the consensus in the Treasury, the Board of Trade, the Bank of England, and the City, as well as in the Foreign Office, was that no good purpose would be served by terminating the 'Anglo-German connection'.

A number of reasons were commonly cited for soldiering on. First, there was the question of exports, which the government was keen to encourage. Quite apart from the general significance of the German market to British companies, it was especially lucrative for exporters of herrings and of finished and semi-finished textiles. Above all, it was a magnet for British coal: by the start of 1939 sales of coal from Britain to Germany took up 20 per cent of the sterling exchange available under the terms of the Payments Agreement.[52] Government concern to foster the recovery of the staple industries guaranteed that the Board of Trade, responsible for industrial policy, would not support any diplomatic gesture which disrupted Anglo-German economic relations. Not

[48] PRO FO 371/23000, C469/32/18, note by Ashton-Gwatkin, 15 Jan. 1939.
[49] See Bank of England file G1/419, covering Norman's visit to Berlin in Jan. 1939. It is not much more informative than its predecessor, except that, first, Norman himself admitted that the contacts with Schacht were 'intended as a first step towards re-establishing contacts between Berlin and London—which had been completely lacking for months past'; and secondly, a pencilled note by 'RC' on 10 Jan. stated that the governor had seen the Reichsbank directors and had discussed the Standstill debts with them.
[50] See MacDonald, 'Economic Appeasement', 121.
[51] PRO FO 371/22951, C2828/8/18, 'Possible effect of economic concessions made by GB to Germany', 3 Mar. 1939.
[52] PRO FO 371/22951, C2861/8/18, memorandum on British exports to Germany, 9 Mar. 1939.

surprisingly, it made clear its opposition to 'any tampering with the Payments Agreement'.[53]

Secondly, the Bank, the Treasury, and the Foreign Office Economic Section were all preoccupied with the importance of maintaining debt-service arrangements for the benefit of 'certain London houses'.[54] Driven by Magowan's claims to justify the arrangement from the perspective of national security, Sir Frederick Phillips argued that termination of the Payments Agreement would 'impede the war preparations of this country'.[55] This argument was initially raised by Leith-Ross, who suggested that under the Agreement Germany was paying 'tribute': about 'one quarter' of its sterling revenues from sales to Britain was devoted to the financing of short and long-term debts. If Germany were able to export the same goods to non-creditors it could realize their full value in imports. So the Payments Agreement weakened Germany, strengthened Britain, and satisfied 'financial morality' at the same time.[56]

The weakness of such arguments was confirmed by Bank of England statistics which showed that German imports from Britain during the second half of 1938 were £2.2 million in excess of the margin allowed for in the Agreement.[57] A report on Anglo-German trade which was circulated within the Foreign Office showed conclusively that the Germans were using the sterling allowed to them under the terms of the Agreement to purchase 'strategic raw materials', highlighting 'copper and other non-ferrous metals; all kinds of scrap, especially iron, other metals, rags, paper and rubber'.[58] There can be little doubt that one source of the government's reluctance to change, let alone denounce, the Payments Agreement was its concern for the welfare of the acceptance houses, as both Norman and Leith-Ross made clear. Prospects of debt repayment by the Germans in 'any measurable time' may have been poor, but at least the Agreement provided leading merchant banks with cash in the form of interest payments and at the same time allowed them to transfer what would otherwise have been losses to the credit side of their accounts.[59]

[53] PRO FO 371/22950, C2581/8/18, minute of 15 Mar. 1939.

[54] This phrase was used by one of the opponents (name illegible) of the Payments Agreement's continuation in a comment recorded in PRO FO 371/22950, C959/8/18, Feb. 1939.   [55] PRO FO 371/22950, C1719/8/18, minute by Phillips, 2 Mar. 1939.

[56] PRO FO 371/22950, C959/8/18, memorandum by Leith-Ross on the future of the Payments Agreement, 24 Jan. 1939.

[57] Bank of England file OV34/206/1170/2, memorandum by the Overseas and Foreign Department, 25 Jan. 1939.

[58] PRO FO 371/22951, C2861/8/18, report on British exports to Germany, 9 Mar. 1939.

[59] See PRO FO 371/22950, C959/8/18, memoranda on the future of the Anglo-German Payments Agreement, 24 Jan. 1939; and PRO FO 371/23000, C469/32/18, note of conversation with Norman by Ashton-Gwatkin, 15 Jan. 1939.

Related to the argument from what Leith-Ross called 'financial moral-ity' was the government's diplomatic purpose in searching for Anglo-German appeasement. As long as there was a Payments Agreement Germany was engaged with the outside world. Its continuation was a sign that the autarkic trend was not irreversible; its machinery pro-vided an institutional mechanism for returning to economic liberalism. Therefore, given the British government's assumption that decontrol and the rise of the 'moderates' associated with such a policy could be taken as evidence of a decision for peace in Berlin, it was accepted that termination of the Payments Agreement 'would be difficult to reconcile with a policy of attempting to improve political relations between this country and Germany'.[60]

This was why the dismissal of Schacht on 20 January 1939 provoked consternation but no change in British policy, despite his almost totemic significance up until that point. In March Tiarks went to Germany to meet his replacement, the current minister for economics Dr Walter Funk, a party man who had served under Schacht at the Reichsbank. Although Funk hardly possessed as impeccable a 'moderate' pedigree as his predecessor, Tiarks (whose first concern was, after all, the interests of the short-term creditors) pronounced himself 'extremely satisfied'. He was encouraged by Funk's apparent willingness to consider both the repayment of at least some credit lines, albeit the ones whose original commercial purpose had expired, and the gradual removal of exchange controls.[61] This was enough to leave Tiarks looking forward to the re-establishment of 'free and active relations . . . between German banks and industry and their London counterparts' in the near future, and he re-turned confident that reason was at last prevailing in Berlin.[62]

Tiarks's mission was well received in the Foreign Office. Funk had made all the signals London had been looking for. As Tiarks pointed out, the man's status in the Nazi Party gave him a credibility with the regime which Schacht, it now appeared, had not possessed for some time. There seemed a good chance that in Funk the British government might have found a conduit to Hitler who was a genuine insider. The conciliatory line on the Standstill debts and exchange controls was taken as evidence that Funk 'might do something useful and is worth cultivating', and

[60] PRO FO 371/22950, C17179/8/18, minute by Phillips, 2 Mar. 1939.

[61] PRO FO 371/23001, C2859/32/18, report by Tiarks on the German economic situ-ation, 8 Mar. 1939.

[62] Tiarks quoted in R. Roberts, 'Frank Cyril Tiarks', entry in D. Jeremy and C. Shaw (eds.), *Dictionary of Business Biography*, vol. 5, *S–Z* (1986); PRO FO 371/23001, C2859/32/18, report by Tiarks.

created hope that the economic counterpart to Munich would soon be settled. The optimistic atmosphere was enough to convince Ashton-Gwatkin that it was not worth taking the deterioration of German relations with the rump state of Czechoslovakia 'too tragically', a matter of days before Nazi troops were marching through Prague.[63]

Economic Appeasement (2): An Anglo–German Industrial *Détente*?

The discussions on trade and payments were paralleled by trade negotiations between the industrial federations of the two countries. The British government encouraged the contacts which were intended to result in agreements beneficial both to British exports and to the prospects of peace. The results were encouraging, and by the middle of March 1939 the prospect of an Anglo-German industrial partnership did not seem too far fetched.

Interest on the part of London in an industrial *détente* in fact went back to the summer of 1938, when the government was becoming concerned about the international economic climate and its increasingly hostile environment for British exports. During the second half of 1937 exporters had faced the consequences of the 'Roosevelt recession'. Their difficulties were intensified by the autarkic policies of the Nazi state, whose commercial practices were characterized both by the official encouragement of bilateral trade deals and by generous subsidies for exports. In September 1938 representatives from the FBI complained to the Board of Trade and to the Department of Overseas Trade that existing industrial agreements, designed to fix prices and guarantee market shares, were being undermined in third markets.[64] British goods on the Continent and particularly in Latin America were being priced out of what had been lucrative markets. Thus, exports to central and eastern Europe fell from 10 per cent of all in 1929 to 8.6 per cent in 1937, while between 1935 and 1938 exports to Latin America dropped from 36.6 per cent of all to 33 per cent.[65] Worst hit were producers of textiles, iron and steel, and

[63] Views of Tiarks and all quotations in this paragraph taken from PRO FO 371/23001, C2859/32/18, report by Tiarks and minute by Ashton-Gwatkin, 8 Mar. 1939.

[64] PRO FO 371/23986, W1049/173/50, 'Decline of British Export Trade, June–September 1938'; R. F. Holland, 'The Federation of British Industries and the International Economy', 1929–39, *Economic History Review*, 2nd ser., 34/2 (1981), 294–5.

[65] Newton, 'The "Anglo-German Connection"', 193.

non-ferrous metals, whose lower overseas sales accounted for over 80 per cent of a £52.4 million drop in domestic exports between 1937 and 1938.[66] Unemployment had peaked at the end of 1937, but during the first half of 1938 its reduction (of 0.3 per cent, to 12.9 per cent of the work-force) was barely noticeable.[67]

How was this disturbing trend in export and employment figures to be reversed? Imperial Preference was an inappropriate vehicle for the expansion of exports. Nor was sterling devaluation seriously considered. Its rate against the dollar slipped during the year, from £1 = $5.02 to £1 = $4.67, largely as a consequence of the American recession although the international political situation and the import bill caused by rearmament were contributory factors.[68] Within both the American financial and business communities there had been throughout the 1930s considerable distrust for British trading practices. This centred on anxiety about the Ottawa system, which was seen as a device for discrimination against American exports to the British Commonwealth and Empire. Given this background of suspicion it is not surprising that sterling's depreciation was believed, albeit incorrectly, to have been engineered in order to achieve an edge in competitive markets.[69] In London, reluctance to provoke the Americans into a retaliatory devaluation combined with the financial and strategic need for a stable exchange rate to rule out the continuation of sterling's fall.[70] Thus, only one course of action remained: the management of international trade. In their meetings with the Board of Trade the FBI representatives had asked for protection from subsidized competition and tariff increases on imports from countries whose purchases of British goods were at consistently low levels, along with withdrawal of most-favoured-nation treatment from their governments. The Board of Trade's response was to accept the case for discriminatory tariff increases but suggest that the issue of subsidized competition in export markets could best be disposed of through both new cartel agreements between the industries of the competing countries and some tightening of the existing arrangements.[71] The FBI welcomed this suggestion, and indeed had already initiated discussions with its German opposite number, the *Reichsgruppe Industrie* (RI).[72] But it hoped for

[66] 'British Overseas Trade', *The Economist*, 134 (21 Jan. 1939), 113–14.

[67] For unemployment figures see *Statistical Abstract for the United Kingdom, 1913 and 1924 to 1937*, Table 127, pp. 142–3.   [68] See Peden, 'A Matter of Timing', 16–17.

[69] Cain and Hopkins, *Crisis and Deconstruction*, 102.   [70] Ibid.

[71] PRO FO 371/23986, W1049/173/50, Board of Trade memorandum, Sept. 1938.

[72] Holland, 'The Federation of British Industries and the International Economy', 297–8.

something more than verbal support for the well-established principle of 'voluntary reorganization' on an international scale.

In fact government backing for the international cartel had already passed this point. During the first half of 1938 the Foreign Office was warning diplomats not to disrupt existing international agreements in foreign countries but to check with the Department of Overseas Trade, which had a complete record of them, first.[73] Robert Hudson, the junior minister at the head of the Department, was strongly committed to the view that the state should intervene to assist British exporters. He was aware of the impact German subsidies were having, but argued that 'a fairly comprehensive understanding' could be achieved by the simple expedient of threatening a subsidy war which the Reich did not have the resources to pursue.[74] Walter Runciman, the president of the Board of Trade, backed Hudson and agreed to use his department's offices to orchestrate conversations between a wide range of British and German industries.[75]

An Anglo-German industrial partnership was the key to reviving exports. The need for such an agreement was dictated by the wide range of sectors where manufacturers from the two countries were competing in third countries, notwithstanding that international agreements already covered many of these. British producers of internal combustion engines, wire rope, telephone and electric cables, printing machinery, agricultural equipment, and pottery were particularly anxious to tighten the existing arrangements.[76] At the same time, the government itself took the view that coal exports would benefit from the establishment of a cartel arrangement.[77] After July 1938 what had been implicit in British economic policy for several months now became open: the need to revive a faltering recovery led to close co-operation between industry and the state in attempts not just to protect existing international cartel agreements

[73] PRO FO 371/21434, A4711/168/9, paper from Davies (Department of Overseas Trade) to Busk (Foreign Office), 14 June 1938. The file also includes the list of international cartel agreements in which British firms were participants.

[74] PRO BT 11/901, note from Hudson to Sir Nevile Henderson, Aug. 1938. See also PRO T 160/866/F15447/021/1, Anglo-German Commercial Negotiations, 1938–9, memorandum by Hudson, 8 July 1938.

[75] PRO T 160/866/F15447/021/2, memorandum by Magowan providing the background to the Dusseldorf Talks between the FBI and the RI, Mar. 1939.

[76] PRO FO 371/22950, C1719/8/18, note by Ashton-Gwatkin, 10 Feb. 1939.

[77] *Documents on German Foreign Policy, 1918–1945*, Series D (hereafter *DGFP*) (Washington, 1953), iv. 325–6, report from the German Economic Mission in Great Britain to the Foreign Ministry, 7 Nov. 1938.

involving British firms but to negotiate new ones in the name of 'orderly marketing'.

From the second half of 1938 the environment became increasingly favourable for Anglo–German industrial discussions. Enthusiasm for an agreement existed not just in London but in Berlin, where the Ministry of Economics was supporting requests from the RI for tariff reductions on German exports. In October Board of Trade officials were handed a list of thirty-four specific items by the same German delegation which had heard Leith-Ross's proposal for a revision of the Payments Agreement.[78] Ruter, leading the German delegation, argued that progress could be made if discussions between the RI and the FBI could be arranged by their respective governments.[79]

The conclusion of an Anglo–German Coal Agreement on 28 January 1939 gave momentum to this search for industrial *détente*. The British call for the establishment of an Anglo–German Coal Cartel had been made early in November. The facts and figures of the case were drawn up in a Board of Trade memorandum handed to the Germans. The document pointed out that sales of British coal on the world market had dropped by 20 per cent since 1933 while German sales had increased by 33 per cent. The ratio between the coal exports of the two countries had shifted from one of 5 : 3 in Britain's favour to 1 : 1 in the period 1933–7. The Board of Trade and the Mining Association of Great Britain (the trade organization of the colliery-owners) believed that one significant reason for this decline was German coal-export pricing policy: 'British coal prices from 1931 to 1936 remained at a figure of 16/- to 16/4d [80–2p] and rose in 1937 to 17/- [85p]; German coal prices decreased from RM 13.70 to RM 9.23. This could only have been achieved by an export subsidy, which must be described as uneconomical.' Price-cutting had resulted in contracts for the German producers to supply the Portuguese railways, electric power stations in Le Havre, and the Cokeries de la Seine. British coal was being driven out of both competitive markets and markets where it had hitherto occupied an unchallenged position. The consequences for employment and for Britain's trade balance with third countries were becoming serious.[80]

---

[78] PRO T 160/866, F15447/021/1, record of informal meeting, 17 Oct. 1938.
[79] Ibid.
[80] See *DGFP*, iv. no. 263, report summarizing Board of Trade paper by the German Economic Mission in Great Britain, 7 Nov. 1938. The figures must therefore be taken as British.

The talks between the Mining Association and its more tightly organized German opposite number, the Rhenish-Westphalian Coal Syndicate, were backed by the respective administrations. The British government had, through the Board of Trade, threatened a subsidy war 'with all its consequences'.[81] Rather than face such protective action the German delegates at the discussions consented to a deal which allocated to the two countries quotas of the total exports of all European coal-exporting countries. The agreement in fact included not only coal but coke, briquettes, and bunker coal and left Germany with a quota of 30 per cent and Britain with one of 50 per cent.[82]

Chamberlain's administration greeted the Coal Agreement with relief. It was the first material sign since Munich that the Nazi regime was prepared to approve of international agreements which were not wholly to Germany's advantage. More significantly from the point of view of the British government, it seemed to be an early indication that the 'moderates' still held a powerful position in the administration after the dismissal of Schacht. Even before this event there had been growing concern at Germany's failure to respond positively to British approaches. When Schacht lost his position after trying to talk Hitler out of an acceleration of the rearmament programme there was great anxiety in London. This escalated into alarm when the Foreign Office received a report from Carl Goerdeler, the conservative mayor of Leipzig and member of the anti-Nazi resistance, that Germany was planning to overrun the Low Countries and use them as a base for air and submarine warfare against Britain.[83] It seemed as if Hitler was preparing to go to war in order to overcome economic difficulties: as Ashton-Gwatkin commented, 'from the economic viewpoint he has chosen the way of despair that will almost certainly lead to violence'.[84] However, when the Coal Agreement was signed and then followed up on 30 January by a speech in which Hitler said that Germany 'must export or die', optimism began to return. Taken together, the Agreement and the speech confirmed a report on 24 January that iron and steel manufacturers had been ordered to accelerate the production of goods for export and slow down work on armaments. The indications were that Berlin had decided to take the peaceful route to resolution of the problems caused by shortages of raw materials: an

[81] See *DGFP*, iv. no. 258, report by the German Economic Mission in London, 7 Nov. 1938.
[82] See *DGFP*, iv. no. 303, Dirksen (German ambassador in Great Britain) to Foreign Ministry, 28 Jan. 1939.   [83] MacDonald, 'Economic Appeasement', 122.
[84] PRO FO 371/23000, C757/32/18, minute by Ashton-Gwatkin, 24 Jan. 1939.

expansion of exports in order to generate the income to finance essential imports.[85]

Having encouraged the talks leading to the Coal Agreement, the Chamberlain government now attempted to exploit what appeared to be an environment favourable to a resumption of the post-Munich drive for an all-embracing settlement with Germany. The opportunity was provided by the industrial discussions involving the FBI and the RI as well as the British and German governments. These culminated in the Dusseldorf Agreement negotiated by the two industrial organizations in March 1939. The Cabinet minister responsible for announcing it to parliament was Oliver Stanley, Runciman's successor as president of the Board of Trade: but the driving force was Hudson at the Department of Overseas Trade, whose enthusiasm for an Anglo-German industrial partnership surpassed even that of the FBI.[86]

Hudson, however, merely acted as a mouthpiece for a government which was becoming increasingly worried about the British domestic and external economic position. The weak export performance of 1938 was reflected in indifferent trade statistics (see Table 2.5 above) and a bad set of unemployment figures for January 1939, when the total rose to 2.032 million, or 14 per cent of the work-force.[87] At the same time the increasing demand for imports generated by rearmament put a strain on reserves of gold and foreign currency. Bank of England statistics reveal a dramatic swing from a net gain of £129 million in 1937 to a net loss of £258 million in 1938, close to one-third of the total figure at the start of the year.[88] During the decade as a whole there had only been one other year when an outflow had occurred—1931, when the figure had been a comparatively modest £34 million (see Table 4.1). A trade agreement with Germany would protect British exports, generate employment, and ease the threatening external position. London's international financial credibility would be preserved. Most of all, by satisfying the national economic interests of Britain and Germany it would create a climate of peaceful

[85] PRO FO 371/23000, C757/32/18, minute by Ashton-Gwatkin, 24 Jan. 1939; and C944/32/18, comment by Leith-Ross on a *Daily Express* report of 24 Jan. by the Berlin correspondent. This received apparent corroboration from H. A. Brassert, an Anglo-American businessman responsible for the construction of the Herman Goering Werke.

[86] *DGFP*, iv. no. 304, Dirksen to Wiehl, 30 Jan. 1939; Federation of British Industries Archive, Modern Records Centre, University of Warwick, MSS 200/f/1/1, minutes of the Executive Committee of the FBI, 8 Feb. 1939.

[87] MacDonald, 'Economic Appeasement', 124.

[88] See R. S. Sayers, *The Bank of England 1891–1944*, III, *Appendices* (Cambridge, 1976), app. 32, Table C.

TABLE 4.1. *Changes in the level of gold and foreign-exchange reserves, 1930–1938* (£ millions)

1930	1931	1932	1933	1934	1935	1936	1937	1938
+7	−34	+29	+122	+10	+79	+211	+129	−258

Source: R. S. Sayers, *The Bank of England, 1891–1944* (Cambridge, 1976), vol. 3, app. 32, Table C.

co-operation which might be the foundation of lasting prosperity. True, the basis of this *détente* would be the cartel rather than the free market: but its achievement would be a signal that Germany had abandoned autarky and replaced it with a commitment to engagement with the international economy.

At Dusseldorf the FBI and the RI put together a framework designed to prevent 'destructive competition'. What this meant in practice was the promotion of formal discussions between individual industries, whose initial object was the fixing of product prices, in Britain and Germany. The FBI and the government correctly hoped that in consequence existing agreements under threat as a result of German subsidy policy would be salvaged. As a result of the successful talks, fifty industrial groups, represented on the British side by the respective trade associations, signified their willingness to enter into negotiations.[89]

Dusseldorf had long-range as well as short-term significance, as became apparent during the course of Anglo-German negotiations in the few months left prior to the outbreak of war. The text of the Dusseldorf Agreement referred to the importance of a joint effort to stimulate international consumption of products made by British and German companies. It followed that Dusseldorf seemed to foreshadow a future characterized by transnational partnership between governments and organized private industry, designed to regulate production and consumption through market-sharing, quotas, fixed prices, and joint development schemes.[90]

The first half of March 1939 was, therefore, a time of optimism in the British government. After Munich Chamberlain had biased his twin-track policy of deterrence and *détente* in the direction of the latter. The only significant gesture towards rearmament had come in February, as a reaction to the scare caused by Goerdeler, when the Cabinet had decided to depart from the principle of 'imperial isolationism' and to prepare the

[89] Ervin Hexner, *International Cartels*, 403.
[90] Holland, 'The Federation of British Industries and the International Economy', 298.

army to fight a war on the European continent.[91] This aside, the period from October 1938 until 16 March 1939 was characterized by a series of British approaches to Germany in which economic co-operation was intended to cement the determination of 'our two peoples never to go to war with one another again'.[92] The day after representatives of the FBI and the RI reached agreement, however, the Nazis marched into what was left of Czechoslovakia. The result of this act of aggression was a modification of appeasement in which during the next few months deterrence was emphasized more than *détente*. But the overall strategy was to remain the same.

[91] See Robert Boyce, 'Introduction', in Boyce and Robertson, *Paths to War*, 21.
[92] The quotation is of course taken from 'the piece of paper' signed by Chamberlain and Hitler at Munich.

5

The Approach of War,
March–September 1939

The Guarantee Policy: The end of Appeasement?

The German invasion of Czechoslovakia was a surprise to the British government, even though it had received a warning of such an eventuality from the Secret Intelligence Service (SIS, otherwise known as MI6) a fortnight earlier.[1] Chamberlain had chosen instead to trust in the reassuring messages emanating from his ambassador in Berlin and from intermediaries such as Tiarks. When the blow against Prague fell his first reaction was to play for time pending a full assessment of Hitler's actions.[2]

It quickly became obvious that so leisurely a response to the new crisis was politically unsustainable. The German move provoked widespread anxiety amongst a public whose willingness to believe in the permanence of the Munich agreement was evaporating fast. In Westminster the government came under pressure from the Labour Party; but for Chamberlain the most alarming development was the open disenchantment with appeasement revealed on his own side of the House. Tory back-benchers regarded the occupation of Prague as a humiliation of the government and of the policy they had so vigorously supported during and after the Munich crisis. Chamberlain very briefly lost touch with parliamentary opinion, moving one close observer to note that 'The feeling in the lobbies is that Chamberlain will either have to go or completely reverse his policies'.[3]

The prime minister quickly recovered the initiative for the government. On 17 March he returned to Birmingham, his political home, to speak mainly about economic recovery and social services. At the last minute he changed his plans. The fall of Czechoslovakia had alarmed the Foreign Office as well as public and parliamentary opinion. The German

---

[1] D. C. Watt, *How War Came: The Immediate Origins of the Second World War* (1989), 166. [2] Ibid. 167.

[3] Ibid. 167. The significance of foreign-policy issues in public opinion and parliamentary alignment at this time has been traced by Maurice Cowling, *The Impact of Hitler: British Politics and British Policy, 1933–1940* (1975).

coup appeared to justify the pessimistic view of Nazi foreign policy held by Sir Robert Vansittart. Lord Halifax shared the dismay of his advisers and warned Chamberlain that the invasion might well mark the start of a new aggressive phase of German expansionism. It was as a consequence of this advice that Chamberlain threw away his prepared text. He replaced it with one which started by justifying the peace-keeping mission at Munich but then became increasingly hawkish. Hitler had promised at Munich that he had no wish to rule non-Germans. He had broken his word. Were his assurances ever to be trusted again? Was the invasion of Czechoslovakia the start of an attempt to dominate the world by force? To growing applause Chamberlain made it clear that Britain and the democracies would resist any such further moves.[4]

The tough line continued when Chamberlain returned to London. A new crisis was looming, or so it appeared. The Romanian minister in London, Virgil Tilea, had persuaded the foreign secretary that the Germans had presented his government with an ultimatum designed to force it into the acceptance of an economic agreement. Were this to be signed Romania would be transformed into a virtual colony of the Third Reich. Berlin was demanding a monopoly of Romanian exports and a halt to its industrial development in return for a guarantee of its frontiers. Tilea wanted to know how Britain would react to German aggression against Romania. He said his government favoured the creation of a new front in eastern Europe, to resist German expansion.

As it happened Tilea's alarming report was not an entirely accurate one. There certainly were German–Romanian economic talks at the time. The German demands were extensive. Berlin was anxious that the production targets set in the Four Year Plan were going to be missed and hoped that the programme could be put back on schedule through an agreement which gave it access to Romanian oil and minerals. Led by Dr Helmut Wohltat, the senior civil servant responsible for the execution of the Four Year Plan, the Germans called for the establishment of a joint German–Romanian petrol industry as well as joint exploitation of Romania's forests and mineral resources. The Romanian arms industry was to be standardized on German lines and German exporters were to be accorded a special status in the Romanian market. There was, however, no ultimatum, no call for a political agreement, and no sign of German aggression. In fact the terms of the economic agreement ultimately signed by Berlin and Bucharest on 23 March were exceedingly vague.

[4] R. A. C. Parker, *Chamberlain and Appeasement* (Basingstoke, 1993).

No immediate transformation of the Romanian–German relationship followed. A year went by before oil exports to Germany exceeded those to Britain. It seems probable that the story was something of a scare engineered by the Romanian government with the purpose of attracting British diplomatic and economic support as a counterweight to German political and commercial influence.[5]

Chamberlain's first move was to gain Cabinet agreement to a proposal he regarded as 'pretty bold and startling', although Halifax thought it 'not very heroic'.[6] Britain cabled its missions in Moscow, Paris, and Warsaw suggesting joint consultation with a view to (unspecified) action in the event of German aggression against Romania. The idea, Chamberlain said, was to threaten Germany with a two-front war. However, this initiative was stillborn. The Soviet Government preferred to wait for Polish and French reactions before replying, and these, when they arrived, were negative. The French said that open association with Moscow would alienate Mussolini and wreck chances of detaching him from Hitler[7] (a line they were soon to abandon). The Poles were not prepared to enter into any arrangements with the Soviet Union, whose ideological and territorial ambitions were regarded with deep distrust in Warsaw (the two countries had fought in 1920). In any case, Colonel Beck, the Polish foreign minister, pointed out that an assault on Romania would have to go through Hungary: there was no common Polish–Romanian frontier. All the Poles were prepared to consider was a secret agreement whereby the British would provide support in the event of German action against Danzig. The agreement would be a bilateral arrangement, concealed, at least initially, even from the French.[8]

British perceptions of the way Polish–German talks over the future of Danzig were developing were crucial in determining what happened next. The port of Danzig had been removed from Germany at Versailles and transformed into a Free City with an autonomous administration under a League of Nations high commissioner. It sat inside a territorial strip, also detached from Germany as a result of the post-war settlement. This was known as the 'Polish corridor', since it was now governed from Warsaw and separated East Prussia from the rest of Germany. Beck, who was if

---

[5] Accounts of the Romanian scare can be found in Kaiser, *Economic Diplomacy and the Origins of the Second World War*; Parker, *Chamberlain and Appeasement*, 202–3; and Watt, *How War Came*, 169–76.

[6] Kaiser, *Economic Diplomacy and the Origins of the Second World War*, 298.

[7] Watt, *How War Came*, 179.   [8] Ibid. 179–80.

anything pro-German, had been negotiating since the Munich crisis with the German foreign minister Joachim von Ribbentrop over the status of Danzig and the corridor. The Germans were now proposing the return of Danzig to the Reich and the construction of an *Autobahn* and multi-track railway through the corridor, with extraterritorial status in each case. In return, Berlin was offering recognition of Polish economic rights in Danzig, a non-aggression treaty for twenty-five years, and a 'common policy in the Ukraine'.[9]

The British were not clear about Beck's response to this offer. They suspected that his suggestion of a secret deal was intended to provide him with a bargaining counter which would strengthen the Polish position in the current talks with Ribbentrop. Lack of information about these discussions was generating anxiety in London that Beck was on the point of coming to some accommodation which, in swinging Poland irrecoverably into the German camp, would create a Nazi-dominated politico-economic bloc running from the French border to the Ukraine.[10] In fact, fears that Beck would connive at such an arrangement were misplaced, largely because neither he nor anyone else in the Polish Government was prepared to give ground concerning the future status of Danzig and the corridor. This became clear after 26 March, when the breakdown of the Polish–German talks became public. In an acrimonious atmosphere the German press began to run familiar stories of how Germans were being ill-treated in Poland. There were rumours of German troop movements towards the Polish border. The government in Warsaw, meanwhile, called up the reservists.[11]

The Chamberlain government was keen to find a way of strengthening Polish resistance to German demands. The Cabinet was, however, uncertain what to do until it received a report on 29 March from Ian Colvin, a *News Chronicle* reporter with SIS connections and good sources in Germany, that a German invasion of Poland was imminent, with Lithuania next on the list.[12] It now appears that the story had been planted on Colvin by well-placed anti-Nazis, probably in the German High Command, in order to provoke Britain into taking tough action designed

[9] See A. J. P. Taylor, *The Origins of the Second World War* (2nd edn., 1964), 258. The background to the Polish crisis is discussed by Taylor on pp. 241–2.

[10] Newman, *March 1939*, 195; Watt, *How War Came*, 180.

[11] Watt, *How War Came*, 193.

[12] Taylor, *Origins of the Second World War*, 260; Watt, *How War Came*, 182 goes into detail about Colvin's intelligence connections.

to restrain Hitler. Chamberlain, calling Colvin's tale 'fantastic', had his doubts from the start, but these were overwhelmed by corroborating reports passed through the American embassy and through Colonel Mason-Macfarlane, the British military attaché in Berlin.[13] The result was everything Colvin's informants could have hoped for: on 31 March, having gained Colonel Beck's agreement, Chamberlain told the House of Commons that Britain and France would lend Poland 'all the support in their power' were its independence to be threatened.[14]

Some historians have seen in the guarantee to Poland a clear break with the policy of appeasement. The guarantee that Britain and France would fight if Polish independence were threatened, a principle extended on 15 April to Romania and Greece, was a clear sign that eastern Europe would not be allowed to become a German colony. Simon Newman has argued that, having failed to contain Germany by peaceful means, the Chamberlain government determined to fight 'to prevent her from reaching full strength'. The alternative was to do nothing, which would allow Germany to build up a position of such power that beside it Britain would face 'relegation to second class status'.[15]

There is certainly some evidence to support this view. On 29 March, even before the guarantee to Poland had been given, the government announced that the Territorial Army would be doubled in size from 170,000 to 340,000. In April it revealed its intention to establish a Ministry of Supply and to institute compulsory military service. This apparent escalation of the rearmament programme was matched by some tough talking. On 6 June the Swedish industrialist Axel Wenner-Gren, owner of Electrolux, part-owner of the ball-bearing giant SKF, and connected to British financial circles through his majority shareholding in the Anglo-French Banking Corporation, met Chamberlain with a message from Goering. Wenner-Gren said that, unlike the Ribbentrop, Goebbels, and Himmler clique, Goering did not want war. The Reichsmarshall 'had been thinking of a 25 year peace pact', satisfaction of all German claims, above all concerning Danzig and the Polish corridor, and then disarmament talks. Goering also favoured what was described, vaguely, as the restoration of international commerce 'to its proper place in world affairs', based on a British initiative to settle exchange problems, spheres of influence, and commercial questions. Chamberlain was frosty. He said that Goering seemed to want 'all give on our side and all take on his':

[13] Watt, *How War Came*, 182–4.
[14] Chamberlain quoted by Parker, *Chamberlain and Appeasement*, 215.
[15] See Newman, *March 1939*, 218.

'something really drastic' needed to happen in Germany before there could be serious talks.[16] The following day Chamberlain made it clear that British public opinion had been 'passionately stirred' by the fate of Czechoslovakia, and the people were now prepared to fight rather than see another nation lose its independence.[17] These firm statements were matched by Frank Ashton-Gwatkin, hitherto a committed advocate of appeasement, when he told Helmut Wohltat that there was no point in discussing an economic settlement based on the Van Zeeland Report until Hitler demonstrated his peaceful intentions.[18]

There was, therefore, an obvious change of emphasis in British diplomacy after Prague. Britain was now presenting Germany with a clear threat to engage it in a two-front war if the pursuit of a formal empire in eastern Europe continued. But it would be mistaken to argue that appeasement, in the form of a twin-track approach based on deterrence and *détente*, had been abandoned. Certainly a good deal of stress was now placed on deterrence—but in the hope that firmness would succeed where conciliation had failed and bring Hitler to the negotiating table after all.

There are numerous indications that the British government did not expect war to follow automatically from the guarantees to Poland, Romania, and Greece. First, the Polish guarantee was, as far as Halifax was concerned, another attempt to help the German 'moderates'. The day after the guarantee was signed *The Times* ran an editorial explaining that the British government was not committed to the defence of 'every inch of the current frontier of Poland'. The paper argued that Chamberlain was prepared to undertake 'free negotiations' even now because he believed 'there are problems in which adjustments are necessary'. The point of the guarantee was to appeal to the Germans' better nature. It was 'an invitation to enter into closer relations if they will conform to normal practices' in relations with foreign countries.[19] Not surprisingly, the Poles were unhappy about this. They expressed their 'surprise' at the attempt to minimize the prime minister's statement and were rewarded with a mealy-mouthed formula from Sir John Simon, who said the editorial was 'unofficial' and 'in no sense inspired from any Government source'. Alastair Parker has suggested that these words implicate George Stewart, Chamberlain's press secretary, or Sir Joseph Ball, head of the Conservative Party Research Department. Whoever was responsible, the

---

[16] PRO PREM 1/328, Chamberlain's record of a conversation with Axel Wenner-Gren, 6 June 1939.   [17] Watt, *How War Came*, 393.
[18] PRO FO 371/22952, C8306/8/18, record by Ashton-Gwatkin of a talk with Wohltat and Weber, 7 June 1939.   [19] Parker, *Chamberlain and Appeasement*, 217.

paper's argument was privately well received: Halifax thought it 'just right'.[20]

Secondly, neither Chamberlain nor Halifax favoured an alliance with the Soviet Union.[21] Initially both seem to have assumed that self-interest would impel the Soviets into a position of benevolent neutrality in the event of a German assault on Poland or Romania. All Halifax asked for was an arrangement by which the Soviet Union provided aid, mostly in the form of weapons, to those countries which asked for it. This, it was believed, should be enough to deter German aggression. If it was not enough then Soviet munitions and material would allow the embattled east European states to hold out long enough for British and French air and ground action in the west, combined with the effects of the blockade, to force a German retreat.[22]

Others were not so sanguine about Poland's chances of surviving a German onslaught in the absence of a full-blown Anglo-French–Soviet alliance. The British chiefs of staff did not believe Polish resistance would last very long. Anglo-French staff talks of 25 April to 4 May in London reached a consensus that the Polish forces would collapse in the early stages of a war with Germany.[23] Strategic logic, therefore, dictated a formal agreement with the Soviet Union. Lloyd George pointed out in parliament that in the absence of a Soviet alliance Britain would be 'walking into a trap' if called on to honour the guarantee.[24] There was cross-bench support for this view in the Commons, coming from the Labour Party, the Liberals, and dissident Conservatives grouped around Churchill. The cause of an arrangement with the Soviet Union was strongly backed by public opinion and, significantly, by a growing number of Cabinet ministers as well as by the chiefs of staff.[25] The conviction was shared in Paris. Putting their concern for Mussolini's finer feelings behind them, the French proposed to the Soviets on 13 April that they provide immediate help to France should it be called on to defend Poland or Romania. In return France would go to the assistance of the Soviet Union if it was attacked by Germany or involved in a conflict with it through helping Poland and Romania.[26] Chamberlain and Halifax, however, stood

[20] Parker, *Chamberlain and Appeasement*, 217; Watt, *How War Came*, 187.

[21] Parker, *Chamberlain and Appeasement*, 219.

[22] Taylor, *Origins of the Second World War*, 311–12.

[23] Watt, *How War Came*, 331.   [24] Parker, *Chamberlain and Appeasement*, 219.

[25] Kaiser, *Economic Diplomacy and the Origins of the Second World War*, 301; Parker, *Chamberlain and Appeasement*, 233, quotes a Gallup poll giving 84% 'yes' replies to the question 'Do you favour a military alliance between Britain and Russia?'

[26] Parker, *Chamberlain and Appeasement*, 223.

by the policy of benevolent neutrality, anxious to keep the Soviet Union in reserve until 'invited to lend a hand in certain circumstances in the most convenient form'.[27]

The Soviets were not impressed. The east European states were militarily weak and anti-Soviet in political complexion. It was a combination which did not augur well in the event of a German *Drang nach Osten*, regarded in Moscow as Hitler's long-term objective.[28] The British proposal of benevolent neutrality on the part of the Soviet Union if Germany invaded Poland or Romania left Soviet security dependent on factors entirely beyond Moscow's control. This was not acceptable, and on 18 April the Soviet government made its own proposal. It suggested the conclusion of a triple alliance between itself, Britain, and France. The arrangement would provide for military assistance on the part of each state for whichever one of them was the victim of aggression in Europe. The three countries would in addition promise to go to the aid of any east European nation on the borders of the Soviet Union were it to be attacked. Once conflict had started, no member of the alliance could make a separate peace: hostilities could only cease by common agreement. The terms of the alliance would be set out in detail in two documents, a political treaty and a military agreement, to be signed simultaneously.[29]

Although London did not like the Soviet suggestion it did not wish to alienate the Russians. With some reluctance, therefore, the British agreed to start negotiations with a view to the conclusion of an Anglo-French–Soviet treaty.[30] The story of these discussions has been told many times and there is no need to repeat the details here. It is enough to say that the talks, protracted over the best part of four months, were a study in futility. Having started out by objecting to the Soviet proposals concerning the defence of states bordering the Soviet Union against aggression, whether in the form of a military assault or of a pro-Nazi coup (called 'indirect aggression') the British by mid-August had accepted most of the Soviet conditions set out in April. The two outstanding issues were, what constituted aggression in the states bordering the Soviet Union, and the right of Soviet troops to enter Polish territory, subject to the agreement of the government in Warsaw. At this point, on 22 August, the Soviets walked out of the talks and concluded a non-aggression pact

---

[27] Watt, *How War Came*, 222–3.
[28] Taylor, *Origins of the Second World War*, 294.
[29] Parker, *Chamberlain and Appeasement*, 223–4.
[30] Ibid. 224; Watt, *How War Came*, 222.

with Germany.[31] Hitler now had what the guarantee policy had tried to avert: insurance against a two-front war.

Why did the Soviet Union join forces with a power which had hitherto identified itself as, and which was to prove to be, the historic enemy of Bolshevism? The answer is still not entirely clear, but it is hard to believe that Soviet policy had no connection with the procrastination displayed throughout the talks by the British government, together with growing indications during July and August that an Anglo-German *rapprochement* was on the cards after all. And these came on top of the exclusion of the Soviet Union from the Munich Conference in September 1938.

There was justification for Soviet distrust of British good faith. Although it was never part of Chamberlain's policy to engineer a Soviet–German conflict, as some Soviet critics have alleged, the British government wanted only an arm's length relationship with the Soviet Union.[32] One of the most important reasons for this was a reluctance on the part of the prime minister and the foreign secretary to alienate the Germans by signing an agreement with the Soviet Union. To this end Halifax rejected an invitation to go to Moscow and Chamberlain turned down an offer from Anthony Eden to undertake a special mission to the Soviet capital.[33] Both Chamberlain and Halifax sought, in A. J. P. Taylor's words, 'to chalk a Red bogy on the wall' in the hope that it would frighten Hitler into a reasonable mood.[34] Neither had any enthusiasm for a formal alliance which would wreck all prospects of Anglo-German accommodation by dividing Europe along ideological lines.

Of course there were other reasons. The absolute refusal of the Poles to countenance right of transit for Soviet troops, even when under pressure to do so from the French and, at last, the British,[35] was one. The unyielding anti-Soviet position of the Polish government was matched in the Baltic states. For some time the British and French floundered in the ideological politics of eastern Europe, afraid that too close a relationship with the Soviets would provoke a pro-Nazi backlash in the very states they were trying to keep out of Hitler's grasp.[36] In addition, Chamberlain could not lose his innate distrust of the Soviet Union. He believed that its long-term ambition was to involve Britain, France, and Germany in a

---

[31] A concise but fairly detailed summary can be found in Parker, *Chamberlain and Appeasement*, 224–45. Taylor, *Origins of the Second World War*, 273–92, covers the ground, as does Watt, *How War Came*, at somewhat greater length.

[32] Taylor, *Origins of the Second World War*, 278–9.   [33] Ibid. 283.

[34] Taylor, *English History*, 546.   [35] Parker, *Chamberlain and Appeasement*, 243.

[36] Newman, *March 1939*, 143, 216.

conflict which would reduce central Europe to such a state of weakness that it would fall into the Soviet orbit. Given that the Soviets were (in Chamberlain's view) militarily weak, it made sense for them to try and manipulate other countries to fight their battles.[37] Although the prime minister became increasingly isolated in this opinion, even losing the support of Halifax by July and August, he believed that a Soviet–German stalemate in eastern Europe suited British interests. In would contain German expansion and keep intact the chances of building a 'peace front' based on an alliance between Britain, France, and the east European states. It is true that Chamberlain was slowly persuaded to move toward the Soviet terms, but this is largely because both he and Halifax believed that the longer the discussions could be spun out the less likely would be a German assault on Poland. The foreign secretary looked forward to the military conversations: 'no great progress would be made' but the talks would gain time for the British and the French. It was important to prevent a breakdown at least until the start of autumn, when the rains would come, muddy the roads, and make any German invasion highly improbable. This was not the policy of a government resolved on a fight for the future orientation of eastern Europe.[38]

The third indication that the British government did not expect war to follow automatically from the guarantees was the rearmament programme. Its escalation was more apparent than real. There was no minister of supply until July, nearly three months after the announcement of the government's intention to establish the Ministry. Hopes that the minister might become the 'grand director of a war economy' were dashed: the Royal Navy and the RAF retained their independence. As a result the new Ministry was responsible solely for the army, and initially at least its main task was the purchase of clothing and equipment.[39] Meanwhile the manner in which the government chose to implement compulsory military service added little to Britain's capacity to fight a European war. Conscription was to apply to future age-groups only, as they reached 20. The first registration of these 'militia men' occurred in June; their call-up took place in July. Service was limited to six months, a training period intended to prepare the conscripts for action, if necessary, two or three years hence.[40] The thinking behind the introduction of compulsory military service was consistent with the government's long-term strategy:

---

[37] See Lord Home of the Hirsel, *The Way the Wind Blows* (1978), 60. Home, then Alec Dunglass, was private secretary to Chamberlain at the time.

[38] Parker, *Chamberlain and Appeasement*, 241.   [39] Taylor, *English History*, 546.

[40] Ibid. 544.

its purpose was not the creation of a large army for engagement on the Continent but the reinforcement of anti-aircraft defence at home. True to his determination to insulate Britain as far as possible from air attack, Chamberlain had determined on the establishment of searchlight sites and anti-aircraft batteries which would be ready to swing into action instantly, at any time of day or night. This could have been achieved by calling out the Territorials or Reservists on the declaration of a State of Emergency. The government decided that such a measure would be seen in Berlin as highly provocative: in consequence, conscription was preferable.[41]

Fourthly and finally, the construction of the guarantee system was not accompanied by any modifications to Montagu Norman's 'Anglo-German connection'. The occupation of Prague and its aftermath had provoked a suggestion from the Foreign Office that another look be taken at the future of Anglo-German payments arrangements. There was, however, no enthusiasm within either the Board of Trade or the Bank of England for a termination of the Standstill. Contact between British and German industrial associations had been officially discouraged in the aftermath of the aggression against Czechoslovakia. But this was seen by the Board of Trade as only a temporary setback, and it cherished hopes of boosting exports through a revival of the Dusseldorf Agreement and of working with individual industries to build on its 'valuable preliminary work ... to the national interest'.[42] Denunciation of existing trade and payments facilities would sabotage the pursuit of this objective.

At the same time the Bank remained sensitive to the interests of the short-term British creditors. These now overshadowed those of all the other nations which had been involved in the Standstill from the very start (Table 5.1). Tiarks's mission to Germany had paid off and the terms of a renewed Standstill Agreement had been reached shortly before the fall of Czechoslovakia.[43] Representatives of the British short-term creditors were due to visit Berlin and finalize the draft agreement.[44] Neither the promotion of exports nor the well-being of leading merchant banks would be served by preventing the departure of the British delegation. The Foreign Office was impressed by these 'very weighty' commercial arguments and decided not to take the issue any further, concerned in any case that given the current international situation, 'the abrogation

[41] Parker, *Chamberlain and Appeasement*, 287.
[42] PRO FO 371/22951, C4981/8/18, Stanley to Halifax, 6 Apr. 1939.
[43] Bank of England file OV34/140, Mar. 1939.
[44] Papers of R. H. Brand, New Bodleian Library, Oxford, file 193A/21.

TABLE 5.1. *Shares of creditor countries in Standstill debts, 10 October 1931 and 28 February 1939* (%)

	10 October 1931	28 February 1939
USA	36.2	26.4
England	28.2	56.3
Holland	13.0	6.7
Switzerland	16.0	8.7
France	4.5	0.7
Belgium	2.1	1.2

Source: Papers of R. H. Brand (New Bodleian Library, Oxford), file 193A/21.

of the agreement and the adoption of a definite policy providing for the economic strangulation of Germany . . . would I think certainly drive Herr Hitler to the desperate policy of provoking war now'.[45] Accordingly the British bankers departed for Berlin in May. The party, led by Frank Tiarks and Charles Lidbury, was composed of directors from Schroder's, the Westminster Bank, Lazard's, and Lloyds Bank. A new agreement was signed on 22 May, carrying the Standstill Arrangements (or so it was intended) from 1 June 1939 to 31 May 1940.[46]

Concern to foster Anglo–German trade and to avoid provocation also influenced the government's attitude to export credits. On 4 July R. S. Hudson at the Department of Overseas Trade was warned by Sir John Caulcutt, chairman of the Export Credit Guarantee Department (ECGD) Advisory Council, that members were becoming increasingly anxious about cover for goods heading for Italy and, above all, for Germany. Caulcutt said that until now he had advised his colleagues 'to proceed on the basis that we should avoid war'. They were no longer disposed to believe him; he wanted advice. He added that if guarantees were refused the flow of exports to Germany from Britain would be progressively brought to a halt.[47]

Hudson argued that, quite apart from its economic implications, the termination of ECGD cover and consequent collapse of Anglo–German trade 'might have a very bad effect politically', convincing Hitler that it was Britain's intention to damage the German economy. The Cabinet agreed: the following day it discussed the subject and concluded that the

[45] PRO FO 371/22951, C4102/8/18, memorandum by Roberts, 6 Apr. 1939.
[46] Papers of R. H. Brand, file 193A/21. Details of the renewed credit agreement can be found in Bank of England file OV34/140, May 1939.
[47] PRO FO 371/22952, C9410/8/18, Hudson's reply to a report by Caulcutt, 4 July 1939.

TABLE 5.2. *ECGD short-term credits: German and Italian shares of all business done and on offer, 28 January–30 August 1939 (£ million)*

	28 Jan.	16 Apr.	3 June	1 July	29 July	30 Aug.
Total business done and on offer	24.9	18.4	28.2	29.5	30.2	24.4
Germany	13.8	10.0	15.5	15.9	16.3	16.4
Italy	4.1	2.6	5.1	5.8	5.9	6.0

Source: Derived from PRO ECG 1/19.

ECGD should not discontinue export credits.[48] It is this decision which no doubt explains why the volume of short-term credits provided for trade with Germany and, albeit on a less remarkable scale, Italy, continued to mount, not merely through the spring but right through the summer of 1939 after the invasion of Czechoslovakia had induced a hiatus (Table 5.2). It was not until 24 August that policy-holders with the ECGD were advised that further cover would not be available for shipment to the Baltic states apart from Poland.[49] This reluctance to disturb existing Anglo-German trade and financial arrangements confirms the impression left both by the talks with the Soviet Union and by the government's attitude towards rearmament in the months prior to the outbreak of war. The guarantee to Poland was never intended to shut the door on a settlement with Germany.

Financial Crisis and the Limits of Orthodoxy

During the summer of 1939 the tense international situation interacted with government anxiety that Britain was running into serious economic difficulties. The result was mounting concern that neither the waging of war nor the maintenance of deterrence into the indefinite future might be possible in the absence of a politico-economic transformation. On 5 July Chancellor of the Exchequer Simon told the Cabinet that the external financial position was becoming increasingly unhealthy. Its deterioration was a function of the defence programme and the provision of aid to Romania and Turkey. The upshot was an adverse balance of trade, which in turn was putting a severe strain on the gold reserves. Now the exchange was under threat and it was becoming increasingly hard for the government to defend a sterling–dollar rate of £1 = \$4.68.[50]

[48] PRO FO 371/22952, C9410/8/18, report of a Cabinet decision, 5 July 1939.
[49] PRO ECG 1/19, minute of a meeting held on 8 Sept. 1939.
[50] PRO CAB 23/100, C. P. 149 (39), 3 July 1939.

Four explanations stand out in the Treasury's analysis of the financial position resulting from rearmament . To begin with, the domestic manufacture of weapons involved importing raw materials worth between 25 and 30 per cent of the value of the order, 'and in these times possibly more'. Secondly, arms and finished goods bought overseas meant lost gold to the extent that they could not be paid for in exports. Thirdly, ability to finance strategically vital imports, whether arms, food, or raw materials (or even American-made machine tools) with exports was likely to diminish, given the need to continue diverting production 'from peaceful enterprise to war preparation'. Fourthly, an average of 25 to 30 per cent of the money provided to foreign countries in loans and credits was spent on purchases in Britain; if the money was spent abroad it added to the gold loss. Either way, overseas aid seemed a bad bargain for Britain at this juncture.[51] All this came on top of the exogenous events which had contributed to the fall in gold stocks. The tense world situation had provoked a capital flight from London, and there had been a trickle of British investments to New York as a result. Far more serious for sterling, however, and for London's position at the heart of the sterling block, was a running down of balances by member states at a rate of £80 million a month, a function of the international crisis as well as of the damage done to Commonwealth economies by the 1937 recession.[52]

The gold drain had cost Britain 40 per cent of its reserves in the fifteen months up to the start of July 1939. The implications for British strategy were alarming. As the paper argued, a continuation of the gold loss would be 'a serious economic anxiety even in peace'. With the possibility of war looming the situation was in danger of becoming critical. The gold reserves, together with assets which might be sold or mortgaged to countries

---

[51] So bad in fact that the Treasury was even then effectively sabotaging Poland's chances of receiving aid from Britain. The Poles had initially requested £60 million in cash for the purchase of weapons and raw materials. After Simon had intervened Chamberlain told Ambassador Lipski that Britain's need to husband resources for a long war made this impossible. The Poles came back with a request for £24 million. The most the government was prepared to consider, however, was £5 million, with an extra £3 million to be provided by the French, and £8 million of export credits. In return the Poles were to devalue the zloty, keep the loan in sterling and francs rather than convert it into gold (which would have been useful for buying from the USA), and use it only for purposes to be agreed with the British and French governments. This was unacceptable to the Poles. For them the whole point of the exercise had been to facilitate a rapid expansion of weapons. The conditions of Anglo-French aid made this impossible. They rejected the deal on 25 July, walking away with only £8 million in export credits (see Kaiser, *Economic Diplomacy and the Origins of the Second World War*, 306–8).   [52] PRO CAB 23/100, C. P. 149 (39), 3 July 1939.

overseas, constituted Britain's sole 'war chest'. At present this was made up of £500 million in gold and £200 million in disposable foreign securities. Given the existing international circumstances there was little prospect of any reduction in the drain, running at a rate of £20 million each month. If a conflict were to break out, the demands on British gold stocks would be greater. It was not easy to see how the 'war chest' would last for the three years of war upon which British military planning was based.[53]

These sobering conclusions were reinforced by an analysis of defence expenditure which pointed out that it was on course to reach £2,100 million between 1939 and 1941, although the Cabinet review of February 1938 had only allocated £1,000 million for the period, a figure revised in September to £1,100 million. Only £910 million could be raised by existing taxation: the balance of £1,190 million would have to be found by borrowing unless taxes were increased. The Treasury was anxious not to raise taxes too far because it knew that in the event of war there needed to be elasticity left in the system to compensate for the loss of revenue from customs-and-excise duties. It therefore reckoned that there was room for tax increases of no more than £100 million in 1940, leaving a borrowing requirement of £990 million.[54] But it was not clear whether the government would be able to find all this (the sum to be found for 1939 represented 9.43 per cent of the Gross National Product for that year)[55] by turning to the capital market. Meanwhile there was a serious risk that inflationary pressures, already present in the south-east,[56] would be intensified by the appearance of a gap between what could be borrowed and what had to be spent. The only option was to fall back on a 'variety of controls'—notably prohibitions of new issues, control of bank advances, of company dividends, and investment policies, and possibly of prices. Such a course of action was currently being studied.[57]

Treasury orthodoxy was being stretched almost beyond recognition by the demands made on Britain by the international crisis, although it was to mount a rearguard action until the introduction of national income accounting in 1941.[58] Simon's paper was itself evidence of a fight-back. It concluded that

[53] PRO CAB 23/100, C. P. 149 (39), 3 July 1939.   [54] Ibid.

[55] Taking the GNP for 1939 to be £5,297,000,000 (see Feinstein, *National Income, Expenditure and Output*, Table 1, T6).

[56] See W. R. Garside, 'The failure of the "Radical Alternative"', *Journal of European Economic History*, 14 (1985); and Peden, *British Rearmament and the Treasury*.

[57] PRO CAB 23/100, C. P. 149 (39), 3 July 1939.

[58] See Newton and Porter, *Modernization Frustrated*, ch. 4.

Purchases abroad of armaments must be avoided to the greatest extent possible. Further expenditure on armaments in this country cannot be undertaken without counting the cost in gold. Indeed, as there is a prospect of the continuance of the present armed peace, if not of the outbreak of war, finality of expenditure (unless for overmastering reasons) should now be declared.[59]

This call for 'finality of expenditure' was made even though it appeared, as Sir Richard Hopkins admitted to the Cabinet, that in the current circumstances Germany was as well if not better placed than Britain to fight a long war. The Third Reich was 'largely self-supporting in food', unlike Britain. German taxation policy and methods of financing state borrowing indicated that there seemed no limit to what could be spent on armaments. Nor was the balance of strength between the two countries likely to tilt in Britain's favour with time, or so it was believed.[60]

The only vaguely positive aspect to the Cabinet discussion was an awareness that it might be in Britain's interest for war to break out sooner rather than later[61] (although the guarantee to Poland had in fact taken the power to decide on the timing of the conflict with Germany out of London's hands). The fundamental problem was that a long war, and even the indefinite preservation of an armed peace, were increasingly seen as incompatible with the maintenance of the politico-economic order which had prevailed since 1920–1. Back in 1937 the Treasury had been forced into recognizing the incompatibility of the balanced budget with rearmament. Now it was obvious that the relatively gentle fiscal stance which had characterized the period since 1920 was unsustainable. Taxes, national insurance, and health contributions had only exceeded 8.0 per cent of all personal income in 1932–3, when the Treasury's obedience to conventional wisdom had led it to balance the budget in the pit of the Depression. Thereafter they had returned to the trend rate of 7.5 per cent before starting to creep back to 8.0 per cent and beyond, with no possibility of a remission in sight (see Table 5.3). If this was going to make life painful for the growing numbers of upwardly aspiring middle and lower-middle class voters it was also hard on the industrialists, about to face a 60 per cent excess profits tax. At the same time the 'variety of controls' referred to in the Treasury paper pointed to a level of government intervention in the capital markets unprecedented since 1918.

The City was, however, facing a problem more serious than the loss of its traditional freedoms. Given the drain of gold and the running down of

[59] PRO CAB 23/100, C. P. 149 (39), 3 July 1939.
[60] PRO CAB 23/100, C. M. 36 (39), 5 July 1939.   [61] Ibid.

TABLE 5.3. *Taxes, national insurance, and health contributions as a percentage of all personal income, 1929–1938 (£ million)*

Year	(1) Total personal income	(2) Taxes, national insurance, and health contributions	% of (1) taken by (2)
1929	4,479	306	6.8
1930	4,426	343	7.7
1931	4,258	328	7.7
1932	4,172	345	8.3
1933	4,220	336	8.0
1934	4,320	326	7.5
1935	4,493	335	7.5
1936	4,730	358	7.6
1937	4,909	392	8.0
1938	5,043	418	8.3

Source: Derived from Feinstein, *National Income, Expenditure and Output* (Cambridge, 1972), Table 10, T28.

sterling balances, it was unclear how the persistence of international crisis could be squared with London's position as an international financial centre. The Treasury recognized that short of abandoning rearmament there were three ways of containing the loss of reserves. Only one, namely the raising of the bank rate, was consistent with the preservation of the old order. This step was duly taken on 24 August: with the gold stock having fallen to £469.9 million, the rate was increased to 4 per cent. But the Treasury knew that the reserves were 'altogether too low already' and that the two other measures would have to be considered.[62]

Here was a choice of evils. The first, a decision to allow sterling to fall until it found its own level against the dollar, might antagonize the Americans and provoke a retaliatory change in the dollar–gold relationship. This would nullify the benefits to be expected from a devaluation of the pound. There was more: the Treasury worried about the implications of a heavy fall on confidence in Britain's economic system. Quite apart from the financial implications of such a blow in encouraging a flight from sterling, there would be 'adverse repercussions on the diplomatic situation'[63]—not least on Anglo-American relations.

The alternative was to impose exchange controls on the German model, a course of action which 'presumably' would allow sterling to keep any rate. But there was nothing else to be said for so drastic a step, which had not even been taken in 1914–18. The Treasury believed that the measure

[62] PRO T 160/877/F16003, brief for the Chancellor, 'Tripartite Consultation in the Event of War', 21 August 1939.　　　　　　　　　　　　　　　　　[63] Ibid.

would, in terminating the automatic convertibility of sterling, mean the end of its status as an international currency. The chancellor, who needed little persuasion anyway, was advised that 'the final loss of much of our financial power might follow'. The absence of controls over international transactions in sterling was one of the props of London's position as a 'great financial and banking centre'.[64] Terminating the liberal regime would undermine Britain's ability to sustain this role. As a result, millions of pounds in invisible income would be sacrificed. According to the Treasury the introduction of exchange controls would transform Britain into the 'different kind of nation' Simon had referred to back in April 1938.[65] Fixing the exchange at an artificial rate could not be allowed to damage exports, which if necessary would require a subsidy from the taxpayer to be sold abroad, while the living standards of the population would inevitably have to be reduced. The picture was one of a controlled economy resembling Nazi Germany or the Soviet Union. In wartime, argued the Treasury, it might be impossible to avoid such an eventuality; in peacetime this radical solution to the diminution of the 'war chest' should be undertaken only in the last resort on the understanding that it was 'a lesser sacrifice than losing a war'.[66]

The lesser of these two evils was clearly a downward float of sterling. At the same time as he informed his Cabinet colleagues of the decision to increase the bank rate, the chancellor therefore asked for authority to change the system whereby the Bank of England supported a sterling–dollar rate of £1 = \$4.68. It amounted to the second sterling devaluation since the decision to return to gold. The first one had been accompanied by stern counter-inflationary steps. This time the government was prepared to take a chance both with investors in sterling and with inflation (not to mention with the Americans) rather than abandon what the Treasury and the Bank evidently regarded as the corner-stone of economic liberalism, or what was left of it. It was a choice which would have been regarded as meaningless by the apostles of orthodoxy at any other time in the post-1918 era, given their conviction that sterling convertibility and sound money were two sides of the same coin.

The government recognized that there was one way of avoiding the need for such fundamental changes to the *status quo*. Assistance from the United States would reduce pressure on the gold reserves. There were, however, two difficulties. First, Washington's hands had been tied by the

---

[64] Ibid.   [65] See Peden, 'A Matter of Timing', 22.
[66] PRO T 160/877, F16003, 'Tripartite Consultations in the Event of War'.

Johnson Act, which prohibited loans to war-debt defaulters (Britain had ceased payments in 1934). It looked as if war would tighten this legal screw. The Neutrality Acts, passed in deference to the popular view that unscrupulous arms dealers had lured the United States into the First World War, forbade the sale of munitions and the provision of credits to belligerent nations. It seemed that these obstacles could only be circumvented if the Americans gave 'us a share of their production without our paying for it'.[67] Such action was in any case likely to be more useful than access to the 'vast gold stocks' of the United States. But although the foreign secretary believed that it would be possible to count on American help, it was clear that a war would have to break out first and then last long enough for attitudes to become 'sufficiently favourable to us to enable us to win . . .'.[68] It was not a comforting prospect as far as the present was concerned, and as Hopkins told the Cabinet, American beneficence could not be assumed even in the event of a long war.

The second difficulty was an ambivalence on the British side about the value of American help. During the years of crisis in the Far East Washington had been long on rhetoric but short on action. With some justification Chamberlain and his colleagues distrusted idealistic diplomacy which left other countries, notably, it was feared, a hard-pressed Britain, fighting battles which were the concern of all the democratic states.[69] But the fundamental problem was anxiety about the price of American help. Tory imperialists such as Lord Londonderry, Leo Amery, and Sir Henry Page-Croft pointed to the post-1918 history of Anglo-American strategic and financial rivalry in Europe and Asia. During the long and painful negotiations for the Anglo-American Trade Agreement in 1938 they urged a belligerent policy on the government: if Washington wanted a modification in tariffs and preferences to accommodate exporters then London should require a drastic cut in the American tariff as a condition.[70] Chamberlain did not share this view. He had taken over the premiership keen to improve relations between Britain and the United States.[71] He was, therefore, concerned to drive the trade talks through to a successful conclusion not because of any prospective economic benefits, which were very small if not non-existent, but because of the strategic implications. The prime minister believed that if American opinion could be educated to act 'more and more with us' the totalitarian states would be frightened.

---

[67] PRO CAB 23/100, C. M. 36 (39), 5 July 1939.   [68] Ibid.
[69] David Reynolds, *The Creation of the Anglo-American Alliance 1937–41: A Study in Competitive Co-operation* (1981), 45.   [70] Ibid. 17–18.
[71] Ibid. 16.

The balance against the 'Berlin–Rome–Tokyo axis' would be redressed; the policy of deterrence would be strengthened.[72]

Chamberlain had continued his efforts to establish an informal alliance with the United States after the signature of the Trade Agreement in November 1938. He was encouraged by President Roosevelt's declaration that 'Great Britain, in the event of a war, could rely upon obtaining raw materials from the democracies of the world'.[73] Chamberlain's concern for Anglo-American harmony was shared by the more progressive elements in the National Government and amongst its parliamentary supporters.[74] The cause was backed by Eden and Churchill, and by Halifax, albeit in a more subdued way, as well as by the Labour and the Liberal leaderships. The view advanced by Wendt, that the prime minister's true ambition was a European politico-economic bloc directed by Britain, France, Germany, and Italy, designed to challenge the industrial and financial power of the United States, is fundamentally misleading. It is based mainly on a series of reports by the German ambassador in London, Herbert von Dirksen, which deliberately exaggerated Anglo-American rivalry in order to influence Berlin in the direction of *détente* with London.[75] Thus there is no evidence that the Dusseldorf Agreement was intended to be the first step on the road to an anti-American European industrial alliance. Rather, it seems as if Chamberlain hoped to draw American producers into the network of inter-industrial agreements as the next stage in the reorganization of trade on the basis of 'orderly marketing'. Dusseldorf might have been a bargaining-counter in this process but hardly a weapon aimed at American capital.[76] As David Reynolds has suggested, existing available evidence does not support the frequently rehearsed argument that fear of American economic imperialism was partly behind efforts to reach *détente* with Germany. Even if industrialists and a senior civil servant such as Leith-Ross did consider playing the anti-American card, there is no sign that the prime minister did so.[77]

It should not, however, be inferred from this that Chamberlain envisaged the type of 'special relationship' which was to characterize Anglo-American relations in the post-war era. Indeed, he wanted to avoid this kind of economic and strategic dependence on the power of the United States. A proposal made by Sir Ronald Lindsay, British ambassador

---

[72] Ibid. 18. [73] Quoted in ibid. 51. [74] Ibid. 16.

[75] B. J. Wendt, *Economic Appeasement: Handel und Finanz in der Britischen Deutschland-Politik* (Dusseldorf, 1971), 526–9.

[76] See C. A. MacDonald, *The United States, Britain and Appeasement, 1936–1939* (1981), 108–10, 130–6. [77] See Reynolds, *The Creation of the Anglo-American Alliance*, 52.

in Washington during the summer of 1939, for a 'debts for bases' deal whereby the British war debt would be cancelled in return for the cession or at least the leasing of certain Caribbean islands to the United States, was vetoed by the prime minister.[78] Treading a path between subordination and an unsustainable financial and strategic independence, the British government hoped for an alliance of equals. But as time wore on and the reserves drained away it began to appear that the price of survival in a three-year war, let alone of keeping the most etiolated version of the *status quo*, might involve submission to the *Pax Americana*.

An Anglo-German Non-Aggression Treaty?

The awareness of looming financial crisis coincided with and may well have inspired a series of attempts at concluding a lasting Anglo-German *détente*. This does not mean that Britain ever wavered in its determination to honour the guarantee to Poland. Nevertheless, the point of all the activity was to persuade Hitler that co-operation with Britain on a broad political and economic front was possible—but only on condition that Germany renounce the use of force as a means of settling international disputes. Such a peaceful turn of events would of course have made the guarantee redundant. The search for such a diplomatic coup led the Chamberlain government to make a number of generous offers to Germany during the course of July and August 1939.

The last fling of Chamberlain's deterrence and *détente* policy was backed by the government's supporters in finance and organized private industry. Even as German demands on Poland poisoned the international atmosphere, representatives from both worlds went to meet leading Nazis. On 22 July E. W. Tennant, the commodity broker instrumental in the establishment of the Anglo-German Fellowship, met Ribbentrop with the government's approval. This had been granted on the understanding that the German foreign minister would not be left in any doubt about Britain's conviction 'that further outbursts by Germany in Europe must cease or they will be met with resistance on our part'.[79] However, Tennant, judging by his own report, seems to have eschewed such robust sentiments. He offered a £100 million credit to the Reich as financial compensation

[78] Reynolds, *The Creation of the Anglo-American Alliance*, 53–4.
[79] PRO PREM 1/335, note of an interview with E. W. Tennant by Sir Horace Wilson, 24 July 1939

for the repudiation of violence and listened, apparently sympathetically, to a tedious piece of self-justification from Ribbentrop.[80]

This futile mission was followed by a meeting between leading British industrialists and Herman Goering. The initiative came from Anglo-Swedish business interests, in the form of Axel Wenner-Gren's Electrolux group, which suggests that the latter's talk with Chamberlain back in June had not been a complete waste of time. The arrangements were made by Birger Dahlerus, managing director of Electrolux Ltd., the British end of the operation, with the help of Sir Harold Wernher, his company chairman.[81] They bore fruit in the encounter with Goering, playing out his dual role as a 'moderate' and economic supremo of the Reich. The composition of the British party reflected a cross-section of industrial and financial interests, including Sir Edward Mortimer Mountain, chairman of Eagle Star Insurance, of the British Crown Assurance Company, and of the Threadneedle Insurance Company; Lord Aberconway, chairman of John Brown (the shipbuilders), Firth Brown Steel, Westland Aircraft, and several large collieries; Charles Spencer, on the board of John Brown and of Associated Electrical Industries and chairman of Edison Swan Cables, a handful of firms involved in electricity supply, and of Lex Garages; and Sir Robert Renwick, a partner in the stockbroking firm of W. Greenwell and a director of electricity supply companies stretching all the way across southern England from Bournemouth to Folkestone.[82] All the industrial firms represented by the British party, apart from Westland, produced commodities whose pricing, distribution, and marketing were covered by international cartel agreements. It was not clear whether these would survive the outbreak of war even in the deep-frozen form which would allow them to be revived after the conclusion of hostilities.

The combination of self-interest with a natural aversion from war did not, however, lead the industrialists into expressing the kind of sympathy for German foreign policy which had been shown by Tennant. Goering asked the industrialists to use whatever influence they had to achieve British mediation in the Polish–German dispute. There would be no need for war if the Poles could be persuaded to back down over Danzig;

[80] PRO PREM 1/335, report on a meeting with Herr von Ribbentrop by E. W. Tennant, 31 July 1939.
[81] PRO FO 371/34452, report by Birger Dahlerus on events leading up to the outbreak of war.
[82] PRO FO 371/22991, C11182/16/18, report of 9 Aug. 1939. The other members of the delegation were Messrs. Albert Holden and S. W. Rason and Sir Holberry Mensforth. The directorships are all listed in the 1939 edition of the *Directory of Directors*.

such a move would reduce international tension and make possible the resolution of the crisis by a Four-Power conference on the Munich model. In reply, the British party defended rearmament and the talks with the Soviet Union: both were measures of security in the face of German expansionism. Hitler's invasion of Czechoslovakia had shown he could not be trusted, and the British government feared that Nazi Germany aimed at the control of central and south-eastern Europe, after which it would turn on the British Empire. Any further aggression would have to be resisted. Significantly, all Goering was able to offer was a spheres-of-interest deal in which Germany's colonial claims were recognized along with its retention of hegemony over the 'near east' as well as central and eastern Europe. In return Berlin would acknowledge British paramountcy over the Commonwealth and Empire. It was a proposition which extended the principle of cartelization to international relations. This was enough for the industrialists to assure Goering that there could be serious Anglo-German talks if London was approached by a negotiator sent in 'good faith'.[83] The message was underlined by the Foreign Office, which confirmed that the British government would participate in any attempt to establish conditions conducive to effective direct conversations between Germany and Poland, a formula with overtones of Munich.[84]

The question was, however, what would produce 'good faith' on the part of the German government? The efforts of the amateurs reinforced the attempts of the prime minister and the Foreign Office to pacify the international situation. These revolved around the offer to Germany of full-blown economic partnership. The origins of this initiative were located in a discussion on 6 June between Sir Horace Wilson and Helmut Wohltat, who was seen by London as a conduit to Goering as a result of his responsibility for the Four Year Plan. When Wohltat returned to London, ostensibly as a delegate to the International Whaling Conference held some seven weeks later, he saw Wilson again as well as Robert Hudson from the Department of Overseas Trade. It was at these talks that the British apparently held out the prospects of an economic *détente* in return for a 'joint . . . declaration that forcible aggression will not be employed by either country as an instrument of international policy'.[85]

[83] PRO FO 371/22991, C11182/16/18, report of 9 Aug. 1939.

[84] PRO FO 371/22991, C11707/16/18, draft note to Goering, 22 Aug. 1939.

[85] *DGFP*, vi. 977–83, Wohltat's minute, written for Goering, of conversations with Sir Horace Wilson, Sir Joseph Ball, and Robert Hudson, 24 July 1939. See also *Documents and Materials Relating to the Outbreak of the Second World War* (Moscow, 1948), ii. 67–72, Dirksen's report of 24 July 1939; and 117–24, Dirksen's minute of a conversation with Sir Horace Wilson, 3 Aug. 1939.

According to Wohltat's account, Wilson proposed a package of measures beginning with 'an agreement on the export of German and British industrial products to the principal markets in the British Empire, China and the USSR'. The evidence of Wohltat, the German ambassador Dirksen, and of Robert Hudson shows that the British were prepared to recognize the economic predominance of the Nazi regime over central and eastern Europe as long as the British were able to keep a share of the region's trade. Hudson ruled out outright colonial concessions but gave another airing to the idea of 'some form of agreement in which Africa would be administrated [sic] jointly by the European powers in trust'. He also suggested loans for the Reichsbank, the 'restoration of the link between the European capital markets', and settlement of the international debt question. Germany's own difficulties with the payment of debts could be overcome by Anglo–American financial assistance.[86] Wilson concluded the talks on 21 July by reminding Wohltat of the potential for economic expansion in a 'common foreign trade policy for the two greatest European states'.[87]

It did not take long for the talks to become surrounded by an atmosphere of confusion and mystery which remains to this day. Historians disagree about the significance of the Wohltat mission. Among recent commentators, Alistair Parker takes the episode seriously[88] while Donald Watt maintains that it has been 'subject to more misunderstanding than any other single question of the years before the war'.[89] The problem is twofold. First, a distorted version of the conversations was leaked to the press. News stories began to circulate to the effect that Britain had offered Germany a massive loan, possibly as much as £1,000 million. Hudson then attempted to set the record straight by publicizing his own version of events, but only managed to intensify the furore. There was an awkward scene in the House of Commons. Chamberlain was evasive about Wilson's contacts with Wohltat and said that Hudson had been acting on his own initiative. Reports of a British loan to Germany were denied.[90] The government argued that the sensationalism of the newspaper accounts had given a status to the discussions which was entirely unwarranted. Both Dirksen's and Chamberlain's versions of this strange chapter, not available until after the war, support the British government's position as far as the loan is concerned. Dirksen told the Foreign Office

---

[86] Hudson's account of his encounter with Wohltat can be found in PREM 1/330.

[87] *DGFP*, vi. 977–83, Wohltat's minute to Goering of 24 July 1939.

[88] Parker, *Chamberlain and Appeasement*, 264–5.   [89] Watt, *How War Came*, 395–6.

[90] Ibid. 401.

that it 'had played no role in the conversations'[91] and the notion was dismissed by Chamberlain, who told his sister that all his critics had 'put two and two together and triumphantly made five'.[92]

Secondly, in support of his claim that the importance of the Wilson–Wohltat and Hudson–Wohltat talks has been grotesquely exaggerated, Watt has argued that Wohltat's and Dirksen's accounts were so far removed from the truth as to be worthless.[93] The two officials deliberately talked up the British approaches in order to convince Hitler through Goering that war was not inevitable and an Anglo-German *détente* still lay within reach. To achieve this impression Wohltat attributed to Sir Horace Wilson a set of proposals which he had in fact been advocating himself for much of the past year. The result was a 'mish-mash of ideas that had been floating around centres of international gossip for a decade'.[94] Hudson's version of his meeting with Wohltat shows that this encounter had not been subject to such misrepresentation: however, if Chamberlain's angry reaction to Hudson's conduct is any guide, the latter's extravagent discourse was an unauthorized, personal initiative.[95]

Watt's dismissal of the affair is, however, unjustified. It is reasonable enough to argue that both Wohltat and Dirksen put a pro-*détente* spin on their reports and played down Wilson's warning that Britain would fight if Germany used force against Poland. But the evidence does not support the contention that it was Wohltat who set the agenda for the meetings. The offer attributed to Wilson represented more than Watt's 'mish-mash': it was the culmination of proposals the British government had been making to Berlin ever since Chamberlain had raised the issue of colonial appeasement, and covered all the outstanding economic issues of the day, notably debt settlement, market sharing, and Germany's foreign-exchange shortage. This was the natural sequel to the Standstill talks, the Anglo-German Payments Agreements, and to the resolutions produced jointly by the FBI and the RI, with the government's backing, at Dusseldorf. The initiative followed from the suggestion made by Wilson himself to Hitler in September 1938, that amongst the 'many things' which ought to be discussed by the British and German governments on the

---

[91] *Documents and Materials Relating to the Outbreak of the Second World War*, ii. (report by Dirksen, 24 July 1939).

[92] Chamberlain quoted by Parker, *Chamberlain and Appeasement*, 262.

[93] Watt, *How War Came*, 396.   [94] Ibid. 402.

[95] PRO PREM 1/330, report by Robert Hudson of a conversation with Helmut Wohltat, 20 July 1939.

resolution of the Sudetener issue were 'arrangements for improving the economic position all-round'.[96]

Nor was the incident an isolated one. The anger expressed towards Hudson by Chamberlain extended to his minister's indiscretion not to his objectives. These were now to be pursued through 'other and discreeter channels'.[97] No time was wasted in opening them. Thus Fritz Hesse, German press attaché in London at the time, recalled in his memoirs how Wilson had spoken to him of Chamberlain's desire for 'a defensive alliance for a period of twenty-five years' between the two countries, an agreement which delimited respective spheres of economic interest, and a loan.[98] At the same time the Labour peer Charles Roden Buxton received the backing of Wilson and of both Halifax and his deputy, R. A. Butler, for a mission to meet senior Nazis, notably Deputy Führer Rudolf Hess, between 8 and 21 August.[99] Roden Buxton called for Anglo-German agreement based on a final settlement of all grievances arising out of Versailles. This meant recognition of German hegemony in central and eastern Europe and the allocation to the Reich of some African territories under a system of international co-operation.[100]

Furthermore, the aftermath of the Wilson–Wohltat conversations does not support Watt's contention that the efforts of Wohltat and Dirksen had been 'all in vain'.[101] After a talk with Dirksen, Wilson himself recorded that Wohltat's information 'had aroused considerable interest' which had been shared by Hitler. Wilson then underlined the importance of peaceful moves on Germany's part; it was up to Hitler to take the heat out of the international situation by removing his troops from the Polish–German border, beginning demobilization, and by announcing his intention to establish home rule for Bohemia and Moravia. If Berlin were to announce 'that there was henceforth to be no aggression on their part, the policy of guarantees to potential victims *ipso facto* became inoperative'.[102]

[96] PRO FO 371/21741, C10822/1941/18, record of a conversation between Wilson and Hitler, 27 Sept. 1938. See above, Ch. 4, p. 85.

[97] See Chamberlain quoted by Parker, *Chamberlain and Appeasement*, 262.

[98] Fritz Hesse, *Hitler and the English* (1954), 68. Given the publication date of this memoir it is inconceivable that Hesse was trying to do anything except set the record straight.

[99] Papers of C. Roden Buxton, Rhodes House, Oxford, 3/4/44, notes for a meeting with R. A. Butler, 1 Aug. 1939; and 3/4/44, report on a visit to Germany, 8–21 Aug. 1939.

[100] Papers of C. Roden Buxton, 3/4/44, 1 Aug. 1939.

[101] Watt, *How War Came*, 403.

[102] PRO PREM 1/330A, report of a meeting with Dirksen by Sir Horace Wilson, 3 Aug. 1939.

The message was a firm one. Unfortunately it was obscured and continued to be so by all that had gone before and by the official approval for the missions of amateurs such as Tennant and Roden Buxton, who were little better than Nazi fellow-travellers.[103] The cumulative effect of Wilson–Wohltat and of the other feelers was to give Hitler the mistaken impression that in Chamberlain's book *détente* counted for more than deterrence to the extent that Britain would not fight over Danzig.[104] In consequence, all the warnings were ignored while attention in Berlin came to be focused on the inducements offered by Wilson, Hudson, Tennant, and Roden Buxton. These provoked Hitler into offering a non-aggression treaty to Britain on the assumption that such a prospect would galvanize London into putting pressure on the Polish government to yield over Danzig.[105] Henderson made a half-hearted effort in this direction with the approval of Chamberlain and Halifax,[106] while Cadogan expressed interest in the possibility of a treaty[107]—but Polish refusal to discuss any compromise finally led to the German onslaught and the honouring of the guarantee.

Although the government's moves towards an Anglo-German non-aggression pact were nullified by its determination to honour its commitment to Poland, its actions over the summer had frightened both potential and actual allies, as well as encouraging enemies. Most historians accept that the Anglo-German discussions were instrumental in persuading the Soviet Union to steal a march on the western powers and insure itself through its own non-aggression treaty with Germany.[108] Meanwhile the

[103] Tennant, for example, wrote of 'the united, dynamic, very young German nation'. He called it 'something tremendous which is definitely there' and recommended 'we should . . . make more attempt to understand it, work with it and accept it. It is now too late to attempt to dam up this terrific force. The last chance of doing that would have been at the time of the march into the Rhineland. We can now only try to guide them, and this we can only begin to do if we can get on to more friendly terms.' See PRO PREM 1/335, report by Tennant of his meeting with Ribbentrop, 31 July 1939. Roden Buxton meanwhile argued 'that we must be prepared to dictate to the Poles to stop Poland becoming arbiter of the fate of the British Empire' and urged recognition of eastern Europe as 'Germany's natural *Lebensraum*'—precisely what Hitler wanted from Britain. What could he have possibly thought of the British government's nerve in the summer of 1939 when it connived at 'unofficial' approaches to Berlin by people like this? See C. Roden Buxton Papers, 3/4/44, 1 Aug. 1939.

[104] See e.g. Parker, *Chamberlain and Appeasement*, 269; Watt, *How War Came*, 405.

[105] PRO FO 371/22978, C12193/15/18, report of a meeting between Dahlerus and Goering, 28 Aug. 1939.   [106] Lamb, *The Drift to War*, 334.

[107] PRO FO 371/22978, C12214/15/18, note of a telephone conversation between Cadogan and Henderson, 30 Aug. 1939.

[108] See e.g. Parker, *Chamberlain and Appeasement*, 270–1. The Soviet Union would have been well aware of what was going on between London and Berlin as a result of reports from its own well-placed agents.

French were alarmed by the talks. The British embassy in Paris reported on 29 July that Foreign Minister Laval now expected '*une trahison* by Great Britain . . . there would not be war because Great Britain would capitulate'.[109] It was a disastrous signal to send to an ally whose own resolution was known to be weak in the first place.

The French thought they knew why the British government had embarked on so counter-productive a course of action. Their perceptive and well-informed ambassador in London, Charles Corbin, linked Wilson and Hudson's meetings with Wohltat to the impact of rearmament on the economy. Growing anxiety about the costs of the defence programme had led the British to consider proposing to Hitler 'against some guarantee of security, the immediate return of German industry . . . to production for peace, a loan for disarmanent which would allow the Reich to stabilize its exchange, buy primary materials and return to a free economy, thus putting an end to the arms' race which is ruining Europe'.[110] This was a fairly well-informed analysis, particularly acute in its reading of opinion inside the Treasury—the same opinion which had led Simon to call three weeks earlier for the declaration of 'finality of expenditure (unless for overmastering reasons) on armaments'.

It can hardly be disputed that the logic of the Treasury's position, let alone that of the government's supporters in finance and industry, pointed not just to the avoidance of war but to the conclusion of a speedy *détente* with Nazi Germany. Interestingly and unsurprisingly, the most hectic phase of Anglo-German contacts and peace discussions since the invasion of Czechoslovakia post-dated the Cabinet meeting of 5 July. In May and June the government had emphasized the deterrence side of its twin-track policy; in July and August the weight was on *détente*. The fact that Anglo-German agreement was never going to be possible should not lead us to underestimate the urgency and intensity of attempts to reach it during the critical weeks of July and August 1939. A world was at stake. How could it be preserved once war had broken out?

---

[109] PRO FO 371/22990, C10521/16/18, report by Campbell on French reaction to conversations of Wilson and Hudson with Wohltat, 22 July 1939.

[110] See *Documents Diplomatiques Français*, 2me serie, *Tome* 17 (Paris, 1984), Document 268, Corbin to Foreign Ministry, 21 July 1939. A report from de Saint-Hardouin, chargé d'affaires in Berlin to Foreign Minister Bonnet of 27 July revealed how the French had been told by a 'well-informed' British journalist that Vansittart had been the source of the leak which had exposed Wohltat's conversations to the press. See Document 331, de Saint-Hardouin to Bonnet, 27 July 1939.

PART 3

War and Peace, 1939–1941

6

Limited War and the Search for a Compromise Peace, September 1939–May 1940

A Phoney War Economy?

The outbreak of war was followed by a flurry of activity on the part of the government. For several months the civil service had been preparing plans for the establishment of a wartime administration. These now came into their own. Chamberlain accepted the resignation of his Cabinet and appointed a new, War Cabinet. New ministries appeared—economic warfare, to conduct the blockade of Germany; food; shipping, to take responsibility for the merchant shipping effort as well as to organize the construction of more ships; and information, to manage propaganda. The War Cabinet authorized the Ministry of Supply to start industrial preparations for a fifty-five division army—the thirty-two British divisions approved a few months earlier augmented by twenty-three recruited from the Dominions, India, and from prospective allies. The Ministry of Labour was given responsibility for national service (it was already operating the registrations for compulsory military service), which was now extended to cover the male population to the age of 41. At the same time a Capital Issues Control Committee was established, to approve issues only for defence purposes or for the maintenance of food supplies. Petrol rationing was established. Exchange controls and import licensing were introduced, to conserve foreign exchange for the purchasing of vital foodstuffs, raw materials, and machine tools, many of them from the United States.

This reads impressively. Yet the reality was very different. The state of mobilization over which the Chamberlain government presided was appropriate to the 'phoney war', a period characterized by virtually no land-based fighting which lasted from the defeat of Poland in September 1939 until April 1940. On 2 September Sir Samuel Hoare, then home secretary and one of the leading proponents of appeasement, told a German journalist that: 'Although we cannot in the circumstances avoid declaring war, we can always fulfil the letter of a declaration of war without immediately going all out."[1] During Chamberlain's remaining time as prime minister these sentiments formed the basis of government policy. The composition of the War Cabinet is enough to give the game away. Chamberlain brought in Churchill as first lord of the Admiralty (his office in 1914) and Anthony Eden as Dominions secretary, but his concession to pre-war critics of the appeasement policy was limited. Simon remained chancellor and Halifax stayed at the Foreign Office. Hoare was moved to the post of lord privy seal but was appointed to the War Cabinet. A long-term supporter of Chamberlain, Kingsley Wood, kept his position as secretary of state for air. When encouraged to approve bombing raids whose purpose would be to set fire to the German forests, he protested on the grounds that such an action represented the wanton destruction of private property.[2] Although the wartime administration appeared to wield more power over the economy and society even than Lloyd George had done in the 1916–18 period, there were no dramatic disturbances to the tenor of life in Britain apart from the evacuation of children away from cities where they would be vulnerable to enemy air-raids. The government refused to initiate food rationing until its hand was forced by the prospect of shortages and the pressure of public opin-ion at the turn of the year.[3] Reluctance to embark on action which might lead to the development of what is now called a 'command economy' led to the rejection of calls from a team of economists, led by Sir William Beveridge and including J. M. Keynes, for tighter state direction.[4] As a result, departments which were central to the war effort, such as the Board of Trade and the Ministries of Economic Warfare, Food, Labour, Ship-ping, and Supply, continued to lead independent lives.[5] For example, in the first months of the war the Ministry of Shipping arbitrarily imposed an import limit of 19.8 million tons a year on the Ministry of Food and one of 23.8 million tons a year on Supply. These quotas, which could not be enforced anyway, were however ignored as both departments embarked on stockpiling programmes, a situation which could only be resolved on the introduction of rationing.[6]

Mobilization by half measure was in fact typical. Thus, the creation of the fifty-five division army, apparently completely at odds with the pre-war trajectory of British strategic thinking, was little more than an

---

[1] *DGFP*, vii. 401, report of *Mitarbeiter* correspondent to Berlin.
[2] See Taylor, *English History*, 560.   [3] Ibid. 565–6.
[4] Paul Addison, *The Road to 1945: British Politics and the Second World War* (1982), 64.
[5] Addison, *The Road to 1945*, 65.   [6] Taylor, *English History*, 565.

aspiration. There was no programme, no deadline except 'as soon as possible'.[7] The scheme, if it can be called one, was surrounded by conditions which could not be met in the present or even in the near future. Meanwhile a small British Expeditionary Force (BEF) of four divisions was packed off to France on 11 September. *The Times*, not for the first time acting as the government's mouthpiece, said the BEF was 'wonderfully prepared',[8] an absurd exaggeration which quickly became obvious. Within three months sixty-two government back-benchers were in the army and reports of shortages in supplies, particularly of munitions, became commonplace.[9]

Progress towards the elimination of these shortages was leisurely. Government spending showed no dramatic increase to meet the emergency of war, rising from £20 million a week in September–October 1939 to £33.3 million six months later.[10] There were still 1 million people out of work in the spring of 1940.[11] As late as the start of May 1940 Churchill was able to lament the fact that manpower in the munitions industry had risen by only 11 per cent since the outbreak of war—one-sixth of what was needed.[12] No great effort was made to secure the co-operation of organized labour in managing a transition from a peacetime to a wartime economy. Anxious not to confront the trade unions yet reluctant to reach a concordat with them, the government had embarked on the conflict with no firm plans for the transfer of workers to war and war-related industry.[13] It is true that a National Joint Advisory Council was established early on, to provide a forum for tripartite consultations between the government, employers, and labour. In addition, following a meeting with a TUC delegation on 5 October Chamberlain issued a circular calling on all government departments to ensure maximum co-operation with the trade unions.[14] But the Ministry of Labour took no effective steps to organize the flow of skilled engineering workers into the munitions industries, where departments of state and private firms were poaching each other's supplies. Nor was any action taken to end the anarchy which characterized the scramble for workers in the construction of military camps, aerodromes, and munitions factories, particularly in the more remote parts of the country.[15] Meanwhile industry carried on producing

[7] W. K. Hancock and M. M. Gowing, *British War Economy* (1949), 96.
[8] See ibid. 96.   [9] Addison, *The Road to 1945*, 69.
[10] Hancock and Gowing, *British War Economy*, 96.
[11] Taylor, *English History*, 567.   [12] Ibid.
[13] Hancock and Gowing, *British War Economy*, 60–2.
[14] Addison, *The Road to 1945*, 58.
[15] Hancock and Gowing, *British War Economy*, 147–9.

luxury goods. Even in June 1940 copper was still being used in large amounts in the manufacture of jewellery, curtain-rails, and bedsteads; the home market was absorbing 50 per cent of all lead supplies; more licences appear to have been issued for the inessential use of jute cloth than for its use either directly or indirectly by the government.[16]

Concern to preserve as much as possible of the pre-war order was the hallmark of budgetary and of foreign trade policy. Simon took a Gladstonian attitude to public finance.[17] Even so, sharp increases in direct as well as in indirect taxation could not cover more than 46 per cent of the government's wartime spending commitments.[18] The government was, of course, prepared to borrow to cover the gap between revenue and expenditure, as it had been since 1937. The Treasury was, however, determined that funds would be raised from the capital market on the voluntary principle.[19] Accordingly there was continuing worry that serious inflation would result if the government's requirement exceeded what the capital market was willing to provide.[20]

These anxieties were justified. In February–March 1940 the government estimated that it would need to borrow between £1,200 to £1,500 million during the next twelve months. It attempted to raise the first slice, a War Loan of £300 million at 3 per cent, in March. The issue was not a success; although total applications exceeded the amount offered, a substantial proportion came from public organizations rather than from private subscriptions, which fell short of the amount hoped for by the Treasury.[21] It was not an encouraging start. And yet the attempt to raise £300 million was nothing compared to what was going to be required in the future on the government's own projections, let alone those of its critics from all parties who favoured an intensification of the war effort.[22] In the meantime inflationary pressures were building with more intensity than had been experienced in the first year of the 1914–18 conflict (Table 6.1).

It was not clear how the war could be financed according to the 'voluntary principle'. Keynes had already suggested an alternative in his pamphlet *How to Pay for the War*. He had shifted attention away from the narrow issue of government funds to the total amount of national income. Calculation of national income and expenditure would

---

[16] Hancock and Gowing, *British War Economy*, 177.
[17] See R. S. Sayers, *Financial Policy 1939–1945* (1956), 34.
[18] Hancock and Gowing, *British War Economy*, 171.
[19] Sayers, *Financial Policy 1939–1945*, 33–5.   [20] Ibid. 42–4.
[21] For details see ibid. 199–200.   [22] Ibid. 35.

TABLE 6.1. *Wholesale prices and wages, August 1914–August 1915 and September 1939–July 1940*

	Wholesale Prices	Wages		Wholesale Prices	Wages
1914	100	100	1939	100	100
1915	129	105/10	1940	142	112/13

Source: A. J. P. Taylor, *English History, 1914–1945* (2nd edn., 1975), 568 (derived from Hancock and Gowing, *British War Economy*, 152, 166).

allow the government to break Gladstonian bonds because it provided a statistical foundation for working out the difference between the value of goods and services produced and total money demand in the economy. Keynes had argued that it was this difference which should be taken as the measure of the inflationary gap rather than the discrepancy between government expenditure and revenue from taxation and voluntary savings. But how was this gap to be closed? Was Britain to repeat the experience of 1914–19, when rising prices had done the job, provoking labour unrest in the process? Keynes suggested that it would be possible to avoid this by controlling demand through higher taxation as well as through the encouragement of increased savings. In particular, he called for forced savings, namely sharp increases in income tax which could be refunded at the end of the war in order to sustain economic activity into peacetime.[23]

These proposals were not taken up by the chancellor for his April 1940 budget. Simon, albeit with some misgivings, clung to the 'voluntary principle' with the full support of his civil servants at the Treasury. Given the disappointing results of the War Loan exercise all the chancellor could do was to manipulate taxes to raise money, treating surtax payers quite sharply as he did so and introducing purchase tax.[24] As *The Economist* understood, this was a budget, and an approach to financial policy, which was different in degree but not in kind from the pre-war days. The journal called for a much more drastic approach to personal taxation in particular—on the Keynesian grounds that it was vital to reduce civilian consumption.[25] Meanwhile the Liberal and Labour parties frequently tried to inject more urgency into the mobilization and Ernest Bevin, general secretary of the Transport and General Workers' Union, accused the prime minister of following a banker's and a *rentier*'s policy.[26] Although neither *The Economist*'s nor the Opposition criticisms were well

[23] Ibid. 33–4.   [24] Ibid. 36–44.   [25] Ibid. 42.
[26] Addison, *The Road to 1945*, 58–62.

received in the Treasury, there was even here a dawning realization that the requirements of fighting and financing a war might very soon force a 'much more full-blooded confiscation of private wealth'.[27]

The most dramatic departure from pre-war orthodoxy had occurred in the field of foreign trade policy, with the introduction of exchange control and of import licensing. Here again, however, appearances were deceptive. From 3 September the sterling area, having emerged into the open after Britain's departure from the gold standard, became a formal trade and currency bloc. Sterling could still be used freely within the area but the automatic right of residents to convert it into other currencies was withdrawn for the first time since the Napoleonic wars. It now became obligatory for residents to surrender specified currencies to the Treasury if they were in Britain, to its equivalent if they were in the Dominions, or to local currency boards if they were in the colonies. The most important of these specified currencies, known as 'hard', was naturally enough the dollar; members of the area agreed to pool dollars and entrust them to the Exchange Equalisation Account in London in return for sterling at a fixed rate of exchange. At the same time the Account issued to each member a hard-currency ration considered adequate to satisfy its economic requirements.[28] It was a system designed to free the British government from anxieties about shortages of foreign exchange: in addition to the restrictions on dollar-purchasing, sterling area members would accept deferred payment for wartime supplies, building up their balances as a result, if they could not be immediately paid in goods, or in cash. By the end of the war Britain's use of food, raw materials, and above all military bases throughout the sterling area was to result in accumulated balances of £2,723 million (almost 31 per cent of the GNP in 1945).[29]

Although these arrangements allowed Britain to fight the war supported by the resources of the sterling area, they did not add up to the construction of an impenetrable ring fence around it. Non-resident sterling was not subject to controls and in the early months of the war foreign holders were able to convert their balances into hard currencies, notably dollars. It was estimated that as much as $737 million was lost to the reserves between September 1939 and early 1940 in consequence.[30] The

[27] Sayers, *Financial Policy 1939–1945*, 35, n. 4.
[28] See Hancock and Gowing, *British War Economy*, 106–12; Sayers, *Financial Policy 1939–1945*, 232–5.
[29] Hancock and Gowing, *British War Economy*, 111. The 1945 GNP figure is taken from Feinstein, *National Income, Expenditure and Output*, Table, 1, T6.
[30] See Newton and Porter, *Modernization Frustrated*, 100.

introduction of dollar-invoicing for exports of tin, rubber, whisky, and furs to the Americas, the Dutch East Indies, Switzerland, and Belgium helped to check the drain. However, this move had an unfortunate side-effect: it limited the market for free sterling to the extent that much of the demand for the currency collapsed and its market rate fell into a steady decline against the official rate, set at the start of the war, of £1 = $4.03. By the end of March free sterling was changing hands at £1 = $3.55.[31] After the explosion of hostilities on mainland Europe in April and May it fell back to £1 = $3.00.[32] This allowed foreign importers to purchase the sterling they needed for all but a narrow range of commodities at discounts of between 20 per cent and 30 per cent and represented a reversal of the terms of trade against Britain at the least opportune moment. Nevertheless, the Treasury and the Bank of England continued to hold out against restrictions on the use of non-resident sterling. They wished to 'preserve sterling, as far as possible, as an international currency after the war',[33] and the chancellor argued additionally that interference with 'the essential liberties which, in the financial and every other field, are traditional in this country' would only act as a disincentive to foreign sterling-holders.[34]

The foreign-exchange difficulties which followed from the lax system of exchange control were exacerbated by the lack of enthusiasm with which the government embarked on the restriction of imports to essential goods. The needs of government departments for foreign exchange became the responsibility of the Treasury's Exchange Requirements Committee (established on 29 August 1939). Private importers were subject to a policy of import licensing, under the control of the Board of Trade. The existence of dual responsibility allowed a significant volume of imports to fall through the net completely, with neither the Treasury nor the Board of Trade taking charge of them. As much as £120 million out of a total import programme of £920 million was left unlicensed in November 1939. No action was taken to reduce the level of what were known as 'uncontrolled imports' until March 1940, when the Ministry of Food agreed to license a long list of privately imported foods.[35] Whether earlier resolution of this difficulty would have led to a significant reduction

---

[31] Sayers, *Financial Policy, 1939–1945*, 244.   [32] Ibid. 245.

[33] Papers of Paul Einzig, Churchill College, Cambridge, 1/18, Hargreaves Parkinson to Einzig, 8 Mar. 1940: report of a talk with Cameron Cobbold (Bank of England). Einzig was a well-connected financial journalist and a passionate opponent of appeasement.

[34] See PRO T 231/77, memoranda and parliamentary statement by Simon on the free sterling market; Sayers, *Financial Policy 1939–1945*, 246–7.

[35] Hancock and Gowing, *British War Economy*, 113.

in leakages of foreign currency is, however, open to doubt. The Import Licensing Department banned very few commodities: even when it came to luxury foodstuffs, importers were allocated a ration on the basis of their past trade.[36]

The weaknesses in the system of exchange and import control assumed growing importance as dependence on the dollar area began to assume unsustainable proportions. On the outbreak of war the government had attempted to concentrate purchases from the USA on foodstuffs and raw materials rather than on manufactured goods. Machine tools formed the main exception to this rule, taking up 17 per cent of the $720 million the British estimated they would have to spend on US supplies during the first year of the war. Only 11 per cent of the total was supposed to be taken up by aircraft and aircraft engines, but this limit was abandoned after French protests in December 1939.[37] The result of what has been described as 'these soaring commitments' was that the prospects of financing a three-year war, the foundation of British strategy, began to appear dim. Two separate analyses of the balance-of-payments situation made early in 1940, one by Lord Stamp and the other by the Treasury, concluded that by the end of the year Britain's external balance was likely to be £400 million in the red. The sterling-area deficit was likely to be of the same order.[38] It meant that Britain could spend no more than £150 million from its reserves of gold and foreign exchange each year if it was to fight the three-year war; it followed that at the present rate of consumption there would have to be a 'vast' contraction of the war effort by the end of the second year of the conflict.[39] In these circumstances the chancellor succeeded in gaining the approval of the Cabinet for an export drive, and for an investigation of the armament programme with a view to a reduction in its size.[40] The government had arrived at an absurd position: in order to be able to continue the war against Germany it would become necessary to de-escalate it—and this before the fighting had seriously begun. Would Hitler oblige?

The Search for a Negotiated Peace: (1) Official

Tighter exchange controls, a tough import-licensing policy, forced saving, industrial conscription, and a concordat with the trade unions might

---

[36] Hancock and Gowing, *British War Economy*, 113.
[37] Reynolds, *The Creation of the Anglo-American Alliance*, 75.
[38] Hancock and Gowing, *British War Economy*, 115.
[39] Ibid. 115; Reynolds, *The Creation of the Anglo-American Alliance*, 75.
[40] Hancock and Gowing, *British War Economy*, 116–17.

well have eased the government's predicament. So might an approach to overseas purchasing characterized by the recklessness demanded by French premier Edouard Daladier in December 1939, when he told the Supreme War Council that he would be prepared to sell every picture in the Louvre if they would buy more American aircraft.[41] The Chamberlain Cabinet was not willing to take these steps because they would have overturned once and for all what was left of the pre-war politico-economic order, undermining Britain's international financial strength and political influence in the process.[42] Chamberlain had gone to war because he had reluctantly been forced to the conclusion that Nazi object-ives threatened international order and British security and influence. Nei-ther he nor his wartime government was prepared to adopt a strategy which put at risk what was being defended.[43]

It followed that Britain's partial mobilization was one half of a 'stra-tegic synthesis'[44] whose objective was not the total defeat of Germany but the destruction of the Nazi regime in a limited war, not least because of concern that a flattened Germany would open the door to Soviet dom-ination of eastern and central Europe.[45] It was believed that the three-year war would follow a pattern. Time was on the Anglo-French side, given the superiority of Allied economic resources over those at the disposal of the Germans. Thus it was expected, as it had been since 1937, that the enemy would attempt an early knock-out blow which would be thwarted by French ground forces and British air power. Thereafter, Allied mobil-ization would peak while German strength was whittled away by the block-ade. Finally, assuming no anti-Nazi coup in the meantime, there would be an Anglo-French offensive. German forces would be defeated, the Nazi regime humiliated, and a new administration in Berlin would sue for peace.[46]

---

[41] Ibid. 114.   [42] Addison, *The Road to 1945*, 62.

[43] See Newton and Porter, *Modernization Frustrated*, 90–3.

[44] For a detailed discussion of this term see Milward, *War, Economy and Society*, ch. 2.

[45] Chamberlain's principal private secretary, Arthur Rucker, went so far as to say that Communism represented a greater danger than Nazi Germany and argued that 'we should . . . not destroy the possibility of uniting, if necessary, with a new German Govern-ment against the common danger. What is needed is a moderate conservative reaction in Germany, the overthrow of the present regime by the Army chiefs.' See John Colville, *Fringes of Power: 10 Downing Street Diaries 1939–1955* (London and New York, 1985), entry for 13 Oct. 1939, 40–1. This view of the long-term danger posed by the Soviet Union was shared by the then deputy to SIS Chief Admiral Sinclair, Colonel Stewart Menzies. Menzies did, however, believe that in the short term the German menace was greater (information received from Kenneth de Courcy).

[46] Hancock and Gowing, *British War Economy*, 72, 99.

For the complex of industrial and financial interests which supported the inter-war *status quo* there was no alternative to Chamberlain's long game, if the war had to be fought at all. Industrialists feared that total war would swing the balance of power on the factory floor towards organized labour, as in 1916–18, while there was anxiety in the City about 'the value of the British currency'.[47] Both constituencies favoured only a limited conflict which could be wrapped up quickly before the pre-war *status quo* disappeared altogether.[48] Most of the liberal imperialists who had supported appeasement during the late 1930s swung behind the war effort, notably *The Times* and the RIIA–Round Table network, one of whose most articulate spokesmen, Lord Lothian, was sent by Chamberlain and Halifax to take up the post of British ambassador to the USA. The strategy was backed by the government's parliamentary supporters, press barons such as Lords Beaverbrook and Harmsworth, by powerful figures in the services, notably Field-Marshall Ironside, chief of Imperial General Staff, Admiral Lord Chatfield, minister for the Co-ordination of Defence, and by the new director-general of the SIS, Stewart Menzies. Menzies himself, who took over the position in November 1939, had a network of connections in the City and multinational industry as well as in the Royal court. This network was dominated by those who had espoused 'imperial isolationism' during the 1930s. It included the Duke of Buccleuch, Lord Steward of the Royal Household and a governor of the Royal Bank of Scotland; Lieutenant-Colonel W. S. Pilcher of the Coldstream Guards; Lord Bearsted, founder of Samuel's (the merchant bank) and chairman of the Nineteen Twenty-Eight Investment Trust as well as of Shell Transport and Trading, the British holding company for Royal

---

[47] See *DGFP*, vii. 363–7, undated report from Baron de Ropp of late 1939. It is almost impossible to provide any detailed account of feeling about the war in the City. In 1989 the author visited the Guildhall library in the City of London in the hope that the archives of leading merchant banks might shed some light on this matter. He discovered that either the papers were not available at all or that, if they were, it was as a rule only for the period before 1914. The American bank, Brown Shipley, was an exception to this, but even here disclosure ceases after 1 Sept. 1939. All that can safely be said is that there was a good deal of uneasiness. This can be intuited from the conduct of particular, influential figures such as Tennant (see Ch. 5 above) and Lords Buckmaster and Bearsted (see below). There are brief sketches of Buckmaster and Bearsted in Scott Newton, 'A Who's Who of Appeasement', *Lobster*, 22 (1991), 7–11.

[48] The FBI even protested to Chamberlain about the impact of his limited mobilization during the first months of the war. They complained that the pick of men and materials were going to munitions, with the result that export orders were being lost. See PRO PREM 1/359, meeting between Chamberlain, Simon, and Stanley, and an FBI delegation, 11 Dec. 1939. For FBI anxieties about total war, see Middlemas, *Politics in an Industrial Society*, 260, 267.

Dutch Shell;[49] Lord Londonderry,[50] like Lothian a member of the Anglo-German Fellowship; Baldwin Raper, the managing director of Shell-Mex; and Sir Robert Renwick, the stockbroker and industrialist who had met Goering shortly before the outbreak of war.[51] All of these individuals had supported the pre-war efforts to achieve a *détente* with Germany; most still hoped it would be possible to achieve one given a change of leadership in Berlin, although Buccleuch did not even see the need for this. The general approach to conducting the war favoured by these circles was expressed by Kenneth de Courcy, another member of the Menzies network, as the pursuit of a 'policy of economic and psychological warfare during a prolonged period of armed attentiveness'.[52]

The government did not, however, do nothing at all except sit back and wait for either a German mistake or the overthrow of Hitler, whichever came first. The search for 'moderates' with whom it could do business continued. Almost from the very start of the war London was in touch with those it felt to be members of the resistance to Hitler, apparently an assortment of generals backed by powerful industrialists such as the steel magnate Fritz Thyssen and by conservative and centrist political figures such as Karl Goerdeler, the mayor of Leipzig (and agent for Robert Bosch, the multinational motor engineering company).[53]

The received wisdom is that the British responded to German approaches but made few if any on their own account. It was the Germans who made the running. There certainly were German feelers,[54] occasionally from Hitler himself (after the conquest of Poland), more often from those purporting to be opposed to the Führer. After the

[49] The author's information on the Menzies network comes from Kenneth de Courcy. See also Padfield, *Hess: The Führer's Disciple*, 112–14. For details concerning Bearsted and Raper see Newton, 'A Who's Who of Appeasement', 7–11.

[50] Londonderry was a large-scale landowner, with extensive estates in northern England and Northern Ireland, and coal-owner (e.g. of the Darlington Collieries) as well as ex-Cabinet minister (air secretary, 1931–5). For further details see Newton, 'A Who's Who of Appeasement', 7–11.

[51] See ibid. Raper's intelligence connections went back to 1918, when he was sent on a special mission to Finland. Renwick was a member of White's, frequently used by Menzies for his networking activities, and his obituarist recorded how he 'became widely recognized as a skilful negotiator in other than ordinary financial and business matters' (*The Times*, 1 Sept. 1973). The information concerning Menzies's connections with Buccleuch and Londonderry was given to me by Kenneth de Courcy himself.

[52] PRO FO 371/24363, C4100/267/62, quoting the Feb. bulletin of the Imperial Policy Group.

[53] See PRO FO 837/1306, report on American Bosch Corporation, note of 28 May 1943.

[54] These have now for the most part been well documented. See e.g. Klemens von Klemperer, *The German Resistance against Hitler* (Oxford, 1992), 154–216.

outbreak of war Dahlerus resumed his peace-broking efforts, again with the encouragement of Goering, but the Foreign Office response was unenthusiastic. The Swedish businessman's objective was, from the British viewpoint, a contradiction in terms. He claimed he was in a position to arrange negotiations with German 'moderates', responsible to Goering, which would produce a basis for a peace settlement. Apparently all this could be achieved with Hitler's approval![55] Chamberlain and Halifax, by December convinced that the German failure to launch an early offensive meant that time was on the side of the Allies and that Hitler knew it, were dismissive. They agreed that Dahlerus was principally concerned with 'saving the face of the present German Government'—a project which could not be squared with Britain's most fundamental war aim.[56]

Another approach came from General Wilhelm Keitel, chief of the Armed Forces High Command (OKW), via an American banker called Henry Mann in November. Keitel said that the German army wished to avoid a war in the west but it would obey Hitler's orders. Was it possible to start talking before there was any military action? This was a thin pretext for discussions, but the government did not ignore Keitel: Lord Bearsted flew out to Paris to meet Mann at the Ritz Hotel.[57] Subsequently the initiative hit the buffers; it was seen in the Foreign Office as part of the pro-Nazi machinations of some American businessmen who claimed to be operating with the support of President Roosevelt, notably James Mooney, European manager of General Motors, an oil millionaire called Rickett, and Ben Smith, who was well known on Wall Street.[58] Lothian confirmed from Washington that Rickett and Smith were 'catspaws of the Nazi Government working to put over the tale' that Goering was plotting against Hitler and that peace overtures should be started through him.[59] Enquiries with the State Department revealed that the Americans had no connections with the White House, and that their tale was 'fantastic'.[60]

[55] PRO FO 371/23100, C20525/13005/18, reports of meetings with Dahlerus on 18 and 27 Dec. 1939.
[56] PRO FO 371/23100, C20525/13005/18, report by W. H. Montagu-Pollock, 18 Dec. 1939.
[57] PRO FO 371/23100, C18837/13005/18, Campbell to Sargent, 17 Nov. 1939.
[58] Ibid.
[59] PRO FO 371/23100, 17219/13005/18, report from Lothian, 24 Oct. 1939. It should be noted that Mooney was a vice-president of General Motors, a post which would have given him the chance to keep in touch with Lord McGowan, chairman of ICI. McGowan, who was known for his pro-Nazi views (he had visited the Nuremberg Rally in 1938), was a director of General Motors.
[60] PRO FO 371/17219/13005/18, report from Lothian, 24 Oct. 1939.

As with the Dahlerus mission, the Keitel feeler led nowhere because it failed to meet what was for Chamberlain, and perhaps less emphatically for Halifax, the two basic conditions of any workable initiative. These were, first, the removal from power of Hitler and all his cronies with the exception of Goering, and secondly, German withdrawal from Poland and Czechoslovakia (excluding the Sudetenland, as agreed at Munich). Both had to be implemented together. As Chamberlain told his sister on 5 November: 'To my mind it is essential to get rid of Hitler. He must either die or go to St Helena or become a real public works architect, preferably in a "home". His entourage must also go, with the possible exception of Goering, who might have some ornamental position in a transitional government.'[61] Goering was still seen as a force for restraint at the heart of the Nazi regime, but there was no possibility that Chamberlain would deal with Hitler again. His feelings of personal betrayal by the Führer's conduct after Munich strengthened the conviction that no agreement with Nazism was possible after all. Chamberlain would not have budged from this position even if Hitler had offered to pull his forces out of Czechoslovakia and Poland.[62] He committed the government to the rejection of any Nazi 'peace offensive', or any neutral one which left the *status quo* in Berlin unchanged, and determined to continue with the blockade.

The British did not, however, play a passive role in this game of peacefeelers. The government made a few of its own during the phoney war, and there is some evidence that it came close to achieving a breakthrough on at least one occasion and maybe twice. The first significant British approach culminated in what has been known subsequently as the 'Venlo incident' of 9 November 1939, when two SIS agents, Sigismund Payne-Best and Richard H. Stevens, were seized by the SS on the Dutch–German border. Having been questioned they were sent to Sachsenhausen concentration camp, where they survived the rest of the war.[63] The background to this fiasco was an apparent negotiation with the spokesman for a group of rebellious generals which had lasted some three weeks. It turned out that the German 'dissident' with whom Payne-Best and Stevens were negotiating was an SS agent by the name of Walter Schellenberg. He was acting throughout with the approval of Heinrich Himmler, the Reichsführer SS; he was ordered to terminate the discussions and bring

[61] Neville Chamberlain Papers, University of Birmingham, NC 18/1/1129, letter to Ida Chamberlain, 5 Nov. 1939. [62] Costello, *Ten Days that Saved the West*, 58.
[63] The best account to date of this murky business is by Callum MacDonald, 'The Venlo Affair', *European Studies Review*, 8 (1978), 443–63. Even now the Public Record Office in London cannot release all the relevant documents.

the British agents over the border on the night of 8–9 November, following the explosion of a bomb at the Burgerbrau beer-cellar. Hitler had only just left, uncharacteristically early, following a commemoration of the failed 1923 *putsch*. The Führer blamed the SIS for the attempt on his life; it was Himmler who ordered the kidnapping. The result was a disaster for the Allies. Dutch neutrality had been breached, giving Hitler a pretext for invasion; SIS networks in the Low Countries and perhaps further afield were blown; and Anglo-French relations had been strained—Paris had only been let into the secret on 7 November.[64]

Was Venlo merely the last move in an intelligence game? There is plenty of evidence to show that for the British the talks were taken very seriously indeed, and some tantalizing scraps hint that the German negotiators may not have been as fraudulent as has been assumed. First of all, Chamberlain and Halifax, on SIS advice, thought they were dealing with a genuine resistance movement centred on the Wehrmacht which would shortly move to overthrow Hitler and establish a new regime. The plotters claimed they were 'strong enough to take a leading part' in the formation of a new administration.[65] Of the Nazi leaders, only Goering would be retained in office. They needed an assurance that Germany's transition from war to peace would receive the co-operation of 'all civilised countries'. The new government would seek the return of Germany 'to peaceful and friendly relations' with the world and would 'be sympathetic to a pan-European policy'.[66] It was all enough to make Cadogan, who had initially been extremely sceptical about the exercise, note that 'there's *something* going on in Germany'.[67] Not even the disappearance of Stevens and Payne-Best was enough to discourage the British, and hopes of success were only dashed when the Gestapo sent out a derisive radio message on 22 November.

The evidence that leads the historian to suggest that German intentions might have been quite serious can be found in the papers of Group-Captain Malcolm Christie. Christie was a businessman who had travelled widely across Europe in the 1930s. His extensive German contacts had led both Sir Robert Vansittart and Claude Dansey, who was appointed Menzies's assistant chief of SIS, to recruit him as an informant.[68]

[64] See von Klemperer, *The German Resistance against Hitler*, 161.
[65] Neville Chamberlain Papers, University of Birmingham, NC 8/29/1, 30 Oct. 1939.
[66] Ibid.   [67] Von Klemperer, *The German Resistance against Hitler*, 161.
[68] Anthony Read and David Fisher, *Colonel Z: The Secret Life of a Master of Spies* (1984). The author was also given information concerning Christie's intelligence activities by Adrian Liddell-Hart.

Interestingly, Christie had a house at Venlo, and at the same time as the two British agents were talking with Schellenberg he was engaged in a negotiation with Max von Hohenlohe-Langenberg, a well-connected Sudeten aristocrat who was apparently acting for Goering but who was later revealed to be an SS member and therefore responsible to Himmler.[69] On behalf of his 'friends' (generals and Gestapo leaders), Hohenlohe offered Goering as leader of a transitionary government which would negotiate a peace deal with the Allies.[70] It appeared that Goering, like the generals, was anxious about the results of an offensive against the west, and there were rumours that Hitler was keen to launch a pre-emptive strike. He shared Allied fears that the only victor in a war between Germany and the Anglo-French would be the Soviet Union.[71] Accordingly, an armistice was essential. Thereafter Goering would be ready to discuss withdrawal from Poland and Czechoslovakia, disarmament under international supervision, the liberalization of the economy, and to undertake in the meantime the establishment of 'a new code and order in Germany'.[72] It was a package which interested the British, and the Reichsmarshall even received 'a Royal invitation to parley'.[73] Christie and his superiors, however, made it clear that the complete removal of Hitler from the political scene was essential first, and it became obvious that Goering was not prepared to contemplate this.[74] How much contact there was between Christie and the SIS negotiators at Venlo is hard to establish, but it does seem that Christie was aware of their discussions, and his own followed parallel lines.[75] In addition, the sequence of events on

[69] See von Klemperer, *The German Resistance against Hitler*, 244.

[70] Christie Papers, Churchill College, Cambridge, CHRS 180/1/28, report by Christie of a conversation with Hohenlohe, 25 October 1939.

[71] Ibid., CHRS 180/1/30, letter to Vansittart of 13 Dec. 1939. This provides details of a memorandum from a 'very first-class source in the German Army', dated 28 Nov. 1939. According to the document, German generals 'claim to have been in touch with British persons of some influence in Royal circles', who advised them that if Germany was badly defeated the UK would not be able to prevent the French from breaking up the Reich. In fact, these circles were reported to have stated that the Reich could only stay intact 'if it developed a basis for peace negotiations prior to a decision in the field', meaning the resignation of Hitler and his replacement by a monarch—perhaps the eldest son of the Crown Prince. For Goering's fears about 'Bolshevism' see also CHRS 180/1/33, 17 Nov. 1939.

[72] Ibid., CHRS 180/1/28, note by Christie of evening telephone conversation with Hohenlohe, 8 Nov. 1939.   [73] Ibid.

[74] Ibid., CHRS 180/1/28, *passim*.

[75] Ibid., CHRS 180/1/28, document 28. This is dated 10 Nov. 1939. It gives Christie's reply to what appears to be a German peace offer and contains in addition a telegram of 13 Oct. from Royall Tyler, League of Nations, Geneva. This states: 'VANLOO RECEIVES NEWS SUNDAY PROPOSE TELEPHONING MI MONDAY BETWEEN FOUR AND FIVE O CLOCK.'

8 and 9 November hints at a connection. When Goering's refusal to move against Hitler was in the open, Christie and Hohenlohe discussed Hitler's 'extinction', which was 'still difficult but might presently be achieved at a price'.[76] This conversation took place on the evening of 8 November; within a few hours German broadcasting had announced the failed attempt on Hitler's life at the Burgerbrau. By the end of the next day Payne-Best and Stevens were under interrogation in Germany. The juxtaposition of events may be coincidental, but it looks as if Christie's talks reached a crisis-point at this stage. Judging by the material in his papers, the discussions with Hohenlohe became much less urgent after 12 November and fizzled out shortly afterwards.

The failure of this initiative and the revelation of SS involvement should not automatically lead us to assume that the Venlo incident was merely a German provocation. It is known that anxiety about Soviet expansion led Himmler to explore peace terms at the start of the war.[77] As early as 13 September the SIS were provided with a remarkably critical assessment of Germany's strategic position, emanating from a very senior level in the SS and typed in the office of a brigade-leader. There is no clue as to the identity of this man, except that he was 'highly placed'. The document accepted that Germany had miscalculated when entering the war. It had refused to believe that the British and French would fight over Poland, had not expected Italian neutrality, and had assumed that the Dominions would keep out of the conflict. Now the British were determined to fight, not for Poland but 'for peace and order in Europe'; they feared German expansionism and after the successive invasions of Czechoslovakia and Poland were unable to believe anything the German government said. Only the presence of Goering at the head not just of a War Council but also of a Peace Cabinet would facilitate the return of confidence in the validity of any negotiations. It was in the Reich's interest to follow such a course, given its poor long-term prospects in the face of British naval supremacy, the Anglo-French war mobilization, and the likelihood of future US intervention on the Allied side. Any peace settlement would have to guarantee respect for treaties, disarmament, ultimate liberation of the Czechs, and the reintegration of Germany with the international economy.[78]

Intentionally or not, the sentiments expressed in this paper represented

---

[76] Ibid., CHRS 180/1/28, report by Christie of an evening telephone conversation with Hohenlohe.   [77] See MacDonald, 'The Venlo Affair', 443–4.

[78] The document can be found in the Christie Papers, Churchill College, Cambridge, at CHRS 180/1/28, dated 13 Sept. 1939.

the agenda for the Venlo talks and for Christie's conversations with Hohenlohe. There seems no reason to believe that they were anything other than genuine. They were not intended for British eyes; a restricted number of copies were sent to Goering, two generals at the most, Gestapo chiefs, Ribbentrop, and a handful of diplomats in the headquarters of the Foreign Ministry.[79] It can therefore be argued that both Christie–Hohenlohe and the Venlo negotiations involved the exploration of a peace deal which had SS support and was none the less authentic for that. However, notwithstanding British optimism, a successful conclusion was always unlikely given the German refusal to specify withdrawal from Poland and to take any action against Hitler, who was to be head of the new, constitutional, post-Nazi government.[80] The German reaction to the Burgerbrau bomb thus gave the *coup de grâce* to a process which was doomed anyway.

Whatever the truth about Venlo and the Burgerbrau conspiracy, one thing is clear: peace-inclined German conspirators who purported to be members of the opposition would have to dispose of Hitler if they wanted Chamberlain to support them. What they wanted from the British above all was a commitment not to take military advantage of any instability which might follow from a coup against the Nazi regime. Talks held in February–March 1940 between Christie and Josef Wirth, an ex-chancellor of Germany, succeeded in eliciting this from London, along with a willingness to provide financial aid to a new German government in which it would be possible to have confidence.[81] The British were even prepared to consider a military diversion if this would help the plotters. The British government was impressed by Wirth. He claimed to speak for the army deputy chief of staff, General Franz Halder, former war minister Otto Gessler, Fritz Thyssen, and for the opposition circle around Robert Bosch. Wirth offered a new government, the federalization of Germany, reduction of Prussia to its component states, and 'a new Polish State and a new Czechoslovak State'.[82] It was all a waste of time. The initiative petered out. The reasons for this are still obscure. It has, however, been plausibly speculated that Wirth's influence was not as great

[79] The recipients are named in a covering note.

[80] This appears to have been Goering's view. The sentiments are reflected in his willingness to 'secure a new code and order in Germany' without removing Hitler (see Christie Papers, CHRS 180/1/28, note of telephone conversation with Hohenlohe, evening of 8 Nov. 1939).

[81] See ibid., CHRS 180/1/35, report on a meeting with Dr Wirth, 13 Feb. 1940. The incident is also related in von Klemperer, *The German Resistance against Hitler*, 163–7.

[82] Von Klemperer, *The German Resistance against Hitler*, quoting Christie, 165.

as he had led the British to believe, and that Halder, along with other generals, found the terms too radical for their taste.[83]

Perhaps the most important reason for the failure of Wirth's conspiracy was Halder's reluctance to strike against Hitler. Halder made this clear himself when he was interrogated after the war. He told Nicholas Kaldor, questioning him on behalf of the US army, that during the winter of 1939–40 he had obtained through the intermediation of the Vatican a written statement of peace terms from the Allies. It 'bore the signature of Lord Halifax, or someone with authority to sign on his behalf'. The terms included the permanent cession of Austria, the Sudetenland, and Danzig to the Reich, 'but involved the elimination of Hitler'. According to Kaldor's report, Goerdeler and General Beck were in favour of accepting the Allied proposals. Halder and his chief, von Brauchitsch, would not, however, co-operate with any attempt to assassinate Hitler at this stage of the war. In consequence, like its predecessors, the plan fell through.[84]

Chamberlain's covert diplomacy had found plenty of well-placed Germans who wanted peace and who were prepared both to sacrifice territorial gains and attempt—or at least say they would attempt—a de-Nazification of the regime in its cause. The problem was to engage with a conspiracy against Hitler which meant business. The impossibility of finding a way around this obstacle proved insuperable and undermined one prop of Chamberlain's long game. There was to be no coup against Hitler by the moderates. It was a difficulty characteristic of an approach to war which was moulded more with with an eye to domestic politico-economic priorities than to the realities of the international situation. Thus the blockade, upon which so many hopes were pinned, was a failure, reduced to an irritation as a result both of the Nazi–Soviet pact and of a steady flow of raw materials from Scandinavia. Meanwhile the three-year war strategy was about to face its greatest test at the hands of a leader whose aim was to finish conflicts within weeks. By the end of June the French

[83] Von Klemperer, *The German Resistance against Hitler*, 166–7.

[84] Papers of Lord Avon (Anthony Eden), University of Birmingham, AP/13/4/23, note of a preliminary talk with N. Kaldor, 22 Nov. 1945. Halder's recollection was slightly mistaken. He told Kaldor that it was Ulrich von Hassell, 'the German Ambassador to the Vatican', who was the agent of the Opposition to Hitler in this affair. In fact the intermediary was Dr Josef Muller, a Munich lawyer. Von Hassell, who had retired from the Foreign Ministry as well as from his diplomatic post (ambassador to Italy, not the Vatican) in 1938, was at the time negotiating with Lonsdale Bryans (see below). In all other essentials Halder's version tallies with the story told by von Klemperer, *The German Resistance against Hitler*, 171–80. After what had gone before the general can be forgiven his confusion.

were beaten and there was an enormous question-mark over the viability of British plans for fighting and winning a war over the long term. It took courage, skill, hard work, luck, and the entry into the war of the Soviet Union and the United States to make up for the fall of France and the collapse of the Anglo-French alliance.

The Search for a Negotiated Peace: (2) Unofficial

Chamberlain rehearsed his distaste for the Nazi regime and his blanket refusal to negotiate with Hitler or any representative therefrom to Sumner Welles, the personal emissary of President Roosevelt, in March 1940. Welles had come on a fact-finding mission, to see whether by talking to political leaders in London, Berlin, Paris, and Rome, he could discover whether there was any common ground which could provide the basis of a peace initiative.[85] Welles, however, was to find out that there were significant voices within the government itself which did not share the prime minister's robust attitude. Both Halifax and Butler, as well as Hoare, hinted that there were other 'constructive forces' which would be prepared to talk to Hitler if they could be convinced that any peace offer he was likely to make was a genuine one.[86]

The expression of such opinions was not confined to ministers. Notwithstanding the wide backing on the Centre-Right of British politics for the government's overall strategic approach, an influential minority of its pre-war supporters in the City, in large-scale industry, and among the landowning aristocracy had never supported the war. After the declaration they worked sometimes openly, sometimes behind the back of the prime minister, for a cessation of hostilities and the rebuilding of the 'Anglo-German connection'.

Very early on the Duke of Westminster organized a group of peers to press the cause of peace on the government. A meeting at Bourdon House, his residence in London, heard the former Conservative MP, Henry Drummond-Wolff, read a highly defeatist paper.[87] Drummond-Wolff was a friend of Goering and a Tory Imperialist who had since 1934 served on the Committee and the Council of the Empire Industries Association (EIA), founded some fifteen years earlier to encourage closer economic links between the countries of the Commonwealth and the

---

[85] See Reynolds, *The Creation of the Anglo-American Alliance*, 82. The official details of the Welles visit can be found in PRO FO 371/24406.

[86] See Costello, *Ten Days that Saved the West*, 72; Reynolds, *The Creation of the Anglo-American Alliance*, 82.   [87] PRO FO 800/317, Hankey to Halifax, 12 Sept. 1939.

Empire.[88] At its height the EIA could count over 200 Conservative MPs amongst its members. Not surprisingly, support for organized markets and planned capitalism, on the model of the cartel, was central to the EIA's economic philosophy. Some of its stalwarts, however, such as Drummond-Wolff, went further. Their dual contempt for *laissez-faire* on the one hand and socialism on the other had led them down the Fascist path. Thus Drummond-Wolff could argue that the press only took the view that it was impossible to have peace with the Nazis because it was controlled 'by the Left and the Jews'. The war had been provoked by 'the money-power'; it would be supported by the United States, 'prototype of the capitalist economy', and the Soviet Union, 'whose dream is world revolution'. The conflict meant hostilities between 'the two races which are the most akin and most disciplined in the world', 'until both are bled almost to death'. Germany was invulnerable on land and at sea, which meant that the issue could only be resolved through the 'beastliness' of air war. Here the planes of the Reich had a clear advantage since London was 'terribly, the best aerial target on the face of the earth'. These sentiments were greeted with assent by the gathering, which incuded the Duke of Buccleuch, the stockbroker Lord Arnold, and landowner Lord Rushcliffe.[89]

The pro-peace cabal met again two weeks later on 26 September, its ranks swelled by the arrival of some MPs as well as of Lord Roden Buxton and his brother Lord Noel Buxton.[90] For the rest of the phoney war this group provided a focus for other Rightist dissenters, such as, for example, Lords Aberconway, Brocket, Buckmaster, and Semphill. These were not fading aristocrats on the margin of British politics. The support of Buccleuch tied them into the Court and City circles which were cultivated by Menzies. Aberconway had been a member of the delegation which had met Goering in August 1939. Buckmaster was on the London Stock Exchange Committee,[91] while Brocket, a landowner, was chairman of the Land Union and before the war had been a confidant of Chamberlain.[92] Semphill, an aviator and industrialist, was a member of the Right Club, an underground pro-Nazi organization founded in 1939 by the

[88] See Anthony Cave Brown, '*C*': *The Secret Life of Sir Stewart Graham Menzies, Spymaster to Winston Churchill* (New York, 1987), 271.

[89] PRO FO 800/317, Hankey to Halifax, 12 Sept. 1939. The government was aware of this group's activities because one of their number, Lord Mottisone, was keeping Lord Hankey, minister without portfolio in the War Cabinet, informed.

[90] PRO FO 800/317, Hankey to Halifax, 26 Sept. 1939.

[91] See Newton, 'The "Anglo-German Connection"', 201.

[92] See Newton, 'A Who's Who of Appeasement'.

Conservative MP Captain A. H. M. Ramsay.[93] Ramsay had little difficulty in recruiting supporters, some of whom included Conservative peers
and MPs. By 3 September 1939 the Club, which had been founded in
May, had 200 members.[94] Not all of these, it is true, were known for their
front-line political activity. No doubt Lord Carnegie and the Duke of
Wellington fall into this category. However, others had more influence:
Colonel Harold Mitchell was vice-chairman of the Conservative Party,
while Charles Kerr and Sir Albert Edmondson were both government
whips. Sir Alexander Walker was not in parliament, but as chairman of
the Distillers' Company, Britain's fifth-largest manufacturing concern by
estimated market value in 1930, and a millionaire, he was in a position to
provide financial backing.[95]

For a good part of the time the peacemongers merely pressed their case
for agreement with Hitler through letters and petitions to the prime minister. On 8 January 1940, for example, Chamberlain was urged to undertake a peace initiative by Lord Arnold.[96] This appeal was supported by
Buccleuch, who expressed his agreement with Hitler that a war would
'play into the hands of Soviet Russia, Jews and Americans', leaving the
British Empire crippled.[97] On 7 March Lord Noel Buxton, supported by
Lords Aberconway, Arnold, Darnley, Harmsworth, Holden, and Ponsonby,
called for a negotiated peace. Hitler was increasingly concerned with 'the
western advance of Russia'; he wanted peace and could be persuaded to
withdraw from the non-German speaking parts of Czechoslovakia and
Poland subject to international guarantees concerning general disarmament and access to food and raw materials.[98]

Hitler's apparent willingness to withdraw from occupied territory and
join an international disarmament pact was cited by Lord Tavistock in
a personal initiative which became public knowledge in March and April.
The peer said that, in addition, Germany was ready to participate in a reformed League of Nations, hold a plebiscite in Austria, and co-operate
with an international body to find a national home for the Jews—on
condition the former colonies were returned. Tavistock, later the Duke of

---

[93] Costello, *Ten Days that Saved the West*, 63.   [94] See ibid. 115.

[95] For Right Club members see Costello, *Ten Days that Saved the West*, 479; for the size
of the Distillers' Company see Hannah, *The Rise of the Corporate Economy*, 102.

[96] Neville Chamberlain Papers, University of Birmingham, private letter from Arnold to
Chamberlain, to be signed by ten peers, 8 Jan. 1940.

[97] Buccleuch's manifesto can be found among the papers of Sir Basil Liddell-Hart,
King's College, London. The document in question is dated 23 Feb. 1940.

[98] PRO PREM 1/443, letter from Lord Noel Buxton.

Bedford, was a one-time supporter of Communism who had by this time become a Nazi sympathizer. Although regarded as an eccentric, he managed to make contact with the German legation in Dublin and claimed that his proposals had its imprimatur.[99]

Tavistock's efforts achieved nothing. In frustration the peer released the story to the press and there was a public furore. Hempel, the German minister in Dublin, denied any involvement in the affair. Such a course of action was not available to Lord Halifax, who had in fact known about Tavistock's initiative since January.[100] The foreign secretary had done nothing to deter Tavistock from continuing with his activities, and indeed had approved a visit to Dublin to check if the terms were authentic.[101]

The Tavistock affair cannot therefore be dismissed simply because its author was a maverick. The connivance of Halifax in the peace-broking of his fellow peer shows that the foreign secretary was prepared to go much further than Chamberlain and act alone in doing so. At the same time as Tavistock was pursuing his Irish connection, a businessman and adventurer of profoundly conservative views, Lonsdale Bryans, was engaged in meeting Ulrich von Hassell in Arosa on the Swiss–Italian border. Hassell was former ambassador to Italy. Having started out as an admirer of National Socialism he was now a member of the German resistance. He associated with the conservative and nationalist Beck–Goerdeler group which at this juncture still hoped to return Germany to democratic government and constitutional rule without removing Hitler, and to negotiate a peace which would leave a reformed Reich the hegemonic power in central and eastern Europe. There was to be no plebiscite for the Austrians and a 'Czech Republic', shorn not simply of the Sudetenland but also, by definition, of Slovakia, was to be established. Poland was to be restored— but on the basis of its 1914 frontier! All the usual noises were made about disarmament and economic liberalization.[102] The territorial provisions of these terms flew in the face of everything the British had been prepared to accept before or during the war. Bryans was nevertheless encouraged to pursue his contact by Halifax, against the advice of his permanent officials, until Cadogan and Vansittart finally prevailed on their chief to abandon this experiment in secret and informal diplomacy.[103]

---

[99] The Tavistock proposals, put together in the form of a memorandum dated 4 Apr. 1940, can be found in the Liddell-Hart Papers, King's College, London. The story of the affair is told in John P. Duggan, *Neutral Ireland and the Third Reich* (Dublin, 1985), 81–3.
[100] PRO FO 371/24406, C3828/89/18, report of a meeting between Halifax and Tavistock, 23 Jan. 1940.   [101] Duggan, *Neutral Ireland and the Third Reich*, 82.
[102] Von Klemperer, *The German Resistance against Hitler*, 168–71.
[103] Costello, *Ten Days that Saved the West*, 472–3.

The failure of open pressure on Chamberlain as well as of covert diplomacy did not deter a number of large-scale industrialists from attempting to cut short the war. The participation of these individuals in cartels and transnational enterprise put them at the heart of networks which included opposite numbers in Germany and which could operate as channels for peace proposals and discussions. The oil, telecommunications, and electrical industries provide three examples. First, executives from Shell-Mex and from the Anglo-Iranian Oil Company were in touch with Goering between October 1939 and February 1940 through contacts in the American oil industry.[104] The culmination of this process was a journey by Baldwin Raper, Shell-Mex's British managing director, to meet an emissary from Goering in Stockholm.[105] Secondly, in November 1939 the Roosevelt administration drew to Chamberlain's attention the peace-mongering activities of a 'substantial element of English big business'. The president specified Lord Inverforth, chairman of Cable and Wireless, linked to Telefunken by its participation in the international telecommunications cartel.[106] Finally, in the first four months of the war Sir Robert Renwick, Charles Spencer, and Birger Dahlerus, having been brought into contact before the war by transnational links in the electrical industry, continued their discussions about the conditions for international peace.[107]

These discussions put the government in a difficult position. It had become policy before the outbreak of war to encourage the spread of 'orderly marketing' throughout all sectors of the economy. To the extent that the industrialists were only trying to salvage such arrangements so that they could be resumed when hostilities had come to an end, it was possible to turn a blind eye to their activities. Thus, after the outbreak of war the Board of Trade and the Department of Overseas Trade were prepared to support the request of the Rolling Stock Manufacturers' Association for continuing membership in the International Rolling Stock Cartel. The Board of Trade took the view that it was desirable to

---

[104] PRO FO 371/24406, C3537/89/18, note of 22 Feb. 1940.   [105] Ibid.

[106] PRO FO 371/23099, C18201/3005/18, report by Lothian of a conversation with Adolf Berle, 9 Nov. 1939. For the wartime activities of Cable and Wireless see PRO BT 64/431, Electrical Machinery and Apparatus Cartels.

[107] See PRO FO 371/23099, *passim*; and PRO FO 371/23100, C20525/13005/18, report of a talk with Dahlerus by W. H. Montagu-Pollock, 18 Dec. 1939, and minute of 27 Dec. 1939. I have discussed the persistence of the cartels into the war and their use as a channel for peace discussions in 'Appeasement as an Industrial Strategy', given as a paper at the conference of the British International Historians' Study Group, University of the West of England, Bristol, 16–18 Sept. 1993. Publication is forthcoming.

maintain British participation in cartel agreements which had involved the industries of more than one country in the pre-war period. These had been made from the point of view of self-interest, namely to limit 'competition from other countries . . . when the war is over the necessity for these agreements may still exist'.[108] Similarly, British electrical manufacturers, notably British Thomson-Houston, were allowed to stay in the International Lamp Cartel. It is true that with the start of the fighting the organization had split in half, one comprising Allied and neutral manufacturers, the other built mainly around industry in Germany and central Europe. British interests were permitted to join the first of these two early in 1940. This did not, however, represent a significant change of policy. Detachment from German manufacturers was largely artificial. The new agreement involved the tacit acceptance by participants that German companies would keep their share of the neutral markets to which they had enjoyed access prior to hostilities.[109]

There was, all the same, a good deal of unease about the exploitation of business connections by industrialists for unofficial diplomacy. This was most strongly felt in the Foreign Office, which had unsuccessfully attempted to block the Rolling Stock Manufacturers' Association from staying in the International Rolling Stock Cartel. The argument had been lost on economic grounds on that occasion. At other times, however, it had been the foreign secretary himself who had overruled his advisers, as he had with the Lonsdale Bryans mission. Both the Renwick-Spencer and the Raper meetings with emissaries of Goering went ahead against the advice of the professionals in the Foreign Office. The second of these at least occurred with the approval of Lord Halifax.[110]

It was this willingness on the part of the foreign secretary to explore every opening which provided the anti-war lobby with a channel into the heart of the government. Lord Brocket's contribution of £200 towards the travelling expenses of Lonsdale Bryans[111] was testimony to this bridge between two fractions of what was now a divided establishment. The consensus in favour of appeasement had been replaced by a fracture between those who repudiated any further attempt to deal with Hitler and those

---

[108] PRO FO 371/23945, W17272/17272/49, memorandum by J. J. Wills (Board of Trade) to Strang, 22 Nov. 1939.

[109] PRO BT 64/53, F8932/39, International Lamp Cartel.

[110] PRO FO 371/23099, C17031/13005/18. The document reveals that Frank Roberts of the Foreign Office Central Department went to John Brown's London offices on 22 Oct. 1939 to discourage the Renwick and Spencer group from proceeding with their meetings with Dahlerus. He failed. As far as Raper is concerned, see Costello, *Ten Days that Saved the West*, 472.   [111] See Costello, *Ten Days that Saved the West*, 471.

who favoured an agreement with Nazi Germany whether or not Hitler was in charge of it. Admittedly the first group was the larger and more powerful of the two, but Chamberlain could not afford to ignore the second. It followed that his room for manœuvre was limited. Although criticized by the Labour Party and the trade unions for a leisurely approach to the war, it is difficult to see how he could have stepped up the effort, even if he had believed it was necessary and desirable to do so, without sacrificing his political base and presiding over a new government dedicated to total war and its corollary, a fully mobilized economy.

Chamberlain certainly rejected the defeatism of the Right-wing fellow-travellers, even to the extent, it now appears, of manœuvring Churchill into the premiership rather than Halifax on 9–10 May 1940.[112] However, he remained confident in his limited war strategy right up to the end, claiming just as the Norwegian fiasco was about to unfold that Hitler had 'missed the bus'.[113] He saw no reason to intensify the war effort and open his government to the Left until the disasters of April and May 1940 wrecked his strategy and his credibility inside parliament and throughout the country at large.

By the time the famous Norway debate had started German troops had begun the offensive which was to end less than two months later with the fall of France. It was now clear that if Britain were not to be defeated it would finally have to mobilize for total war. Chamberlain was not the man to preside over an administration dedicated to this task; his fate was sealed when the Labour leadership made it clear they would not serve under him. On 10 May Churchill, opponent of appeasement and advocate within the War Cabinet of a more offensive strategy, whatever the cost, succeeded to Number 10.[114]

---

[112] See ibid. 461–4.   [113] Taylor, *English History*, 573.
[114] The events are reconstructed in Addison, *The Road to 1945*, 92–102.

Total War and the Search for a
Negotiated Peace, 1940–1941

The Politico-Economic Consequences of Mr Churchill

The three-year, limited-war strategy could not survive the collapse of France. The Maginot Line and the French army had failed utterly to hold up the German advance. Following the signature of the Franco-German armistice on 22 June 1940 the British confronted a European politico-economic bloc either directly controlled or dominated by Nazi Germany. All of the north and west European coast from the Arctic Circle to the mouth of the Loire was in hostile hands. Britain's old ally was reduced to a neutral rump, its army shrunk to 100,000 men. The Italian entry into the war opened a second front in the Mediterranean and east Africa; there was concern about Japanese expansionism in the Far East. So not only had the foundations of the strategy for defeating Germany been destroyed but the nightmare of an isolated Britain engaged in a three-front war was now a serious prospect.

The government was left with a stark choice between peace with Germany, on Hitler's terms, or fighting on with the minimum objective of strengthening its bargaining power in any negotiation and with the more hopeful, maximum one of prolonging the conflict until American aid and maybe participation made victory certain. History records that the Churchilll coalition refused to treat with Hitler. Having taken the decision, it needed to overcome first a German attempt at subjugation from the air and then the Italian challenge to its imperial lines of communication. Britain surmounted both of these hurdles with the resources of technology, particularly radar, men, and munition which had been organized in Chamberlain's day.[1] These were, however, completely inadequate for a war to which no time-limit could now be attached.

All the same the government believed there was light at the end of the tunnel, largely because it was operating on the quite mistaken assumption that the German economy was seriously overstretched. In particular, the

[1] Hancock and Gowing, *British War Economy*, 210.

Ministry of Economic Warfare stressed the German shortage of oil.[2] In fact the German economy did not reach peak mobilization until 1943–4, and synthetic production ensured that lack of oil was not a problem until the last stages of the war.[3] This fantasy, however, propped up morale and justified a reformulated strategy. It was argued in the autumn of 1940 that German control over the Continent would ultimately collapse if the British knocked the Italians out of the war and tightened the blockade with precision bombing against key industrial targets as well as with acts of sabotage by resistance groups whose activities could be co-ordinated from London. Once the breakdown of German authority, morale, and co-ordination had become obvious British forces, along with those raised by the Allied governments-in-exile, could engage the enemy in direct combat on the Continental mainland.[4]

It followed that there needed to be a rapid and significant expansion of all the armed services, as well as of the merchant marine, in order to keep the flow of supplies coming to Britain. Thus the government committed itself to a front-line aircraft strength of 6,600 by mid-1942.[5] Merchant shipping production, which had all but collapsed in the Depression, was in late 1940 set a figure of 2 million deadweight tons per annum.[6] The aspiration to create by mid-1942 an army of thirty-two divisions supplemented by twenty-three from the Dominions, the Empire, and Allies, having been regarded as over-optimistic in May 1940, was confirmed in September.[7]

There was no chance that these targets could be met if the government stuck to the economic policy which had guided it through the first eight months of the war. Fulfilment of the programme demanded an increase in public spending incapable of being matched by funds raised through taxation and on the voluntary principle. It required a rise in the volume of imports from the United States at a time when Treasury fears about diminishing hard-currency reserves had led it to argue for cuts in overseas purchasing so that gold and foreign-exchange resources were used up at a rate of only £150 million a year. Even before the fighting had started in Scandinavia and the Low Countries they were being run down at a rate of between £200 million and £250 million a year.[8] Yet in view of the determination to continue fighting there was no alternative to total war and its corollary, the abandonment of financial caution along

---

[2] Taylor, *English History*, 625.   [3] Ibid. 625.
[4] Hancock and Gowing, *British War Economy*, 214–15.
[5] Ibid. 213.   [6] Ibid. 255.   [7] Ibid. 213.
[8] PRO T 160/992/F17002, minutes by Waley and Phillips of 13 and 15 May 1940.

with a return to the interventionist policies of the Lloyd George coalition between 1916 and 1919. Treasury fears were overridden: the import
programme continued to expand and on the fall of France was extended
to include all outstanding French orders, worth $600 million.[9] What was
left of the post-reconstruction macroeconomic framework had to be
jettisoned, along with its central assumption that the national interest was
only compatible with policies designed to deliver 'sound finance' and the
maintenance of sterling's role as an international currency. Defence of the
national interest now called for a new economic policy which emphasized
the full employment of resources.[10]

The Churchill coalition offered such a definition of the national interest. Of necessity repudiating the Tory-liberalism which had dominated
the political agenda between the wars, it received the backing of those
who had fought against economic orthodoxy. The result was a government
which in the circumstances was greeted with a groundswell of popular
enthusiasm, both because it offered hope for the future and because its
composition was more genuinely 'national' than its predecessors. True,
there was no great purge of appeasers. Simon was appointed lord chancellor and replaced by Sir Kingsley Wood, while Sir Samuel Hoare was
sent to Madrid with the 'special mission' of keeping Spain out of the war.
None the less, the new administration contained Tory imperialists (for
example, L. S. Amery and Lord Beaverbrook), Britain's most powerful
trade-union leader (Ernest Bevin), key members of the Labour Party
(Clement Attlee, the leader, along with his deputy Arthur Greenwood,
A. V. Alexander, Hugh Dalton, and Herbert Morrison), and Lloyd George
Liberals such as Sir Archibald Sinclair. What united these men was commitment to full mobilization. Most of them, particularly on the Left,
had been advocates of planning and intervention since the late 1920s.
Beaverbrook and Amery had never supported the international economic
liberalism of the British establishment. Imperialists, trade unionists, socialists, and radicals were all from their different perspectives committed
to maximum production for the war.[11] The absolute priority of this objective was finally signalled by the absence of the chancellor from the War
Cabinet for five months. Meanwhile the power of the Treasury in the
Whitehall bureaucracy was reduced. Until 10 May the Economic Policy
Committee and the Food Policy Committee had both been chaired by the
permanent under-secretary to the Treasury. When Churchill took over in

[9] Reynolds, *The Creation of the Anglo-American Alliance*, 97.
[10] PRO T 160/992/F17002, EPC 40/30, 17 May 1940.
[11] Newton and Porter, *Modernization Frustrated*, 90.

Downing Street he replaced the civil servant with Greenwood (minister without portfolio) and Attlee (lord privy seal).[12]

The first steps towards the abandonment of the old, limited-mobilization policy had in fact been taken by the Chamberlain government on 9 May. Then it was accepted that financial considerations could not be allowed to stand in the way of a rapid and substantial improvement in British defences. However, it was easy enough to jettison a policy;[13] but a replacement had to be found. It was one of the achievements of the Churchill coalition to develop an economic strategy which was determined by the war effort rather than the other way around.

The starting-point was a massive increase in public expenditure. Some of this was already programmed, but the decision to stand by a thirty-two division army and an air-force of 6,600 front-line planes by mid-1942 accelerated and intensified the expansion. Over the war as a whole public spending was increased from £1,933 million in 1939 to £5,565 million in 1945; the government pumped £900 million into capital investment in the munitions industries.[14] From 1940 to 1945 its outlays accounted for over 50 per cent of GNP; although they fell after 1945, they never returned to pre-1939 levels (Table 7.1). The process was financed by abandoning the last vestiges of Gladstonian finance and substituting for it Keynesian national income accounting.

Although national income accounting allowed the government to make full use of the country's financial resources and pursue an anti-inflationary policy at the same time, the new 'stabilization budgets' were not in themselves adequate to cover the gap between goods and services produced and the high level of demand in the economy. Unemployment disappeared. Consumption goods became relatively scarce. Market forces bid up prices in the first year of the war with the result that the cost-of-living index rose by 21 per cent, wholesale prices by 44 per cent, and the index of wage rates by 13 per cent.[15] The response initially took the form of piecemeal measures to extend rationing, and of price controls. For the most part these measures covered foodstuffs. But the cost-of-living index was not calculated solely on the basis of food prices. Between June 1940 and March 1941 fuel prices rose from 116 to 119 while clothing prices leaped from 137 to 168 (August 1939 = 100). As early as November 1940 it was obvious to the prime minister's advisers in the Economic Section

[12] Hancock and Gowing, *British War Economy*, 217.
[13] Reynolds, *The Creation of the Anglo-American Alliance*, 97.
[14] Newton and Porter, *Modernization Frustrated*, 90.
[15] PRO T 230/12, paper by James Meade on 'Principles of War Finance', 25 Nov. 1940.

TABLE 7.1. *Central government expenditure as a percentage of GNP, 1931–1951 (£ million)*

Year	Expenditure	GNP	% expenditure of GNP
1931	884	4,063	21.6
1932	868	3,913	22.2
1933	822	3,927	20.9
1934	813	4,173	19.5
1935	851	4,380	19.4
1936	885	4,543	19.5
1937	960	4,912	19.5
1938	1,110	5,177	21.4
1939	1,538	5,478	28.1
1940	3,378	6,878	49.1
1941	4,637	7,921	58.5
1942	5,228	8,540	61.2
1943	5,729	9,080	63.1
1944	5,878	9,140	64.3
1945	5,194	8,754	59.3
1946	3,669	8,855	41.4
1947	3,154	9,458	33.5
1948	3,291	10,517	31.3
1949	3,495	11,133	29.8
1950	3,539	11,737	30.2
1951	4,519	12,958	34.9

Note: Statistics do not include expenditure by public corporations or by local authorities.
Source: Derived from Feinstein, *National Income, Expenditure and Output*, T8, Table 2 and T31–2, Table 12.

of the Cabinet Secretariat that a comprehensive counter-inflationary strategy would be necessary for the sake of social justice and stability. Accordingly, in the winter of 1940–1 new schemes of rationing, based on the allocation of points to limit demand for food and clothing, and of price controls, giving the Board of Trade power to fix maximum prices and margins, were drawn up. They were formally introduced in the spring.[16]

These measures guaranteed that no citizen would be short of the basic requirements of a civilized existence. Additionally, given the central place of labour in a war where production held the key to victory, controls were an essential part of the government's bargain with the trade unions. Bevin quickly understood that a formal wages policy would be unacceptable. It was, however, equally obvious that wage restraint was crucial to the maintenance of price stability in a fully employed economy: this was achieved because organized labour was prepared to exchange pay demands for physical action against inflationary pressures.[17]

[16] Hancock and Gowing, *British War Economy*, 334.   [17] Ibid. 333–40.

This concordat between the Churchill government and the trade unions signalled the resurgence of corporatism. After May 1940 the trade unions were more effectively integrated into decision-making than ever before. The presence of senior Labour Party figures in the War Cabinet had much to do with this, but most important was Ernest Bevin's appointment to the Ministry of Labour. Bevin's responsibility for manpower policy made him the most significant figure on the home front. His past career guaranteed him the confidence of trade unionists—a vital asset given the importance of industrial conscription to the war effort. Bevin's central task was the allocation of workers to the most essential industries—munitions, coal, steel, electricity, agriculture. This was achieved by 'manpower budgeting', and between mid-1941 and mid-1943 Britain added 2 million people to the forces and to the munitions industries.[18] Output in arms and arms-related industries such as aircraft, vehicles, engineering, and metal manufacturing expanded. Aircraft production per annum rose from a total of 7,940 in 1939 to 26,263 in 1945. Launchings of Royal Navy ships and landing craft increased from 94,000 deadweight tons in 1939 to 600,000 deadweight tons in 1943.[19] In the radio and electronics industry the output of valves grew from 12 million a year in 1939 to more than 35 million in 1944.[20]

Control of manpower was a necessary but not a sufficient condition for these achievements. Equally significant was the co-operation of the trade unions, which was secured partly as a result of the Ministry of Labour's concern for the welfare of each worker and partly as a consequence of institutionalized co-operation between government, industry, and labour. The mechanism was the National Joint Advisory Council, where civil servants met with employers and trade unionists to co-ordinate regional and national planning for the war effort. At the same time the organization of the productive effort required the development of a partnership between government and industry. The process was reflected in a significant expansion of civil servants involved in liaison with industry. Before the war their number had stood at 14,700: by the time of its conclusion there were 113,000.[21]

In these circumstances some erosion of the autonomy enjoyed in the era of 'industrial self-government' was inevitable. The allocation of imported raw materials, it is true, was organized by trade associations. But these operated within a framework of official supervision conducted after

[18] Newton and Porter, *Modernization Frustrated*, 96.   [19] Ibid.
[20] Pollard, *Development of the British Economy, 1914–1990*, 165.
[21] Newton and Porter, *Modernization Frustrated*, 97.

early 1942 by the Ministry of Production. Industrial sectors which did not perform as efficiently as the government wished were liable to drastic reorganization. Thus, in 1943 the Ministry of Aircraft Production forced firms with a poor production record to change all their controlling personnel.[22] At the same time it became necessary to curtail the output of consumer goods in order to release capital and labour resources for the war effort. Accordingly, civilian industry was cut back and concentrated in a handful of factories working round the clock. Between March 1941 and March 1944 about 290,000 workers were released from 'non-essential' activities and directed into munitions and other war-related industries.[23]

The British determination to carry on fighting Germany alone necessitated the rapid construction of a command economy best characterized by the term 'war socialism'.[24] Essential to this process was the transformation of the sterling area into a discriminatory economic bloc where foreign trade and payments were lifted out of the market altogether and placed under the control of the government. The loss of foreign exchange from the central reserves and the problems created by the low free sterling rate in New York led during the period May–July 1940 to the deliberate suspension of sterling's status as an international currency. Recognizing the need to 'reconsider' the economic situation in the light of 'the enemy's resolve to seek immediate victory', the government overrode Treasury misgivings and introduced a series of bilateral payments agreements with its suppliers. It correctly anticipated that the substitution of direct for multilateral settlements would minimize the loss of foreign exchange provoked by the sterling rate in New York. In effect, Britain followed the German example: trading partners would be paid for exports in limited amounts of their own currencies drawn from the Control and considerably larger sums of sterling which could not be used outside the sterling area.[25]

These controls on the use of non-resident sterling, supplemented by regulations which forbade the sale of sterling securities, could not, however, prevent the continuing outflow of hard currency which, together with the accumulated sterling balances, left Britain in 1945 as the world's greatest debtor. While the reduction of Britain's sterling liabilities could be postponed until after the end of the war, payment of gold and dollars for imports from the United States could not. Churchill managed to buy

---

[22] Milward, *War, Economy and Society 1939–1945*, 205.
[23] Newton and Porter, *Modernization Frustrated*, 96.
[24] See Taylor, *English History*, 205.   [25] Sayers, *Financial Policy 1939–1945*, 296.

time by taking the option which had been considered and rejected a year earlier—namely, the exchange of strategic bases throughout the Caribbean and in Newfoundland for destroyers, now to assist with anti-invasion as well as with anti-submarine patrols. The British reserves were, however, seriously depleted in late summer when they were used to finance large orders for aircraft and tanks. By mid-October the Treasury had come to the conclusion that Britain would be unable to fund purchases from the United States after December.[26]

Churchill was hopeful that it would be possible to avoid such a crisis, largely because he believed that the re-election of Roosevelt in November 1940 guaranteed a pro-British policy in Washington. Whilst this was a correct assessment of the president's loyalty, it was a highly unrealistic one of his political position. Roosevelt was hedged around with isolationist sentiment and neutrality legislation; it was impossible for him to lead the United States into taking a more active part in the conflict, as Churchill had hoped. Nor was FDR able to arrange the massively generous programme of credit the British needed. Ultimately, of course, the difficulty was surmounted by the introduction of Lend-Lease and the extension of US anti-submarine convoy escorts across most of the Atlantic during 1941.[27]

The prime minister called Lend-Lease 'the most unsordid act in history'. On one level it was certainly an act of remarkable generosity. As Roosevelt had said, it removed the dollar sign from British war requirements and allowed access above all to American ships, aircraft, munitions, petroleum, and food worth a total of $27,023 million (£6.7 billion, equivalent to the total British Gross Domestic Product by factor cost in 1940).[28] Yet although no payment was required, conditions were attached. As a gesture of good faith the British had to realize assets in the United States. In particular, they were forced to sell American Viscose Corporation (AVC), a Courtaulds subsidiary, at half-price, the Treasury itself having to compensate Courtaulds, within a week of the Lend-Lease bill's signature by FDR.[29] Secondly, the British were not permitted to re-export any Lend-Lease material they did not require, and they also had to agree not to export any commodities they produced themselves which were similar to those received under Lend-Lease. All this contributed to a fall in British exports from a level of 100 in 1938 to 29 in 1943.[30] Finally,

[26] Reynolds, *The Creation of the Anglo-American Alliance*, 147.   [27] Ibid. 147–50.
[28] Hancock and Gowing, *British War Economy*, 353; see also Feinstein, *National Income, Expenditure and Output*, Table 3, T10.
[29] Reynolds, *The Creation of the Anglo-American Alliance*, 163–4.
[30] Taylor, *English History*, 624.

the British were compelled to sign a 'consideration' that, in return for American aid, they would commit themselves to co-operation with Washington in the post-war creation of a multilateral world economic order, of necessity built on the principles of non-discrimination in trade, currency convertibility, and fixed exchange rates. This spelt trouble ahead for Imperial Preference and the sterling area as it had developed during the war.[31]

The political impact of total war was profound. Just as in 1914–18, the bargaining power of organized labour was enhanced by full employment and by its presence in the institutional machinery of tripartite collaboration. State action strengthened collective-bargaining arrangements in areas where workers had hitherto been poorly organized: a statutory minimum wage was fixed for agricultural workers and a National Reference Tribunal was established to arbitrate in unresolved disputes between both sides of the mining industry.[32] Trade union membership expanded from 6.25 million to 8 million during the war years; weekly earnings rose from an index of 100 in 1939 to 180.5 in 1945. Reinforced by progressive taxation and by price controls, these wage rises facilitated an increase of £900 million in the share of the national income taken by wage-earners between 1938 and 1947 (1947 prices). During the war there was a mild redistribution of income to the working class, whose after-tax income rose by 9 per cent, while middle-class income after tax fell by 7 per cent.[33]

The combination of full employment, greater political power, and relative prosperity fired the self-confidence of organized labour. A new agenda began to develop, from a comparatively early stage in the war, which reflected long-standing aspirations to job security, comprehensive health care, town and country planning, and equal access to educational opportunity. These proposals had their roots in the reconstruction movement of a generation earlier; they had been supported by the marginalized coalition of planners and trade unionists during the late 1920s and 1930s. It was, therefore, unsurprising that in January 1941 an entire edition of *Picture Post* was devoted to the creation of a new, socially just Britain after the war.[34] This commitment to the eradication of poverty and gross inequality was reinforced by a growing faith in the power of interventionist economics to deliver the basis for prosperity. The passage of the Education Act and a succession of White Papers in 1944 ensured that whoever was in power once the enemy had been beaten would be committed to the establishment of secondary education for all to the age

[31] Reynolds, *The Creation of the Anglo-American Alliance*, 274–82.
[32] Newton and Porter, *Modernization Frustrated*, 103.
[33] All figures quoted in ibid. 103.   [34] Ibid. 101.

of 15, a national health service, a planned urban and rural environment, and a permanently high level of employment, to be achieved by the deployment of Keynesian economics.[35] It was a scenario in which the Bank of England figured not as a defender of sterling's world-wide role and of zero inflation but as a promoter of economic growth and of closer links between the City and industry. For the last three years of the conflict the Bank conducted an unsuccessful rearguard action against plans for its nationalization. This was an act of public ownership to which even Conservatives such as Churchill himself had no objection.[36]

It was fitting that Churchill should fail to oppose the nationalization of the Bank. In 1925, as chancellor of the exchequer, he had reluctantly followed the advice of the Bank and the Treasury in returning Britain to the gold standard. His action had confirmed the hegemony of orthodox economics and its proponents, who were at the core of the post-reconstruction liberal–conservative coalition. Now, as prime minister in charge of a total war which could not be fought without the repudiation of inter-war conventional wisdom and the political marginalization of the interests which had supported it, Churchill was preparing the ground for a new politico-economic order.

It must be admitted that the prime minister was not enthusiastic about some of the most critical items in the reconstruction programme. He tried to play down the significance of the Beveridge Report, for example, arguing that fighting the war took precedence over social engineering.[37] But Churchill's efforts to water down reconstruction were undermined by the need for support from the Left and by the growing popularity of the agenda for post-war Britain. The arrival of the sea-change was confirmed in 1945. A coalition of planners, technocrats, trade unionists, the liberal professions, and returning servicemen and women voted for a Labour Party which was seen as the vehicle best equipped to fulfil the hopes for a better future and the completion of the work which had been so peremptorily brought to a halt after 1918.[38]

Halifax's Peace Bid, May–September 1940

Neville Chamberlain had remained in government after his resignation as prime minister. He took over as lord president of the Council until

---

[35] See Addison, *The Road to 1945*, 244–7.
[36] Newton and Porter, *Modernization Frustrated*, 106. Churchill abstained in the parliamentary vote on nationalization of the Bank of England.
[37] See Addison, *The Road to 1945*; and Newton and Porter, *Modernization Frustrated*, 102.   [38] Addison, *The Road to 1945*, 270–8.

ill health compelled his retirement in September (he died two months later). The ex-prime minister was prepared to accept and endorse the implications of fighting on. But many who had supported his policy of appeasement were not. The King had wanted Halifax to take over the premiership.[39] His anxieties about Churchill's judgement and policies, and about the new premier's supporters across the political spectrum, were shared by many within the Conservative Party. Not the least of these was Lord Halifax, who described Churchill and his associates as 'gangsters'. The term met with the approval of R. A. Butler, who consoled himself and the exiled Hoare with the thought that Churchill could be brought to heel by the powerful 1922 Committee of back-benchers if he forgot that 'the Government depends upon the Tory squires for its majority'.[40]

The remarks of Halifax and of Butler reflected a belief that Churchill's commitment to total war threatened strategic disaster for the British Empire. As it became increasingly obvious that Britain would fight on, whatever happened to France, this became a conviction strong enough to override the two ministers' loyalty to the government of which they were members. They reckoned it was futile to struggle on alone: Britain risked the loss of its navy and the collapse of its position in the Middle East, given the increasing likelihood throughout May 1940 that continuing war against Germany meant conflict with Italy as well. A strategic disaster of this magnitude would not only mean the loss of access to oil but in addition the severing of communications with the Indian Empire as well as with the Far Eastern territories currently held by Britain. Defeat on such a scale would leave Britain at the mercy of the Axis powers; there would be no possibility of peace with honour. In these circumstances the survival of Britain as an independent state, let alone of the Empire, would be at Germany's discretion.[41]

Halifax's and Butler's profound misgivings about continuing the war if there was any chance of escape with dignity put them at the centre of a peace movement which was connected to all the core institutions of the Conservative Party. The presence within it of Queen Mary, the Dukes of Westminster and Buccleuch, Lords Aberconway, Bearsted, Brockett, Buckmaster, Harmsworth, Londonderry, Mansfield, and Rushcliffe, as well as of at least thirty MPs, demonstrated the enduring nature of the lobby's links to the court, the City, large-scale industry, and to the land-owning aristocracy—Butler's Tory squires.[42] It was more than anxiety

---

[39] Costello, *Ten Days that Saved the West*, 47.   [40] Ibid. 52–4.   [41] Ibid. 206–7.
[42] Kenneth de Courcy, 'The Late Lord Butler, KG', *Special Office Brief*, 2 Apr. 1987; interviews with Kenneth de Courcy, 4 Aug. 1989 and 23 Feb. 1990.

about the future of the Empire *per se* that united this group, although that was genuine enough. All its members shared a profound fear that the domestic and international order which had sustained liberal–imperialist Britain was about to be irretrievably overturned. Already the war had begun to transform the relationship between the state and society. With some justification it was believed that total war meant the socialization of Britain and a ruinous conflict in the heart of Europe from which only the Soviet Union would benefit. US ambassador Joseph Kennedy reported to his president that Montagu Norman believed 'Britain as we have known it was through', while Halifax reckoned the war 'will mean Bolshevism all over Europe'.[43]

Churchill could not fail to be aware of this political reality which rendered his position vulnerable. The Conservative MPs who had supported appeasement to the bitter end were still in the House of Commons. When Churchill entered the chamber with Chamberlain after forming his new administration it was the former prime minister who received the bigger cheer. Churchill warned several radical journalists looking for a dramatic purge of the 'Guilty Men' that if he 'trampled on these men . . . they would set themselves against him' and in that strife lay Germany's best chance.[44]

Nevertheless, the new prime minister did take some radical steps against his opponents on the Right. By May 1940 it was obvious that the British Union of Fascists (BUF) was part of a network which linked the Nazi Party in Berlin to the Right Club and another pro-Nazi organization known as the Nordic League.[45] There was plenty of evidence to indicate that both the Right Club and the Nordic League were using access to military secrets to pass extremely sensitive material to Germany, including details of British plans for the invasion and defence of Norway in April.[46] At the same time it was clear that the two groups were in the process of merging with the BUF. As early as 11 September 1939 the ruling council of the Nordic League had agreed that it should join the BUF, looking to Sir Oswald Mosley as their leader.[47] For months Special Branch and MI5 had observed BUF, Right Club, and Nordic League activity. In May 1940 the authorities pounced, the pretext being the liaison of Right Club member and Nazi agent Anna Wolkoff with a cipher clerk at the American Embassy, Tyler Kent. Kent had shown

---

[43] Costello, *Ten Days that Saved the West*, 141.
[44] Reynolds, *The Creation of the Anglo-American Alliance*, 103.
[45] Pauline Henri, 'Verge of Treason', *Searchlight*, 192 (1989), 9–11.
[46] Ibid. 10.　　[47] Ibid.

Wolkoff copies of Churchill's correspondence with Roosevelt in the first months of the war. These had been copied and sent on to Rome and Berlin. Kent, meanwhile, seemed to be waiting until the start of the presidential campaign before releasing the information to the press in an attempt to wreck Roosevelt's prospects of re-election by revealing him to be in league with the British to put an end to US neutrality.[48]

Churchill was sufficiently alarmed by evidence of this pro-Nazi activity to persuade the Cabinet to approve Defence Regulation 18b, which gave the Government powers to arrest and detain potential dangers to British security. The bill completed all its parliamentary stages in a single day and received the Royal Assent at 6.00 p.m. on 22 May. It was followed by a crack-down on the far Right: during the following three months 1,769 people were arrested, including Sir Archibald Ramsay, MP, Anna Wolkoff, former director of Naval Intelligence Sir Barry Domville, Sir Oswald Mosley, and leading BUF members.[49] The Duke of Buccleuch was at the same time dismissed from his post as lord steward of the Royal Household and placed under surveillance;[50] the director-general of MI5, Sir Vernon Kell, was sacked on the grounds that he had been too indulgent towards the Fascist underground; Churchill himself took the unusual step of appointing his own personal intelligence adviser, Sir Desmond Morton. Morton, a veteran of Churchill's Focus group and possessing an SIS background, was seen by the prime minister as rather more committed to the anti-Fascist cause than Kell had been or Menzies was reputed to be.[51] It all amounted to a warning to opponents of the war effort and meant that advocates of peace with Germany would have to tread very carefully if they were to be left free.

It is of course true that there were a handful of Leftist MPs in the peace group, and that along with one of its parliamentary organizers, R. R. Stokes, this faction looked to Lloyd George as leader of an alternative administration.[52] The motivations here were diverse: following the Communist Party line, which was to denigrate the war as 'imperialist' throughout the time of the Nazi–Soviet pact; pacifism; or, as in the case of Stokes himself, an extraordinarily naïve Germanophilia. Yet this

[48] For a detailed account see Costello, *Ten Days that Saved the West*, ch. 5.

[49] Ibid. 115; Henri, 'Verge of Treason', 10–11.

[50] Costello, *Ten Days that Saved the West*, 184.

[51] Padfield, *Hess: The Führer's Disciple*, 118–20.

[52] See R. R. Stokes Papers, New Bodleian Library, Oxford, Box 1. Papers here include approaches to Beaverbrook (4 Apr. 1940) and to Lloyd George (19 June 1940) with a view to starting peace negotiations. A paper of 19 July provides a list of peers and MPs keen for Churchill to make a conciliatory reply to Hitler's peace offer. The names are familiar.

progressive wing of the peace party did not possess the influence of the larger and better connected Conservative centre. Its chosen leader lacked Halifax's sense of desperation; Lloyd George, far from being the British Pétain, supported the decision to fight on. The old Liberal did believe that a peace would have to be negotiated in the end, because he did not see how Britain could win the war in the absence of American or Soviet intervention, preferably both, and in the circumstances of 1940 neither seemed very likely. But for the present it was necessary to prove Britain's invulnerability to Nazi attack. Only when this had been achieved should talks be contemplated: respectable terms required the frustration in open combat of German designs on Britain.[53]

Despite the existence of some Left-wing support for the peace movement it was, as Churchill knew, from the Right that threats to his government would emerge. Only a little more than two weeks after taking over as prime minister Churchill faced a serious challenge in Cabinet from Lord Halifax on the issue of whether or not to approach Mussolini with a view to using Italian offices to broker a European peace conference. The initiative was supported by the French, with whom the foreign secretary wanted to keep in step.[54] Halifax believed that the failure of the French forces meant the war was effectively over. It was now his duty to take steps to negotiate a peace on the best terms available. He reckoned that with Italian help it would be possible to extract from Germany a deal which left Britain fully independent, its Empire and its navy intact. In return Halifax would give ground to Italian expansion in the Mediterranean by agreeing to the internationalization of the Suez Canal, Malta, and Gibraltar.[55]

The question was discussed by the Cabinet for the best part of three days, 26–8 May. The debate has been vividly reconstructed in recent years by Martin Gilbert and John Costello in particular and there is no need to repeat the exercise.[56] It is enough to say that Churchill argued against the foreign secretary in favour of fighting on alone if necessary. Halifax, feeling his premier to be talking 'the most frightful rot', threatened resignation—an act which would probably have led to the fall of the government. Churchill was supported by Attlee and Greenwood, and by Sinclair. But the outcome was uncertain until Chamberlain committed

---

[53] Letter to the author from Adrian Liddell-Hart, Dec. 1988; interview with the same of 13 Dec. 1988. The Stokes Papers (New Bodleian Library, Oxford, Box 1) show that Lloyd George did not respond to the entreaties of the peace party during the summer of 1940.

[54] Costello, *Ten Days that Saved the West*, 198–9.

[55] Reynolds, *The Creation of the Anglo-American Alliance*, 103–4.

[56] See Costello, *Ten Days that Saved the West*, ch. 9; Martin Gilbert, *Winston S. Churchill*, VI: *Finest Hour, 1939–1941* (1983), 404–8.

himself to his successor's side, believing that air power would permit Britain to carry on regardless of France's fate 'until other forces can be mobilised perhaps in the USA'. Halifax was isolated, and Churchill took care to reinforce his own position by a successful emotional appeal to the determination and patriotism of junior ministers. The foreign secretary gave way: there was to be no appeal to Rome. The battle had revealed the fault-line in British politics and society to be running across the Cabinet table: Greenwood had warned that 'the industrial centres of Britain would regard anything like weakening on the part of the Government as disaster'. Churchill's dependence on the support of Labour Cabinet ministers and the provincial Britain of the producer which they represented showed which way the balance of forces was moving.[57]

Halifax had been rebuffed, but he did not give up. During the summer he initiated at least two and perhaps three separate attempts to bring about a negotiated end to the conflict. On each occasion, with the support of Butler but not his Foreign Office staff, he attempted to draw from Germany terms which would leave the British Empire undisturbed while conceding to Hitler hegemony over the Continent. This formula commended itself to the large number of imperial isolationists in the peace party. It is not surprising, therefore, that one of the key players in the first approach was Kenneth de Courcy.[58]

The story begins not in June but in February 1940. While in France on a mission for Butler, de Courcy gained access to the details of a secret memorandum written for the French Cabinet by General Weygand. It was, in de Courcy's own words, 'a prepared alibi for a separate peace'.[59] Thereafter Butler shared de Courcy's conviction that the French would quickly drop out of the war once the real fighting started. Butler had never been committed to the war anyway and this piece of news strengthened his belief that it should be brought to a halt. Like his chief, the junior minister took it as axiomatic that Britain and France should not part company: it was better to settle with Germany before events took over and precipitated catastrophe. Unfortunately for Butler, however, Chamberlain would have nothing to do with this suggestion, while Halifax's attempts to engineer a deal had not achieved anything by the end of the phoney war.[60]

---

[57] See Gilbert, *Winston S. Churchill*, vi. 417–21.

[58] The account of this initiative presented here owes much to interviews with de Courcy on 4 Aug. 1989, 23 Feb. 1990, and 22 June 1992. There is a concise summary of events in de Courcy, 'The Late Lord Butler'.   [59] De Courcy, 'The Late Lord Butler'.

[60] Interviews with de Courcy; id., 'The Late Lord Butler'.

By the middle of June the disaster de Courcy had foreseen in February was obviously only a short matter of time away. Now Halifax and Butler moved quickly. The French decided to request an armistice on 16 June. The following day Butler met the Swedish minister in London, Bjorn Prytz, and made it clear that Churchill would not be permitted to obstruct the search for peace: 'no diehards will be allowed to stand in the way', he said. Prytz was then taken to see Halifax who reinforced the message and told the Swedish diplomat that 'commonsense and not bravado' would prevail. Two recent biographers of Butler and Halifax, Anthony Howard and Andrew Roberts, have suggested that Butler encountered Prytz by chance and that the episode had no profound significance.[61] But the meeting was not accidental. Prytz was singled out quite deliberately as the neutral postman who could relay the message to Berlin that Britain was prepared to talk. He fulfilled this task and reported the sentiments of Halifax and Butler to Stockholm in a message which anticipated that if there were to be talks a possible start could be made after 28 June.[62] He concluded by referring to conversations 'with other members of Parliament' which indicated an expectation that 'Halifax might succeed Churchill . . . if and when negotiations begin'—a sign that the foreign secretary and Butler were not operating in complete isolation. By 19 June at the latest Prytz's information was under consideration in the German Foreign Ministry.[63]

While Halifax and Butler were in touch with Prytz, de Courcy, with their approval, had approached Joseph Kennedy. This was de Courcy's idea. Convinced that 'wild men' were 'dragging this Empire towards disaster',[64] he had persuaded Butler that no peace settlement would be acceptable or lasting unless it was guaranteed by Washington. The agreement as envisaged by de Courcy depended on a German withdrawal from occupied territory in western Europe but a free hand in the east. The British Empire would be left intact. If Hitler failed to keep his word and re-entered evacuated territories the United States would join Britain in a declaration of war.[65]

The imperial solution had of course been canvassed for some time by

---

[61] See Anthony Howard, *Rab: The Life of R. A. Butler* (1987), 96–100; Andrew Roberts, *The Holy Fox* (1991), 231–6.

[62] The telegram is quoted in an unpublished memoir by Sir Peter Tennant, whom the author interviewed on 29 Mar. 1989.   [63] Memoir by Tennant.

[64] Costello, *Ten Days that Saved the West*, 310.

[65] De Courcy, 'The Late Lord Butler'; interviews with de Courcy. The story is also told by Costello, *Ten Days that Saved the West*, 308–11, and by Padfield, *Hess: The Führer's Disciple*, 123–4.

military strategists and by the peace party. There was enough support for it within the Royal Navy for one of its serving officers, Captain Russell Grenfell alias 'T-124', to publish in the summer of 1940 a robust defence of British isolation from Continental land engagements.[66] This scenario was supported by Butler, who was prepared to go further than de Courcy and suggested conceding the mouth of the Rhine to Germany. De Courcy found this unacceptable and refused to include the proposal in the package he put to the American ambassador. The SIS chief Stuart Menzies was another sympathizer, though not necessarily for the same reasons as Buccleuch, Londonderry, and Westminster. Menzies, who was throughout this time in touch with de Courcy, did not believe that an Anglo-German pact in 1940 would be the prelude to a permanent reduction of international tension. He argued that Britain should take advantage of a de-escalation in hostilities to concentrate on a programme of massive investment in sea and air power, including nuclear weapons, in conjunction with the USA. In the meantime Germany would almost certainly exploit the opportunity provided by peace in western Europe and the 'free hand' in the east to assault the Soviet Union. There would be a mutually destructive and exhausting Nazi–Soviet struggle. Finally, armed with the atomic bomb, the Anglo-Americans would be able to name their terms for a final settlement. With Germany and Russia weak and impoverished, Britain, with American support, would have retained its international status and position. Both the Bolshevik and the Nazi challenges would have disappeared without the politico-economic consequences of total war having transformed Britain into a semi-socialist state dependent on the United States.[67]

It is doubtful whether Ambassador Kennedy appreciated such nuances. However, he was enthusiastic about the scenario de Courcy had put before him. Kennedy wasted no time in meeting Halifax and agreed to pursue the initiative with the president. He was optimistic about its

---

[66] Interview with Adrian Liddell-Hart, 22 June 1989; Padfield, *Hess: The Führer's Disciple*, 265.

[67] This interpretation of Menzies's views is provided in a very cryptic fashion by Padfield, *Hess: The Führer's Disciple*, 113–14, and within *Special Office Brief*, 2 Apr. 1987. The expanded, detailed version presented here was given to the author by de Courcy in the interviews of 4 Aug. 1989, 23 Feb. 1990, and 22 June 1992. Research into the development of atomic weapons was being pursued at the time in Britain, France, and Germany. For example, French heavy water was smuggled out on the SS *Broompark* in June 1940 via the mouth of the Gironde and taken to Britain along with a consignment of industrial diamonds. It was a triumphant SIS operation conducted by the Earl of Suffolk, his two female assistants, and Frank Foley. Suffolk and his partners went home; Foley stayed on to watch the German mechanized divisions arrive (information from Andrew Rosthorne, 22 June 1994; Arnold Kramish, *The Griffin*, 1987).

chances of success, with some reason. Berlin was very shortly to receive news of the Butler–Prytz conversation. Already Hitler was thinking about how to end the conflict with Great Britain and his ideas were practically identical to those of the imperial isolationists, though without the sub-text they contained for Menzies. On 22 June Hitler told Goebbels that 'negotiations were under way' via Sweden.[68] Like Kennedy, the Führer must have been confident: finally it seemed as if the British were going to take the step he had believed they would take in September 1939—leave Europe to the Germans and concentrate on the Empire. If Washington was prepared to organize a peace conference then a rapid de-escalation could begin. On 25 June the Swedish banker Marcus Wallenberg met Victor Mallet, the British minister in Stockholm, and told him that the Germans were 'keen to negotiate' with Halifax.[69]

It never happened. Prytz's telegram was leaked to the British press attaché in Stockholm, Peter Tennant, by two Social Democratic politicians. Tennant reported the matter to his own Legation and told the *News Chronicle* correspondent Eric Dansy about it. Dansy wrote a story which never made it past the censor, but the information found its way back to the prime minister. Churchill acted quickly. De Courcy, who had been asked by Halifax to meet Kennedy again, was unable to do so because on 18 June he was warned off and threatened with detention under Defence Regulation 18b. He learned that Churchill was threatening to lock up Halifax and Butler if they pursued the initiative.[70] On the same day the prime minister publicly committed Britain to fighting on. When Gunther, the Swedish minister for foreign affairs, questioned Mallet about the Prytz telegram he was referred to Churchill's robust declaration. No reply ever came to Wallenberg's message of 25 June and the affair fizzled out.

Halifax had been thwarted again. Neither he nor Butler ever came closer to achieving a negotiated peace. But they continued to try. Clearly it was now too dangerous to attempt any feelers via the representatives of neutral missions in London. The search for a settlement therefore moved abroad, both to Switzerland and to the United States. In both countries the senior British diplomat, respectively Sir David Kelly and Lord Lothian, favoured talks with Hitler. Kelly was authorized by Butler to make con-tact with Max von Hohenlohe to see what terms Hitler was prepared to offer. The answer came back after a meeting between the two men on 14 July. Hohenlohe had said that Hitler wanted a 'concord' with Britain based on the familiar division of spheres between the Continent and the

---

[68] Costello, *Ten Days that Saved the West*, 322.   [69] Memoir by Tennant.
[70] *Special Office Brief*, 2 Apr. 1987. Churchill was alerted to the incident either by the leak to Dansy or by monitoring of Swedish diplomatic traffic (or both).

Empire.[71] He warned, however, that time was running out and that Britain faced the possibility of invasion if its leaders did not start talking soon. In Washington meanwhile Lothian attempted to use the Quakers as go-betweens with Germany. Ernst von Weiszacker, the permanent official at the head of the German Foreign Ministry, believed Lothian had received Halifax's authorization for this move.[72]

The foreign secretary's manœuvres convinced Hitler that there were powerful groups in Britain which would be able to displace Churchill or at the very least force him into a negotiation if the appeal from Berlin was couched in moderate and statesmanlike tones. This view received apparent confirmation from the Swiss ambassador in London who told Berlin, with some justification, that there was growing hostility towards Churchill from court and financial circles as well as from a section of the Conservative Party itself. The prime minister's support was now limited to junior ministers, 'Conservative diehards and the Labour Party, which wishes to continue the war on ideological grounds'. In an attempt to capitalize on what he understood to be the strength of the peace party, Hitler therefore made a public 'appeal to reason and commonsense [an echo of Halifax's message to Prytz] in Great Britain' on 19 July.[73]

Hitler's 'appeal to reason' fell flat. It did provoke some interest on the part of the MPs and peers who had grouped themselves into a parliamentary peace lobby on Churchill's accession to the premiership. But it made no headway within the government. Indeed, Churchill used the occasion to demonstrate his mastery in the Cabinet by ordering Halifax to deliver a public rejection despite the foreign secretary's desire to explore the offer seriously. Meanwhile a parallel attempt to destabilize the Churchill coalition by mobilizing against it the Duke of Windsor, known to be committed to Anglo-German *détente* from his time as king in 1936, also failed. Concerned about the effect the Duke's popularity might have in England, the prime minister moved him from temporary exile in Lisbon to the other side of the Atlantic: he appointed him governor of the Bahamas, out of reach (so it was hoped) of German agents and the temptation to meddle in British politics.[74]

Throughout August the lines of communication between the Germans and the peace party in England seem to have been quiet. Hitler attempted

---

[71] Costello, *Ten Days that Saved the West*, 345; *DGFP*, x. no. 188, Hohenlohe to Hewel, 18 July 1940. See also PRO FO 371/24407, C7578/189/18, report by Kelly, 18 July 1940.
[72] Costello, *Ten Days that Saved the West*, 346–8.
[73] For views of Swiss Ambassador and for Hitler's offer see Padfield, *Hess: The Führer's Disciple*, 126–7.   [74] Brown, *'C': The Secret Life of Sir Stewart Menzies*, 273–6.

to settle the issue by force, having failed to persuade the British government to negotiate. By all accounts the Führer took the view that an invasion of Britain would be an extremely risky and hazardous undertaking. But Churchill's refusal to talk and the inability of the prime minister's opponents to unseat him had left Hitler no alternative except the military option if the war was to be concluded on terms completely satisfying to Berlin.[75] The key to a successful assault was of course mastery of the skies, and this was what the Luftwaffe tried to achieve during the period from the very end of July until mid-September. By then it had become obvious that air superiority had not been attained; indeed Fighter Command had narrowly but decisively outperformed the Luftwaffe. On 17 September Hitler acknowledged defeat in the Battle of Britain by postponing the invasion, codenamed Operation Sealion, indefinitely.[76]

On 5 September, as the Battle approached its climax, the Foreign Office learned that an emissary from Hitler was in Stockholm. This man, a Berlin lawyer and Security Service official, was Dr Ludwig Weissauer. He wanted to meet a representative of the British government to discuss peace terms. Mallet in Stockholm was instructed to let Weissauer know through Dr Eckburg, president of the Swedish High Court of Appeal, that the British government was not interested.[77]

Weissauer was offering the usual division of interests between the Continent and the Empire, although he added that Hitler had also characterized this scenario as one of a world divided 'into two economic spheres'. Germany was, in addition, talking about the reconstitution of 'a Polish state' though not of a Czechoslovakian one. The future status of Egypt and the Mediterranean as well as of the French and Belgian colonial territories was to be up for negotiation.[78]

It was an interesting appeal, reflecting discussions on the future of west European heavy industry currently being undertaken by the New Order Planning Staff headed by State Secretary Gustav Schlotterer of the Ministry of Economics. In the views attributed to him by Weissauer, Hitler had called for 'an end to the economic division of Europe', a sentiment which echoed the planner's enthusiasm for a Continent-wide 'rationalization of industry' and customs union. The removal of barriers to trade was being proposed, but not in the name of economic liberalism: the aim was an organized market in which producers 'would have a

[75] See Winston S. Churchill, *The Second World War*, II: *Their Finest Hour* (rev. edn., 1951), 278. [76] Churchill, *The Second World War*, ii. 297–8.
[77] See PRO PREM 4/100/18, summary of peace-feelers, Sept. 1939–Mar. 1941.
[78] Ibid.

quota to be bought, sold, traded, increased or diminished as required by changing circumstances.'[79]

The proposal was designed to appeal to industrialists as well as the court and financial circles whose pro-peace sentiments were well known in Berlin. Hitler was holding out the prospect of a cartel-makers' peace, however fleeting his references, which would leave German interests paramount on the Continent while Britain's non-European trading arrangements would be unaltered. All the same, it was intended to honour the spirit if not the letter of the Anglo-German Coal Agreement negotiated in 1939. A place would be offered to British coal and coke producers in the reorganization of the European coal and steel industry under consideration by the Planning Staff. The idea was attractive: reports reached the German Foreign Ministry a few weeks later that 'a few British industrialists' were inclined to a compromise peace and in its pursuit were attempting to keep links open with the Third Reich.[80]

This approach has been understood by historians to reflect Hitler's willingness to negotiate.[81] There is certainly not much doubt that Hitler would have preferred to strike a peace deal with Britain which would have left him free to concentrate on the east. But it is not clear that the Weissauer feeler was instigated by the Führer. Indeed, German documents suggest that it was provoked by the British. A memorandum of 23 October from the chief of Security Police and Security Service, to whom Weissauer would have been responsible, to the Foreign Ministry, stated that Berlin had learned through Swedish connections how Mallet 'had expressed himself in a most intimate circle to the effect that this Government might possibly be prepared to ascertain unofficially whether Germany was prepared for peace negotiations'. Weissauer had travelled to Stockholm in response to this information, to indicate Germany's willingness to bargain. It does appear true that the initiative was abandoned after the Cabinet had discussed Weissauer's offer, although for good measure Mallet, under instruction to return a negative reply, let the Germans know through Eckburg that the government had been divided.[82]

---

[79] John Gillingham, *Industry and Politics in the Third Reich* (1985), 147–8.

[80] *DGFP*, x. 791, Consul-General (Geneva) to Foreign Ministry, 5 Dec. 1940. Gillingham, *Industry and Politics in the Third Reich*, 145–7.

[81] See Costello, *Ten Days that Saved the West*, 398.

[82] Ibid. 398; *DGFP*, x. 381–2, Chief of Security Police and Security Service to Foreign Ministry, 23 Oct. 1940, provides the German version of this episode. Interviewed on 29 Mar. 1989, Sir Peter Tennant, during the war working for Special Operations Executive (SOE) under the cover of press attaché in Stockholm, called Mallett 'a terrible defeatist. He was convinced the war would end in the Autumn of 1940.' The minister 'went behind our backs; the cipher girls told us what he was up to'.

Could Mallet alone have been responsible for an approach from Hitler and its discussion by the British Cabinet? It seems very unlikely. Mallet's suggestion that 'his Government' might want to know whether Germany was prepared to talk, his report of an argument within Cabinet, and his position inside the Foreign Office all constitute evidence pointing towards Halifax.

The failure of the Mallet–Weissauer initiative marked the effective end of British efforts, inspired directly or indirectly by Halifax, to make peace with Hitler. It has been argued that Churchill was prepared to let the feelers go out in order to convince Hitler that invasion was unnecessary since a peace party was in the background, waiting to pounce.[83] There is a limited amount of evidence for such a deception on Churchill's part, although the prime minister never believed a landing to be very likely. Halifax and his supporters in the continued prosecution of appeasement were, however, genuine. In the spring and summer of 1940 they thought the situation confronting both the Empire and British society to be so urgent that they were willing to go beyond what Chamberlain had envisaged and settle for accommodation with a Continent under the domination of a Germany led by Hitler.

Bartering Hitler against Churchill?

The German failure in the Battle of Britain helped to make Churchill's position more secure, a process which was confirmed by his assumption of the Conservative Party leadership on Chamberlain's retirement in September.[84] The first of these two developments strengthened the peace party's faith in British bargaining power to the extent that the replacement of Hitler became central to the concessions it expected to win from German negotiators. The second forced the group to become increasingly indirect and conspiratorial in its approaches to Germany, to preserve its security.

Thus, on 27 November Sir William Wiseman, the former senior SIS officer in the United States, now a partner in the merchant banking company of Kuhn Loeb, discussed peace terms with Fritz Wiedemann, once Hitler's adjutant and now consul-general in San Francisco, and Stephanie Hohenlohe-Waldenberg. Both were Nazi agents. They worked for the *Ausland* Organization (AO), whose superficial task was to retain contact with German nationals living abroad. In fact the AO was devoted

---

[83] Interview with Adrian Liddell-Hart, 13 Dec. 1988 and 22 June 1989; Padfield, *Hess: The Führer's Disciple*, 126.   [84] See Churchill, *The Second World War*, ii. 439.

to the dissemination of pro-Nazi propaganda and to intelligence gathering. Its head in Berlin was Ernst Wilhelm Bohle, and he reported to Deputy Führer Rudolf Hess. However, the AO was actually run and its activities financed by Max Ilgner of I. G. Farben, itself used as an espionage network by Walter Schellenberg, whose master was the Reichsführer SS, Heinrich Himmler.[85]

The meeting was held in the Mark Hopkins Hotel, San Francisco.[86] Wiseman announced himself the spokesman for 'a British political group headed by Lord Halifax, which hopes to bring about a lasting peace'. He added that Halifax represented a 'very strong' political party in the Houses of Parliament which believed in co-operation between the British Empire, Germany, and the United States. But any arrangement would have to be made with a 'Hitlerless' Germany controlled by a regime capable not only of making agreements but of sticking to them. Hitler, stressed Wiseman, was simply not trusted by the British. In reply the Germans took a sympathetic line and suggested a monarchist restoration under the Crown Prince, or an administration run by Heinrich Himmler, himself a monarchist. Wiseman did not demur at any of this. He advocated a meeting between Halifax and a representative of the monarchist party. Discussion about conditions for peace, the removal of Hitler aside, was fairly vague. The only other specific detail mentioned was a restoration of France on the Polish model, in other words, shorn of the provinces considered by the Germans to be rightfully theirs.

During the meeting Wiseman claimed a semi-official role for himself. He said he was working for Halifax and that he would send a record of the discussion, not to be circulated around the Foreign Office, directly to the foreign secretary.[87] Subsequently William Stephenson, who as head of British Security Co-ordination during the period 1940–5 was following in Wiseman's footsteps as senior SIS officer in the United States, claimed

[85] See Charles Higham, *Trading with the Enemy: How the Allied Multinationals Supplied Nazi Germany Throughout World War Two* (1983), 188; Padfield, *Hess: The Führer's Disciple*, 71–3.

[86] There are published accounts of this meeting in Costello, *Ten Days that Saved the West*, 399–403; and in Higham, *Trading with the Enemy*, ch. 11. My own information comes from Adrian Liddell-Hart who very kindly supplied me with photocopies of the original FBI documents. These include a letter from Director Hoover to Berle in the State Department; a memorandum dated 30 Nov. 1940 based on electronic surveillance of the encounter at the hotel; an intercepted letter from Hohenlohe-Waldenberg to Wiseman, dated 17 Dec. 1940; a paper concerning the background and activities of the princess; and a statement by Wiseman.

[87] All references to the meeting as well as to direct and indirect quotations made by the participants are taken from the FBI report of 30 Nov. 1940 unless otherwise stated.

that Wiseman was an *agent provocateur* responsible to him. John Costello has argued that it was Lord Lothian who was in fact behind Wiseman's activities. Charles Higham, however, maintains on the basis of US army intelligence records that Wiseman's behaviour was 'neither condoned nor supported by any government': the banker was completely on his own.[88]

The most plausible explanation for Wiseman's conduct is that he was indeed an SIS *agent provocateur* who exceeded his brief because he allowed his own political commitment to a negotiated peace to run away with him. Sir William had in fact never left the intelligence community after 1918. Between the wars he had been a member of the Room and the Walrus Club, two private organizations which drew together stockbrokers, bankers, and academics from the north-east of the United States. Representative figures were Nelson Rockefeller, Winthrop Aldrich (president of the Chase Manhattan Bank), and Nelson Doubleday, the New York publisher, as well as Vincent Astor, a member of the American branch of the British family.[89] This community had in common their Anglophilia and commitment to the vision of a liberal-capitalist world community under the guiding influence of the Atlantic powers which was common to the Round Table, the RIIA, and the Council for Foreign Relations (CFR), of which Rockefeller was a member.[90] Wiseman became the main point of contact between the American group and its equivalents in Britain, namely the Ends of the Earth Club and the 16 Club.[91] Both drew together individuals from the British financial and intelligence networks: Menzies and Rex Benson, of Robert Benson and Company, Ltd., the merchant bank, were members, as was Wiseman.

After 1918 the Room had concentrated on monitoring Japanese naval expansion in the South Pacific as well as political and economic conditions in Peru, the Caribbean, and in the Panama Canal zone. On the outbreak of war, however, it switched its focus to counter-espionage. Using the contacts furnished by its banking members it checked accounts which might be used as sources of finance for foreign intelligence and sabotage operations within the United States. Vincent Astor became Roosevelt's chief source of intelligence until 1940–1, when he was replaced by John Franklin Carter.[92] In addition, regulars of the Room and the Walrus Club such as David Bruce and the successful Wall Street

---

[88] See Costello, *Ten Days that Saved the West*, 399; Higham, *Trading with the Enemy*, 192–3.   [89] See Brown, *'C': The Secret Life of Sir Stewart Menzies*, 123.

[90] Shoup and Minter, *Imperial Brain Trust*, 61.

[91] Brown, *'C': The Secret Life of Sir Stewart Menzies*, 123.

[92] Phillip Knightley, *The Second Oldest Profession* (1986), 211–12.

lawyer Bill Donovan later became central to the OSS (Office of Strategic Services, Roosevelt's version of SIS, established in 1941). Donovan was appointed its chief and Bruce took up the post as head of its London station in 1942.[93]

Membership of such a network explains how Wiseman could operate informally and independently while simultaneously keeping contacts with Lords Lothian and Halifax as well as with Stewart Menzies. It locates him within an ideological context of hostility to total war and its implications but well-disposed towards the concept of the strategic peace favoured by Menzies. Indeed, the outlines of such a settlement can be discerned in Wiseman's remarks about collaboration between the British Empire, the United States, and Germany at the meeting with Wiedemann and Hohenlohe-Waldenberg.

Wiseman's contacts were, however, not able to prevent a fiasco. The FBI had bugged the meeting. Wiseman was placed under close surveillance. An attempt was made to deport Hohenlohe-Waldenberg (it failed after she started an affair with the director of the Immigration and Naturalization Service).[94] In the meantime Lothian died unexpectedly before 1940 was out, leaving Wiseman 'rather confused as to what to do'.[95] Early in the New Year Churchill decapitated opposition to him within Britain when he dispatched an unwilling Lord Halifax to Washington as Lothian's replacement. The premier told his private secretary, John Colville, that the foreign secretary 'had no future in this country' because of his reputation for appeasement.[96] The peace party had been rocked, and during 1941 its opportunities for using the United States as a base for clandestine negotiations became very limited. In mid-June all Nazi consulates were closed; Wiedemann was forced to leave the country in July.[97]

Wiseman's initiative had ended ignominiously. But it set out an agenda which coincidentally or not attracted a section of the resistance to Hitler during the first months of 1941 in particular. The nucleus of the group in question was composed of Carl Goerdeler, the highly conservative Johannes Popitz (formerly minister of finance in Prussia) and Generals Beck, Halder, and von Brauchitsch. On the outer circle of the conspiracy were Hjalmar Schacht as well as Admiral Canaris, head of the Abwehr (German Military Intelligence) and the chief of its Central Department,

[93] Brown, *'C': The Secret Life of Sir Stewart Menzies*, 123, 396.
[94] See Higham, *Trading with the Enemy*, 199–200.
[95] Costello, *Ten Days that Saved the West*, 403.
[96] Gilbert, *Winston S. Churchill*, vi. 953.
[97] Higham, *Trading with the Enemy*, 199–200.

Hans Oster.[98] This was the Right-wing anti-Nazi coalition with which the British had been in covert contact since the outbreak of war. Wiseman's meeting with Wiedemann and Hohenlohe-Waldenberg was another chapter in a familiar tale; the Englishman's own record makes it clear that the two Germans were part of the von Hassell–Beck–Goerdeler–Halder network.[99] All of the group's members were committed to German hegemony in central and eastern Europe, even though they were prepared to support a withdrawal from occupied territory in the west. They repeatedly made clear their determination to return Germany to constitutional government and contemplated, as Wiseman had learned, a monarchist restoration featuring either the crown prince of Prussia or his son. Until the spring of 1940 the conservative revolutionaries had accepted that their plans required the removal of Hitler from active politics, either by forcing him to retire or by appointing him head of a post-Nazi state with no more than honorific powers, or even by assassination. After the triumphs of May and June, however, the Führer's position had become much stronger and talk of replacing him died away, as indeed did the plotting of his opponents. Now, with Britain unexpectedly still fighting and the war in a position of stalemate, the German peace party had begun to revive. By January 1941 it was understood that no settlement with Britain would be possible as long as Hitler presided over the Reich. As a *quid pro quo* German dissidents suggested that Churchill should be replaced also: the two leaders should be bartered against each other.[100] Although Wiseman had not gone so far as this in his conversations with Wiedemann and Hohenlohe-Waldenberg it was an idea obviously implicit in his declaration of loyalty to Halifax.

Wiseman had not been the only point of contact between the British peace party and the German resistance during the turn of 1940 into 1941. Another channel ran through Spain. It was opened by Albrecht Haushofer, a member of von Hassell's group, through Heinrich Stahmer, a German diplomat in Madrid. Haushofer's intention was to open a dialogue with Samuel Hoare, the British ambassador. From time to time Hoare had

[98] Von Klemperer, *The German Resistance against Hitler*, 20–5.

[99] According to Wiseman's statement, Wiedemann was by his own account in contact with Halder, Beck, and Schacht. Other contacts were the industrialist von Siemens and Count von Helledorf, chief of the Berlin police. All favoured a monarchist restoration; the Crown Prince was 'in touch with them all'.

[100] PRO FO 371/26542, C1118/324/18, 8 Jan. 1941: report from Istanbul of a New Year speech by Franz von Papen, the German ambassador. It was von Papen, not generally associated with resistance activity at this stage, who suggested bartering Hitler against Churchill.

been spoken of as a possible replacement for Churchill; Halifax's departure to the United States made such a scenario more plausible by January 1941 than it had been a few weeks earlier. Stahmer duly approached Hoare through the offices of the Swedish Embassy. The upshot was agreement by Hoare and Haushofer that no armistice could proceed without the removal from power of both Hitler and Churchill.[101]

This was no conspiracy of outsiders. Most of the participants had been supporters of National Socialism and still retained close connections with the regime. Haushofer, for example, was the son of a famous geopolitician whose ideas had attracted Hitler and his deputy, Rudolf Hess, back in the 1920s. With Hess's patronage young Albrecht Haushofer had acquired a position of influence in Nazi foreign-policy making circles; currently he was working under Ribbentrop.[102] It had been Hess who had, with Hitler's blessing, given Haushofer responsibility for contacting the British;[103] like his chief the Deputy Führer was convinced that Churchill could not in the end prevail against the powerful interests within industry, the City, and the Conservative Party who were known to be in favour of calling a halt to the war. Haushofer's work for Hitler and Hess provided excellent cover for his pro-resistance activities. But the ambiguity surrounding this man and indeed the entire conspiracy does not end here. Haushofer had been drawn into the von Hassell–Popitz group as a result of his close friendship with another member, the lawyer Carl Langbehn. Langbehn, however, was a friend and neighbour of Heinrich Himmler.[104] And Himmler would have been aware of the meeting between Wiseman, Wiedemann, and Hohenlohe-Waldenberg and of the views expressed there.

By early 1941 the Reichsführer SS had also concluded that peace with Britain was necessary but impossible as long as Hitler stayed in position. Through Langbehn he was able to exploit the external connections of the resistance and use its network as a front for the SS coup against Hitler which had first been considered in the early weeks of the war. In the spring of 1941 'one of Himmler's confidential agents', probably Langbehn himself, approached Carl Burkhardt of the International Red Cross to ask the Swiss official if he could find out whether the British would be prepared to make peace with Himmler rather than with Hitler.[105] On

[101] Padfield, *Hess: The Führer's Disciple*, 161; Wolf-Rudiger Hess, *My Father Rudolf Hess* (1986), 80–1.   [102] Von Klemperer, *The German Resistance against Hitler*, 35–7.
[103] Padfield, *Hess: The Führer's Disciple*, 138–43; Hess, *My Father Rudolf Hess*, 80.
[104] Hess, *My Father Rudolf Hess*, 72–3; von Klemperer, *The German Resistance against Hitler*, 36.
[105] Ulrich von Hassell, *The von Hassell Diaries 1938–44* (1948), 205, entry for 18 May 1941.

28 April Burkhardt was in touch with Haushofer, to assure him that the British wanted peace—but not with the present government and perhaps not for much longer.[106]

What kind of regime would have replaced Hitler's? The composition of the anti-Hitler movement makes it most unlikely that any successful move against the Führer during the first months of 1941 would have opened the door on to a democratic Germany. The key forces in the conspiracy were all beneficiaries of the Nazi revolution: senior army officers, the Abwehr, industrial corporations such as Krupp's,[107] circles within the Foreign Ministry, and leading figures in the SS including the head of the organization himself. Some of these, such as von Hassell, Popitz, Canaris, Beck, and Halder, were content that the nationalist, anti-Versailles agenda of the post-1918 period had been executed and were now revolted by the barbarism inherent in the Nazi state. Others, notably Himmler, were anxious about the prospects of the forthcoming invasion of the Soviet Union in the absence of peace with Britain. Intelligence reports suggested that Soviet strength was greater than had been anticipated. Military resources currently tied down in the Mediterranean, North Africa, and western Europe could be of vital importance to the success of Operation Barbarossa.[108] Varied though the motivations of each element in this coalition might be, however, they were united in the growing conviction that Hitler's conduct of the war was likely to jeopardize all the successes of the years since 1933.

An armistice which revolved around the replacement of Hitler and Churchill was attractive to the British peace party. During the last part of 1940 and the first months of 1941 there was mounting anxiety about the prime minister's policies, conduct, and strategy, most of it coming from the Right. Thus, in December the US military attaché in London, Raymond E. Lee, learned that the City was 'ready for appeasement at any time'; it was irritated since it had 'no hold on Churchill', who seemed to have no concern for the Empire. The prime minister was unpopular with the 'country', meaning the Tory squirearchy, and relied overmuch on detention without trial.[109] At the end of April 1941 Anthony Eden, who had replaced Halifax at the Foreign Office, met a small deputation of

---

[106] Ibid. 207, entry for 18 May 1941.
[107] See PRO FO 371/26542, C1884/324/18, report by Knatchbull Hugessen (ambassador to Turkey) dated 29 Jan. 1941 to Nichols of a meeting of Germans in Istanbul. Most of those present had been connected to Krupps. All agreed that 'Hitler should be got out of the way'.   [108] Hugh Thomas, *Hess: A Tale of Two Murders* (1988), 163, 207.
[109] James Leutze (ed.), *The London Journal of General Raymond E. Lee, 1940–41* (Boston, 1971), 165–6, entry for 8 Dec. 1940.

leading Conservatives led by Erskine Hill, chairman of the 1922 Committee. Hill and his colleagues expressed fears 'at the party political situation', as well as concern that 'much socialistic legislation will be passed under the guise of war needs'.[110]

These expressions of dissent were fuelled by a series of military setbacks. In North Africa British forces had by the end of April lost most of the ground taken from the Italians to newly arrived German troops under General Rommel. An attempt to protect Greece against the Germans failed miserably and wasted resources which would have been better used against Rommel's Afrika Korps. In the first weeks of May British forces were driven off Crete, albeit at great cost to the Germans. All the time shipping losses in the Atlantic mounted; between June 1940 and December 1941 total losses of British flag tonnage were 7 million deadweight tons or 36 per cent of the merchant fleet as it stood at the start of the period.[111] The toll of oil-tankers was particularly heavy and by the early summer British oil stocks were only about 4.5 million tons. Capacity was 7 million tons; this was danger level.[112]

It all led to increasing frustration with the prime minister. He was accused of running the war as if he were in charge of 'a complete dictatorship'. What made this criticism more serious than most was its origin within the government itself. It was made by Lord Hankey, minister without portfolio in Chamberlain's War Cabinet. Churchill had demoted Hankey in 1940, appointing him chancellor of the Duchy of Lancaster. But Hankey's long career in the Whitehall machine made him a natural confidant for disenchanted officials. He claimed in a letter to Halifax of 1 May 1941 that four senior officials, a top civil servant, and the Australian prime minister Robert Menzies had all approached him with their anxieties. The complaints made by Hankey received a public airing and elaboration on 7 May when the Commons debated a motion of no confidence in the government, although Churchill won with ease (447 votes to 3).[113]

The disenchantment with Churchill, both recent and long-standing, was reflected in continuing peace-feelers from the British side. Burkhardt's conversations with von Hassell and Haushofer provide some evidence of these. More can be found in the anxiety of the Duke of Buccleuch,

---

[110] Anthony Eden Diaries, University of Birmingham, entry for 30 Apr. 1941.

[111] Hancock and Gowing, *British War Economy*, 250.   [112] Ibid. 257.

[113] David Day, *Menzies and Churchill at War* (1986), 168–9. Hankey had served as secretary to the Committee for Imperial Defence from 1912 to 1938 and to the Cabinet from 1919 to 1938.

expressed in two letters to Butler of 15 and 22 February, that Lonsdale Bryans be reactivated and provided with the means to meet von Hassell. According to Bryans such an encounter might possess 'vital importance'; Buccleuch was keen for the matter to be pursued. Butler's response was, however, cool. Although the junior minister did not adhere to Churchill's injunction of January and maintain 'absolute silence', he did warn Buccleuch to go 'very slow' and passed the file on to Cadogan, who blocked any further action.[114]

Cadogan could not prevent Hoare from meeting German agents. Following the agreement with Haushofer that there could be no peace unless Hitler and Churchill were both removed, the ambassador met Max von Hohenlohe either at the end of February or at the start of March 1941. Hoare reported to London that Hohenlohe had made the case for a settlement with Hitler. Hoare had not been impressed and had made it clear that 'no one in England believed Hitler's word . . . we were not prepared to accept any European dictatorship.'[115] But a very different version of this conversation reached the Italian ambassador in Madrid, Lequio. There is no reason to believe that the diplomat invented any aspect of his report in which Hoare is quoted as having told Hohenlohe that

the position of the British Government cannot remain secure. Despite recent American legislation providing for aid to Great Britain Churchill can no longer count on a majority . . . sooner or later he [Hoare] will be called back to London to take over the government with the precise task of concluding a compromise peace . . . he will only take this mission on condition that he has full powers.[116]

Hoare went on to explain that he would have to remove Anthony Eden from the foreign secretaryship and replace him with Butler.

The Hoare–Hohenlohe conversation, along with the information reaching Burkhardt, undoubtedly encouraged both Hitler and his opponents in their search for a settlement with Britain. On 6 March, the day Hoare told the Foreign Office about his meeting with Hohenlohe, it was reported from Stockholm that 'high officials' in Berlin believed Germany to be 'ready for peace'. The news came from Princess Wied, wife of the German minister; she suggested a meeting be held in Sweden between

[114] PRO FO 371/26542, C1954/324/18, letters by Buccleuch to Butler of 15 and 22 Feb., together with Butler's brief note for Cadogan.

[115] PRO FO 371/26542, C2505/324/18, 6 Mar. 1941.

[116] *Documenti Diplomatici Italiani*, 9th ser., vol. 5 (Rome 1984), Lequio to Ciano, 14 Mar. 1941. This version also squares with one subsequently reported to Churchill.

Montagu Norman and Hjalmar Schacht after another four or six weeks had passed.[117] And certainly the pace quickened during the following month. On 18 April General Aranda, commandant of the Spanish War College and an SIS informant,[118] told the British military attaché in Madrid about Goering's conviction that the longer the war lasted the bleaker Germany's prospects would become. The Reichsmarshall was anxious to discuss peace possibilities and was sending Max von Hohenlohe to London on the following day to sound out the situation 'in this respect'[119]—an initiative which, given the aristocrat's neutral status as a citizen of Liechtenstein, was certainly feasible.

Whether Hohenlohe flew to London is unknown. But shortly afterwards the Foreign Office was disturbed by a rumour that Rudolf Hess had gone to Spain on Hitler's behalf. The story first appeared in the Vichy press,[120] but was then corroborated by King Carol of Romania,[121] who was resident in Seville at the time, via the British Embassy in Lisbon.[122] Hoare received a rather pointed inquiry from London about the accuracy of this report. It took the ambassador three days to reply, most ambiguously, that if Hess had come 'his arrival has been kept remarkably secret and his presence in town is not even rumoured yet'.[123]

Neither the Spanish government archives now available nor records within the British Foreign Office confirm Hess's journey. The former are, however, exceedingly disorganized and incomplete; in the latter there are still papers suppressed until 2017. One of these covers developments in Spain from 20–2 April, the time when Hess is supposed to have been there.[124] Nevertheless there are two strong pieces of supporting evidence. The first surfaced in the House of Commons on 19 June when the Labour MP for Nelson and Colne, Sidney Silverman, claimed that Hess had undertaken a diplomatic mission to Madrid and had considered flying to a meeting in Gibraltar.[125] The second took the form of a *Sunday Dispatch* newspaper article by Andre Guerber, dated 30 September 1945. The story, written from documents in the Reich Chancellery archives

[117] PRO FO 371/26542, C2287/324/18, report from Stockholm, 6 Mar. 1941.

[118] See Brown, *'C': The Secret Life of Sir Stewart Menzies*, 312.

[119] PRO FO 371/26945, C4235/306/41, report of a conversation with Aranda by Torr (military attaché), 18 Apr. 1941.

[120] PRO FO 371/26945, C4140/306/41, request from Major Bright of MI3a to Foreign Office to discover more about this, 22 Apr. 1941.

[121] Ibid., C4147/306/41, Campbell (Lisbon) to London, 22 Apr. 1941.

[122] Spanish Ministry of Foreign Affairs Archives, Madrid, file R1913/12.

[123] The request for comments from Hoare can be found in PRO FO 371/26845, C4147/306/41, 22 Apr. 1941. Hoare's reply: C4613/306/41, 25 Apr. 1941.

[124] See Padfield, *Hess: The Führer's Disciple*, 174.   [125] Ibid. 273

which have since disappeared, stated that Hitler had sent Hess on a 'secret mission' to Madrid in April 1941.[126]

Despite the absence of official confirmation, the weight of evidence, both contemporary and later, tips the balance of probability in favour of a mission to Spain by Hess. Why should the Deputy Führer have gone there? The Foreign Office at the time was concerned about German pressure on the Spanish government to let troops march all the way through the country to attack Gibraltar.[127] Such an operation, if successful, would have cut Britain off from the Mediterranean, North Africa, and the Middle East. A question-mark would have been placed over its ability to continue the war. It is therefore unsurprising that most of the speculation about Hess's reported visit concerned the threat to Gibraltar. But as Silverman was to hint and Guerber to maintain quite explicitly, the journey had another purpose—to contact the British through General Franco as well as through their own agents in order to discuss terms for a negotiated peace.[128] Since Hess had set up a link with Sir Samuel Hoare through Albrecht Haushofer in the autumn of 1940 this can only mean that he was aiming to reach the ambassador, whose sentiments were of course well known in Berlin.

According to Guerber, whose information included the transcript of a meeting involving Hess, Hitler, and Goering on 4 May, the Deputy Führer returned to Berlin convinced that the British would make peace. Hitler was sufficiently impressed to authorize an approach to the British so that they would drop out of the war before the assault on the Soviet Union. This, then, appears to be the background to Hess's famous flight. Yet ambivalence lurks below the surface. Before Hess left Augsburg he had been told by his own agent, Haushofer, that the British would not deal with Hitler.[129] In the Guerber report, however, there is no sign that Hess was aware of such a reservation: he appears to have believed that the key to a settlement with Britain was a demonstration of German 'sincerity about peace'. If Churchill found this unacceptable, 'the British people will rise up' and force him to make peace.[130] So did Hess disregard Haushofer's advice and remain loyal to the Führer, while shielding his informant from the consequences of treasonable sentiments? Or had the Deputy Führer used his connection with Haushofer to join with the coalition of forces which had now concluded that Hitler must be

---

[126] PRO FO 371/46780, C6601/44/18.   [127] See file PRO FO 371/26945, *passim*.

[128] See Guerber's report in PRO FO 371/46780, C6601/44/18.

[129] See e.g. von Klemperer, *The German Resistance against Hitler*, 222.

[130] PRO FO 371/46780, C6601/44/18/, Guerber, 30 Sept. 1945.

overthrown? Was the mission of 10 May genuinely on behalf of Hitler or the start of what was supposed to be a palace coup?

After more than fifty years the details of the Hess affair are still obscure. Despite Hess's well-known devotion to Hitler in the past there are grounds for suspecting that his loyalty was not absolute by this time. There are also compelling reasons to doubt whether it was Rudolf Hess who landed at Eaglesham on the evening of 10 May:[131] the pilot had no trace of the scars and lesions which Hess carried as a result of injuries sustained in combat during the 1914–18 war.[132] The mystery is compounded by aeronautical evidence: the plane which left Augsburg was a D type Me 110, aviation number 1545. The plane which landed was an E type, the latest model and indeed just off the production line. Its aviation number was 3869. After taking off the D type was monitored by German radar and was last seen flying past the island of Terschelling, off the Dutch coast. Its track (not to mention its fuel capacity) indicates that the destination was not Scotland but Aalborg in north Denmark, at the time a German air-base.[133]

Two aspects of the Hess affair stand out amidst the confusion, which was not resolved by the release of all but one of the relevant Foreign Office papers in June 1992. First of all we can be reasonably clear about the terms to be offered to the British. According to Guerber's article the proposal was described as the 'Plan ABCD Number S 274K': there was a copy amongst the documents in the Reich Chancellery archives upon which his story had been built. It was designated ABCD simply because there were four parts: (a) to persuade the British government with documentary evidence that continued pursuit of the war was 'useless'; (b) to guarantee the independence and integrity of the British Empire in return for an undertaking 'not to meddle in any way' with

---

[131] The whole issue of Hess's identity, one which many commentators either dodge or dismiss with unwarranted flippancy, has been dealt with exhaustively by Hugh Thomas in *Hess: A Tale of Two Murders*.

[132] As reported by Lt.-Col. J. Gibson Graham (RAMC) after a medical examination of the prisoner on 13 May 1941. See PRO PREM 3/219/7.

[133] See Thomas, *Hess: A Tale of Two Murders*, ch. 3; information provided to the author by aviation historian Douglas MacRoberts, 19 May 1994. One interesting piece of information which may of course be coincidental is that on 9 May Sir Samuel Hoare was involved in a row with Spanish customs officers. The issue was a 177 kilo tub of aircraft engine lubricant which he was seeking to have released for his own personal use. It was about 1.5 times as much as would have been necessary for a return flight to Stockholm. The ambassador does not seem to have been successful in persuading the authorities to be accommodating towards him. See archives of the Spanish Foreign Ministry, Madrid, file R1912/11, 9 May 1941.

the internal or external affairs of Continental states; (c) an offer of a twenty-five year alliance with the Reich; (d) benevolent neutrality on the part of Britain during the forthcoming German–Russian conflict. The details of the package were consistent with those of all previous attempts to reach Anglo-German *détente*, both during the war and before its commencement. The only minor variation on its predecessors was the call for 'benevolent neutrality' in a Nazi–Soviet war, but even this was no more than a contemporary version of the old demand for a 'free hand in the east'.[134]

Secondly, the initiative failed, although there is some evidence to suggest that it was examined more carefully than most commentators have hitherto appreciated.[135] But it was Churchill, along with a very small circle of advisers and senior Cabinet ministers, who considered and rejected the plan. German hopes that the British peace party would be able to use the proposals in their political struggle with the prime minister were never fulfilled. Churchill shrouded the entire affair in the tightest secrecy so that very little leaked out.[136] In any case, despite his somewhat embattled position in early 1941 the prime minister was more strongly placed than most of his internal opponents, whose political influence had been seriously weakened by the crack-down of May–July 1940 and then by the aftermath of the Wiseman–Wiedemann fiasco at the end of the year. Surveillance was extensive: the Duke of Buccleuch complained about it in his February letters to Butler, while Churchill kept a file on Hoare, receiving reports on his movements in Spain from an agent with the code-name of Harlequin.[137] It follows that the prime minister was aware of the Hess mission and its ramifications in advance of the event, and that this intelligence allowed him and not the peace party to control developments, suppressing or manipulating all relevant information in the process. He was, therefore, able to reject the German offer without provoking what might have become a damaging, even destabilizing, public row.

The decisive factor in Britain's refusal to deal with Germany was foreknowledge of Operation Barbarossa. This had been gained through decrypts of German code and cipher traffic; it was confirmed in Plan ABCD Number S 274K.[138] Far from facilitating a *rapprochement* between London and Berlin against the Bolshevik enemy, it reassured Churchill

[134] PRO FO 371/46780, C6601/44/18, Guerber, 30 Sept. 1945.
[135] See Padfield, *Hess: The Führer's Disciple*, 368–70.   [136] Ibid. 369.
[137] For Buccleuch see PRO FO 371/26542, C1954/324/18; for reference to the file on Hoare see PRO PREM 4/23/2368, 19 Apr. 1943.
[138] Brown, *'C': The Secret Life of Sir Stewart Menzies*, 340–1.

that Britain would soon have a formidable ally in the war against Nazism. Any doubts about the prime minister's enthusiasm for welcoming the Soviet Union back to the anti-Nazi cause were stilled by his broadcast on the night of the invasion.[139]

The failure of the Hess mission one year to the day after Churchill had become prime minister drew a line under the era of Anglo–German appeasement. There was to be no *détente* founded on a division of territory, markets, and raw-material resources throughout Europe, Africa, and some of the Far East. Prospects of such an arrangement, pursued with tenacity by Chamberlain's government up to the outbreak of war, had initially been wrecked by the nature of Nazism itself: an unstable mixture in which familiar German imperialism was in reality overshadowed by revolutionary, racist expansionism. No agreement with Hitler had been possible. After the outbreak of war Chamberlain still hoped an Anglo–German settlement might be achievable on condition it was with a new regime in Berlin, maybe authoritarian but certainly non-Nazi. Yet even in the first months of the war sections of the British establishment had continued to explore the feasibility of a deal with Hitler's Germany. When the Allied military effort was overwhelmed by disaster in May and June 1940, Halifax and Butler came close to such a breakthrough. Their failure amidst Churchill's general crack-down on the pro-German Right seriously weakened the British peace party. Churchill became powerful enough to frustrate subsequent efforts to end Anglo–German hostilities, whether or not they were on the basis of Hitler's replacement. After the Hess fiasco there were to be no more. Within six weeks the war was to be widened by the invasion of the Soviet Union. The prospects of victory over Nazism, however long-term, were enhanced by the Soviet entry into the conflict. Now the peace lobby's most powerful argument, namely that the war had become a futile and wasteful stalemate, had collapsed. The struggle was to continue, and the Leftward shift of British politics and society became irreversible.

---

[139] For the text of Churchill's speech see Winston S. Churchill, *The Second World War*, III: *The Grand Alliance* (1950), 331–3. For the impact of the broadcast on attitudes see Kim Philby, *My Silent War* (1989), 73.

Conclusion

The Hess affair marked the last serious attempt to reach a specifically Anglo-German *détente*. But it did not mark the end of underground contacts designed to explore the chances of terminating hostilities. Representatives of the British, and after 7 December 1941, American governments were frequently on the receiving end of approaches from Germany. These took place in neutral capitals and were frequently on the initiative of forces claiming commitment to the overthrow of Hitler.

Up to early 1944 most of the offers presented to the Anglo-Americans were true to the nationalist, anti-Communist agenda of the German Right. Thus, at the start of December 1941 Victor Mallet recorded a feeler from a Baltic banker whose interests had 'international ramifications'. This individual, identified as a 'Mr X', trotted out the usual litany: big-business circles and senior officers would overthrow Hitler and establish a military regime as a prelude to constitutional rule—on condition that they were supported by the Allies first. The peace settlement would provide for the exploitation of western Russia 'by European or international colonization' as well as for 'complete evacuation of other territories'.[1]

'Mr X' was vague about his sponsors. But reading between the lines of Mallet's report it is possible to detect the hand of the SS. The Balt had been prompted to make his journey to Stockholm by 'a very prominent lawyer with strong connections in the biggest business circles'.[2] This sounds like Carl Langbehn, who himself approached the Americans on behalf of the Reichsführer SS twice, in December 1942 and in September 1943.[3] Meanwhile Hoare continued to dally with the Germans, meeting Hohenlohe again in May 1942. Eden told the ambassador that 'he should

---

[1] See PRO FO 371/26597, C13631/13631/18, record made by Mallet on 1 Dec. 1941.
[2] Ibid.
[3] For details see von Klemperer, *The German Resistance against Hitler*, 323–7. The later of these two missions ended in disaster for Langbehn. The Gestapo intercepted a coded cable from an unidentified Allied mission in Berne which reported on Langbehn's activities in Switzerland. On his return to Germany the lawyer managed one meeting with Himmler before he was arrested. Himmler, most anxious to prevent the full story behind the affair leaking out, then turned round and denounced his agent for 'treachery'. Langbehn was executed.

have nothing to do with this man'—but there was another approach from the aristocrat a year later.[4] On 25 July 1942 Roosevelt warned Churchill about a report from Madrid that Montagu Norman was establishing contacts with Hjalmar Schacht through the services of Tiarks.[5] Late in 1943 Walter Schellenberg, now head of Amt VI, the SS foreign intelligence section, journeyed to Stockholm where he had long and detailed conversations with an OSS agent called Hewitt.[6]

Common to most of these peace-feelers was a German hope that the western Allies would recognize a Reich led initially at least by Himmler and run by the SS, as a prelude to the cessation of hostilities and an evacuation of occupied territory—in the west. There was no talk of a de-escalation on all fronts. Despite the decision at Casablanca in January 1943 that there could be no peace in the absence of unconditional surrender to the Soviets, British, and Americans, discussions revolved around the prospect of a separate deal between a reformed government in Berlin and the western Allies.[7]

There is no evidence that either Roosevelt or Churchill was remotely sympathetic to any of this. It is true that Churchill had some doubts about the unconditional surrender policy, largely on the grounds that it might generate solidarity in Germany and so prolong the war. But both the prime minister and the Cabinet were prepared to recognize the reality behind the commitment to unconditional surrender: the policy came from Roosevelt and there was nothing to be gained by an argument with

[4] Avon Papers, University of Birmingham, vol. 27, SP/42/22, Hoare to Eden, 11 May 1942; SP/42/25, Eden to Hoare, 2 June 1942; SP/43/27, Hoare to Eden, 5 July 1943.

[5] Avon Papers, University of Birmingham, W(g) 42/87, top copy of a report from Roosevelt to Harry Hopkins, dated 25 July 1942. It was put in a locked box and handed to the prime minister who then informed Eden. The foreign secretary then questioned Norman, who denied having seen Schacht 'for more than a year' and said that Tiarks was now living incommunicado in the country. Churchill minuted Eden on 31 July: 'We have been at war for over $2\frac{3}{4}$ years. Can he extend his assurance to cover the whole period?' The documents contain no such assurance; in fact there is no reply. On 2 Aug. the Americans were sent a reassuring cable which, on the basis of the material in the file, was not at all justified. It is perhaps worth recalling that in Mar. 1941 Princess Wied, wife of the German minister in Stockholm, suggested a meeting between Schacht and Norman after 'four or six weeks' (see Ch. 7 above).

[6] Schellenberg interrogation, PF 606,561 National Archives, Washington, Statement no. 6, handed in 16 July 1945. I am most grateful to Mr Hugh Thomas for allowing me to photocopy this material, which was declassified in Oct. 1990.

[7] Schellenberg's conversations with Hewitt followed this track and were characteristic of most feelers (see ibid.). According to Schellenberg Hewitt was quite responsive. Subsequently the US chargé d'affaires in Stockholm became extremely disturbed by Hewitt's activities and arranged for him to be taken out of Sweden on a British plane early in Jan. 1944. See *Foreign Relations of the United States* (1944), i. 489–93.

Washington. And there were points in favour: after Versailles German nationalists had blamed their own politicians and the Allied powers for what they claimed to have been a humiliating settlement. Additionally, the president and the prime minister were keen to allay Soviet suspicions, fed by reports from their agents in western intelligence services, that the capitalist nations might sink their differences behind an anti-Bolshevik peace.[8]

Why, given official disapproval in London and Washington, did members of the German resistance, whether they were SS members such as Schellenberg, conservatives such as Goerdeler, or democrats such as Otto John, persist in trying to make an arrangement with the Anglo-Americans? One reason must be the German awareness of strong anti-Communist sentiments at high levels in British society above all. Throughout the summer of 1941 the Spanish ambassador in London, the Duke of Alba, was reporting the existence of profound misgivings about the Anglo-Soviet alliance. An unnamed junior minister at the Foreign Office (possibly Butler before he was moved to the Board of Education) told Alba about 'disgust in Conservative circles'.[9] On 17 September Admiral Chatfield, a member of Chamberlain's War Cabinet until dismissal in April 1940, spoke of his anxieties about the consequences of a defeat for the Axis powers. There would 'be no country in the world with an army strong enough to withstand the Soviets', said the admiral, whose opinions were reiterated by a group of senior army officers as well as by the secretary of state for war David Margesson (chief whip under Baldwin and Chamberlain) three days later.[10] During the second half of the war the Germans continued to believe that there was a substantial and well-placed opposition to Churchill, one source of their information being Karl-Heinz Kraemer, the Amt VI agent in Stockholm, believed by Schellenberg to have good contacts in Britain.[11]

The unconditional surrender policy intensified fears about Soviet

[8] For the genesis of the unconditional surrender policy and for Churchill's attitude towards it see von Klemperer, *The German Resistance against Hitler*, 240.

[9] Spanish Foreign Ministry Archives, Madrid, R1912/11 (covering the dealings of the Gabinete Diplomatico with the British Embassy from 1939 to 1945), Alba to Foreign Ministry, 18 July 1941. Alba's extremely well-informed reports were passed by the Foreign Ministry to von Stohrer, the German ambassador in Madrid.

[10] Ibid., Alba to Foreign Ministry, 17 Sept. and 20 Sept. 1941.

[11] See National Archives, Washington, Schellenberg interrogation, Statement no. 6, PF 606,561, 16 July 1945, App. XXIII, section 11; and National Archives microfilm 1270/18, Schellenberg testimony to Lt.-Col. Smith W. Brookhart, Jr., Hersbruck, Germany, 8 May 1946.

expansionism and at the same time antagonized Stewart Menzies and Bill Donovan, respective heads of SIS and of the OSS.[12] Both Menzies and Donovan maintained covert links with the enemy. Menzies was in regular contact with Admiral Canaris, while Allen Dulles, OSS station head in Berne, supplied Donovan with regular and plentiful information on the German resistance.[13] There were at root three reasons for the existence of these clandestine links. First, the Allied intelligence chiefs were concerned about the strategic impact of a Soviet advance into the heart of Europe. They believed that it would be possible, by offering discreet aid to Hitler's enemies, to terminate the war before Germany's collapse turned eastern and central Europe into a power vacuum which only the Soviets could fill. Secondly, underground connections with the German resistance provided the Allies with valuable information. In 1943, for example, Fritz Kolbe, a well-placed official from the German Foreign Ministry, walked into Dulles's offices in Berne with a suitcase of classified material which he continued to replenish thereafter. Kolbe's intelligence was of the highest quality, containing information about the V-1 and V-2 rockets, German troop deployment along the Channel coast in the summer of 1944, and the exact location of the Führer's headquarters at Rastenberg.[14] Thirdly, from Dulles's point of view at least the extension of feelers into Germany allowed the United States to identify the groups and individuals it would wish to support in a post-war German state and society dedicated to liberal-capitalist principles—a resurrection of the Wilsonian approach to Germany's reconstruction a generation before.[15]

None of this should be surprising. Before the war Dulles, like his chief, had been a highly successful Wall Street corporate lawyer. He had developed contacts in multinational industry and finance, with ITT

---

[12] Von Klemperer, *The German Resistance against Hitler*, 242. For Menzies in particular see Phillip Knightley, *Philby: KGB Masterspy* (1988), 105–6. Philby told Knightley early in 1988 that Menzies 'was in touch with Canaris via a cut-out in Sweden'. Kenneth de Courcy told me that Menzies and Canaris actually met during the war, once at least, in Spain. On the night of Canaris's execution in Apr. 1945 de Courcy met Menzies at White's. The Duke of Buccleuch was also present. The SIS chief was drinking. He had heard about the death of his opposite number and said: 'My best friend has been murdered' (interviews with de Courcy, 4 Aug. 1989, 23 Feb. 1990, and 22 June 1992).

[13] Von Klemperer, *The German Resistance against Hitler*, 315–27.

[14] Knightley, *Philby: KGB Masterspy*, 121–2; von Klemperer, *The German Resistance against Hitler*, 321–3, 400 n.

[15] *Lies of Our Times*, May 1994, interview with Christopher Simpson, 14–15. Simpson is the author of *The Splendid Blond Beast* (New York, 1993), an examination of the Armenian massacres and of the Holocaust. One theme of his book is why such acts of genocide 'go largely unpunished and how demands for social justice get thwarted—and by whom'. I am grateful to Robin Ramsay for sending me the photocopy of this article.

and Schroder's, for example.[16] He was a member of the CFR.[17] Thus, even while official policy in Washington was concerned with how to purge Germany of the industrial and financial élites who had supported Hitler, Dulles was compiling lists of eminent bankers and industrialists whom he wished to see rehabilitated in the context of a pro-western, anti-Communist state. Two examples are Karl Blessing, a director of the Reichsbank and associate of Himmler, and Herman Abs, a board member of forty-five major companies including the Deutsche Bank, Mercedes Benz, and I. G. Farben. After the war Blessing became chairman of the Bundesbank while Abs began his rehabilitation as an administrator inside Germany of Marshall Aid. He finished it as head of the Deutsche Bank.[18]

During the war, however, it was not possible for either Dulles or Menzies to help the anti-Hitler forces anything like as much as they would have wished. The resistance moved to the Left during the first half of 1944 and accepted that the assassination of Hitler could not be made conditional on Allied support or on separate peace deals with the Anglo-Americans. None the less, there were contacts between the conspirators in the Stauffenberg plot against Hitler and the Anglo-Americans. Dulles appears to have promised them presidential backing, air-raids on the Nazi stronghold at Berchtesgarten, the selective bombing of towns which, under Nazi and Gestapo influence, refused to join the revolt, and leaflet drops.[19] It was all in vain. When the bomb went off on 20 July Roosevelt showed no interest. British intelligence does not seem to have followed Dulles's example. It offered no encouragement to the plotters. However, Churchill was in touch with Stauffenberg through Stockholm,[20] and Spanish Foreign Ministry papers from April 1944 refer to 'peace talks between the Allies and the Germans'.[21] The prime minister referred to the plot in guarded terms on 12 July. He seems to have taken the view that while no commitment could be made before the overthrow of the regime and

---

[16] Higham, *Trading with the Enemy*, 112–13.
[17] Shoup and Minter, *Imperial Brain Trust*, 61.
[18] See *Lies of Our Time*, May 1994, interview with Simpson, 15–16.
[19] Von Klemperer, *The German Resistance against Hitler*, 422 n.
[20] Ibid. 383, 425 n.
[21] Spanish Foreign Ministry Archives, Madrid, R1373/9, 8–30 Apr. 1944. The file reveals that the Spanish authorities worked very hard to ascertain the identity of an agent, said to be from 'Hess', who was travelling from Britain through Portugal and Spain to Germany in connection with the 'talks'. They finally singled out a Swiss banker called Rudolf Pfenninger. The index to British Foreign Office correspondence in the Public Records Office, London, reveals that arrangements were in hand for a journey by Pfenninger at this time. Unfortunately it has not yet been possible to locate the file. The reference given is Y 4550/2200/652.

the death of Hitler, a successful conspiracy would create a new situation. 'We'll see', is about as far as Churchill was prepared to go.[22]

The failure of the bomb plot meant war to the end. It also marked the collapse of the German resistance, as most of its members were rounded up by the SS. From the summer of 1944 until May 1945 almost all peace-feelers from Germany were made at the behest of Himmler and Schellenberg, a process which culminated in Himmler's ill-fated attempt to negotiate a surrender to the western Allies at the end of April. Hitler heard about this and ordered that the Reichsführer SS be placed under arrest.[23] By this time it was all academic. Soviet troops were in Berlin, Anglo-American forces had reached as far as Lübeck in north Germany and had taken Munich in the south. Hitler committed suicide on 30 April and the war ended with the unconditional surrender of German forces on all fronts on 8 May 1945.

The end of the war brought with it the scenario the peace party had feared. In July 1945 the British electorate, radicalized by total war, elected a majority Labour government for the first time. There was to be no repeat of the post-1918 experience. This time the reconstruction agenda was carried through against weak opposition from a demoralized Conservative Party. By 1950 Britain had a National Health Service. Town and country planning was established. Economic expansion had reduced unemployment to below 3 per cent of the work-force. A shift in manufacturing production and export composition away from the old staples in favour of the new industries which had received a stimulus from the war —electrical goods, electronics, aerospace, and vehicle manufacturing— was under way.[24]

The experiment had not been wrecked by a premature move to decontrol; the political power of the Bank, the City, and of large-scale industry was for the time being in eclipse. The Bank was taken into public ownership. Meanwhile sterling remained inconvertible, except for a brief and unhappy interlude in the summer of 1947, and wartime payments arrangements remained in force along with import restrictions, rationing, and licensing throughout the 1945–51 period. This left very little room for the resumption by merchant banks and discount houses of their traditional international activities. They were driven to dealing in short-term gilt-edged stock and especially in Treasury bills issued by the

---

[22] Von Klemperer, *The German Resistance against Hitler,* 380.

[23] The story was told by Schellenberg in his interrogation (National Archives, Washington, Statement no. 6, PF 606,561, 16 July 1945). It can also be found, told briefly, in Martin Gilbert, *The Second World War* (rev. edn., 1989), 676.

[24] Newton and Porter, *Modernization Frustrated,* 115–17.

government to mop up savings. The latter increased from £892 million in 1939 to £3,680 million in 1945, and both were a function of the vast expansion of public expenditure necessitated by the war effort.[25]

It is true that the post-war Labour governments were strong believers in managed markets and in co-operation with industry. But the rules had changed. Even by 1943 it was clear that the attitude of the state to cartelization was no longer favourable. An example of the new climate was the dispute between the government and the British partners in the International Lamp Cartel. First the Treasury, citing the priority of supplying the home front, banned bulb exports from Britain for six months (under the agreement British companies had exported 17.5 million bulbs out of a total production figure in 1938–9 of 100 million). Then the transfer of money to enemy or related members of the cartel, notably Philips, was banned. The government defended this action on straightforward national-interest grounds, but it also pointed out that 'these type of agreements' flew in the face of the emerging national and international consensus on domestic and external economic policy.[26] After 1945 full employment replaced restrictionism. Government faith in the efficacy and desirability of 'industrial self-government' collapsed in the face of enthusiasm for public investment, a competition policy, and nationalization, which embraced by 1951 coal, steel, the railways, road haulage, Cable and Wireless, and the public utilities.[27]

Victory in war and success in reconstruction were, however, accompanied by dependence on the United States. The Labour government, facing what Keynes called a 'financial Dunkirk' when it came to power, negotiated a $3.75 billion loan from the United States to cover the likely current-account deficit up to 1950. The terms involved acceptance by the British of a much shorter time-scale than they had anticipated in embracing the objective of currency convertibility at a fixed rate of exchange to which they were committed as a result both of the Lend-Lease 'consideration' and the Bretton Woods Agreement. This was the background to the experiment with liberalization in the summer of 1947. In view of the international demand for dollars at the time, it is not surprising that the result was almost a disaster. Britain's trading partners took their chance to get out of sterling into dollars; by 20 August, the dollar drain from the

---

[25] Richard Roberts, 'The City of London as a Financial Centre in the Years of Depression, the Second World War, and Postwar Official Controls, 1931–61', in A. Gorst, L. Johnman, and W. Scott Lucas (eds.), *Contemporary British History 1931–61* (1991), 70.

[26] PRO BT 64/53, F8932/39.

[27] See Jim Tomlinson, 'Mr Attlee's Supply Side Socialism', *Economic History Review*, 46 (1993), 1–22.

central reserves running at an annual rate of $650 million, it was obvious that convertibility would have to be suspended.[28] Failure to have done so would have resulted in the exhaustion of the American credit within weeks. Britain would have been left with gold and hard-currency reserves too meagre to permit the continuation of reconstruction.

After 20 August 1947 controls were reimposed and the foreign-exchange position was eased after 1948 by Marshall Aid. Thereafter American pressure on the Labour government to set about dismantling Imperial Preference, import restrictions, and exchange controls became significantly weaker, although politically motivated speculation against sterling did play a part in the 1949 devaluation which brought the currency's value against the dollar down from £1 = $4.03 to £1 = $2.80. When the decontrol of sterling started in earnest, with the return of a Conservative government in 1951, the initiative owed much more to desperation inside the Treasury, the City, and the Bank than it did to American insistence.[29]

Britain's international economic power as the centre of a discriminatory trade and currency bloc provides part of the explanation for Washington's softer line after 1947. An Anglo-American quarrel over the future of international reconstruction risked splitting the western world into two currency zones, one centred on the dollar and one on sterling. Prospects of a world financial and trading order based upon the principles of Article VII would have receded almost to vanishing-point. At the same time the onset of the Cold War precipitated a rapid revision inside Washington of the value of the British Empire. During the war Churchill had struggled against the anti-colonial radicalism of Roosevelt and his New Dealers, who regarded the Empire as an oppressive anachronism (and as a barrier to the free flow of US trade and investment). From 1946–7 at the very latest the Department of State and the new Department of Defense came to see the Empire as a bulwark against what they believed to be Soviet-inspired Communist expansion in the Far East and in the Middle East. And Britain itself began to play an increasingly important role in the organization of west European defence against perceived Soviet expansionism, a performance which culminated in the establishment of the North Atlantic Treaty Organization (NATO) in 1949.[30]

The inescapable truth is, however, that although Britain could have

---

[28] Newton and Porter, *Modernization Frustrated*, 110–11.

[29] See Scott Newton 'Operation ROBOT and the Political Economy of Sterling Convertibility, 1951–1952', *European University Institute Working Paper* 86/256 (Florence, 1986).

[30] See Scott Newton, 'Britain, the Sterling area and European Integration, 1945–50', *Journal of Imperial and Commonwealth History*, 12 (1985), 164–80.

survived without American aid after 1945 the cost would have been very high. Dramatic cuts in overseas investment and in foreign military commitments would have been necessary. Living standards would have fallen because lack of dollars would have reduced food and raw material imports from the western hemisphere to what could be afforded in bilateral deals. But in 1945, with exports running at 33 per cent of their 1938 level, what could the British have bargained with? True, the colonies provided non-dollar resources, such as tobacco, cocoa, cotton, rubber, and ground-nuts which could be exploited for the benefit of the British factory and the British consumer. However, the benefits to be derived from a programme of investment in colonial development were clearly not going to be instant. In the meantime the British people themselves would be subject to rationing more intense than during the war, and reliance on home-grown sources of food would be heavy enough to require the use of schoolchildren in gathering in the harvest. The Treasury and the Cabinet contemplated such a doomsday scenario on three occasions, in the summers of 1945, 1947, and 1949, by which time the consequences of autarky would have been less severe in view of the successful export drive. Nevertheless, even then they rejected the isolationist option in favour of the economic and strategic benefits to be gained in solidarity with the United States. Dependence on Washington was a political choice: it followed from the Attlee government's commitment to liberal rather than to Gosplan-style socialism, and from its mounting concern about Soviet foreign policy.[31]

Dependence on the United States, the presence of Soviet forces in the heart of Europe, as well as Britain's own turn to the Left were all products of the war. The other nightmare of the Right, decolonization, also unrolled over the subsequent generation, starting with Indian independence in 1947. It was a function not so much of American anti-imperialism as of the growing political and financial costs involved in policing an Empire at a time of militant colonial nationalism. Nevertheless, the war was a catalyst, forcing promises out of the British throughout Asia as they bid for the help of local populations against the Japanese, and disrupting the economies of hitherto quiet African colonies.[32]

The course of British, and indeed world, history since 1945 has led

---

[31] The economic and strategic background to the post-war 'special relationship' is explored in detail in C. C. S. Newton, 'Britain, the Dollar Shortage, and European Integration', unpublished Ph.D thesis (University of Birmingham, 1982).

[32] Cain and Hopkins, *Crisis and Deconstruction*, 275–91; J. A. Gallagher, *The Decline, Rise and Fall of the British Empire* (Oxford, 1982).

some younger historians to question the sacrifices made in the 1939–45 war. An example is Andrew Roberts, author of a recent sympathetic study of Halifax. Roberts is incorrect to argue that Halifax abandoned appeasement after the *Anschluss*, but he is right to identify it with a struggle to 'preserve some of the best elements in the British way of life'. The failure of Halifax and the peace party to achieve their goal 'obliterated for ever' these elements. The war revealed imperial weaknesses and led to the break-up of the Empire. Britain became a middle-ranking power. In other ways, too: 'Much of what Halifax feared has come to pass. Today Hickleton Hall is a hospital for the insane, "The Dorch" is owned by an Arab, Temple Newsam is a museum, 88 Eaton Square has been split into flats and the beautiful Little Compton Manor, where the Halifaxes spent so many happy weekends in 1940, is now a College of accountancy.'[33] The notes struck here by Roberts suggest that he, like his subject, identifies the 'best elements in the British way of life' with what the cultural historian Martin Wiener has called the 'southern metaphor'—in other words, the pastoral, gentlemanly values of Consumer's England, now buried by the National Health Service, cosmopolitanism, and commerce.[34]

Unquestionably the war delivered a massive blow to the old order. In central and eastern Europe this took the form of the installation of Communist regimes under instruction from Moscow. Yet unpleasant though the period of Soviet hegemony in eastern Europe was for most who lived under it, very few indeed would say that Nazi supremacy, involving continuing oppression and genocide, would have been better. And in the circumstances of the time what other choice was there? By the early 1990s the Soviet Union had ceased to exist. Russian forces had left most east European countries, which had abandoned one-party rule for pluralist democracy.

In Britain the war heralded the hegemony, albeit temporary, of Producer's England. For a time the full employment of capital and labour and the pursuit of economic growth rather than the maintenance of a balanced budget, zero inflation, and the widest possible use of sterling as an international currency, became objectives of macroeconomic policy. From the sacrifices of 1940–5, and from the values which underpinned the anti-Nazi struggle, there emerged a belief that it was possible for society to organize its resources in a way which would guarantee each

[33] Roberts, *The Holy Fox*, 306.
[34] Martin Wiener, *English Culture and the Decline of the Industrial Spirit* (Cambridge, 1981).

member a job, a house, medical treatment free at the point of need, and education up to the age of 15. For more than thirty years after the end of the war successive governments struggled to meet these aspirations. Despite growing economic difficulties, they generally succeeded and in so doing presided over an increase in living standards unparalleled in the experience of the British people. Surely, the destruction of Nazi and Fascist power and these faltering steps towards social democracy were for many an improvement on a 'British way of life' which appears to have revolved around country houses, Eaton Square, and the Dorchester Hotel.

Bibliography

INTERVIEWS

Kenneth de Courcy: 4 August 1989; 23 February 1990; 22 June 1992.
Adrian Liddell-Hart: 13 December 1988; 22 June 1989; 26 March 1990.
Sir Peter Tennant: 29 March 1989.

UNPUBLISHED COLLECTIONS FROM OFFICIAL AND INSTITUTIONAL ARCHIVES

Bank of England, London.
Federation of British Industries, Modern Records Centre, University of Warwick.
Ministry of Foreign Affairs Archive, Planta baja, Palacio de Santa Cruz, Plaza de la Provincia, Madrid.
Public Record Office, London: Board of Trade (BT)
                                   Cabinet (CAB)
                                   Foreign Office (FO)
                                   Home Office (HO)
                                   Prime Minister (PREM)
                                   Treasury (T).

PRIVATE COLLECTIONS OF UNPUBLISHED PAPERS

Lord Avon (Manuscripts and Rare Books Reading Room, University of Birmingham).
R. H. Brand (New Bodleian Library, Oxford).
C. Roden Buxton (Rhodes House, Oxford).
Neville Chamberlain (Manuscripts and Rare Books Reading Room, University of Birmingham).
Group-Captain Malcolm Christie (Churchill College, Cambridge).
Kenneth de Courcy (Hoover Institution on War, Revolution and Peace, Stanford, California).
Paul Einzig (Churchill College, Cambridge).
Basil Liddell-Hart (War Studies Library, King's College, London).
R. R. Stokes (New Bodleian Library, Oxford).

PUBLISHED ARCHIVAL COLLECTIONS

Documents Diplomatiques Francais, 2ᵐᵉ ser.
Documenti Diplomatici Italiani, 9th ser.

Documents on British Foreign Policy, 3rd ser.
Documents on German Foreign Policy, ser. D.
Foreign Relations of the United States.

REFERENCE WORKS

(Unless otherwise stated, place of publication of all books is London.)

Directory of Directors, 1940 (1940).

Statistical Abstract for the United Kingdom, 1913 and 1924 to 1937 (1939).

FEINSTEIN, C. H. (ed.), *National Income, Expenditure and Output of the United Kingdom, 1855–1965* (Cambridge, 1972).

League of Nations, *Europe's Trade* (Geneva, 1941).

United Nations, *A Study of Trade between Latin America and Europe* (Geneva, 1953).

——*A Survey of the Economic Situation and Prospects of Europe* (Geneva, 1948).

Who's Who, 1940 (1940).

SECONDARY WORKS

ADDISON, PAUL, *The Road to 1945: British Politics and the Second World War* (1975).

ALLEN, G. C., *The Structure of Industry in Britain: A Study in Economic Change* (2nd edn., 1968).

ASTER, SIDNEY, ' "Guilty Men": The case of Neville Chamberlain', in Boyce and Robertson, *Paths to War.*

BARKEI, A., *Nazi Economics: Ideology, Theory, and Policy* (Oxford, 1988).

BLANK, STEPHEN, *Industry and Government in Britain: The Federation of British Industries and the International Economy* (Farnborough, 1973).

BOND, BRIAN, *British Military Policy Between Two World Wars* (Oxford, 1980).

BOYCE, ROBERT W. D., *British Capitalism at the Crossroads 1919–1932: A Study in Politics, Economics and International Relations* (Cambridge, 1987).

——and ROBERTSON, ESMONDE H., (eds.), *Paths to War: New Essays on the Origins of the Second World War* (Basingstoke, 1989).

BROWN, ANTHONY CAVE, *'C': The Secret Life of Sir Stewart Graham Menzies, Spymaster to Winston Churchill* (New York, 1987).

CAIN, P. J., 'J. A. Hobson, Financial Capitalism and Imperialism in Late Victorian and Edwardian England', in A. N. Porter and R. F. Holland (eds.), *Money, Finance and Empire 1790–1960* (1985).

——and HOPKINS, A. G., *British Imperialism I: Innovation and Expansion, 1688–1914* (1993).

——*British Imperialism II: Crisis and Deconstruction, 1914–1990* (1993).

CARR, WILLIAM, *Arms, Autarky and Aggression: A Study in German Foreign Policy, 1933–1939* (1972).

CHURCHILL, WINSTON S., *The Second World War*, II: *Their Finest Hour* (rev. edn., 1951).

——*The Second World War*, III: *The Grand Alliance* (1950).

CLARKE, PETER, *The Keynesian Revolution in the Making* (Oxford, 1988).

COLVILLE, JOHN, *Fringes of Power: 10 Downing Street Diaries 1939–1955* (London and New York, 1985).

COSTELLO, JOHN, *Ten Days that Saved the West* (1991).

COWLING, MAURICE, *The Impact of Hitler: British Politics and British Policy 1933–1940* (1975).

CROUZET, FRANÇOIS, *The Victorian Economy* (1982).

CROZIER, ANDREW, 'Prelude to Munich: British Foreign Policy and Germany 1935–38', *European Studies Review*, 6 (1976), 357–81.

——*Appeasement and Germany's Bid for Colonies* (1988).

DAVENPORT-HINES, R. P. T., 'McGowan, Harry Duncan', in D. J. Jeremy and Christine Shaw (eds.), *Dictionary of Business Biography*, 4 (1984).

DAY, DAVID, *Menzies and Churchill at War* (1986).

DE COURCY, KENNETH, 'The Late Lord Butler, KG', *Special Office Brief*, 2 Apr. 1987.

DIAPER, STEPHANIE, 'Merchant Banking in the Interwar Period: The Case of Kleinwort, Benson and Sons, Ltd.', *Business History*, 28 (1986), 55–76.

DUGGAN, JOHN P., *Neutral Ireland and the Third Reich* (Dublin, 1985).

EICHENGREEN, B. J., 'Sterling and the Tariff, 1929–1932', *Princeton Studies in International Finance*, 48 (Princeton, NJ, 1981).

FISK, ROBERT, *In Time of War* (1983).

FORBES, NEIL, 'London Banks, the German Standstill Agreements, and "Economic Appeasement" in the 1930s', *Economic History Review*, 2nd ser., 40 (1987), 571–87.

GILBERT, MARTIN, *The Second World War* (rev. edn., 1989).

——*Winston Churchill*, VI: *Finest Hour 1939–1941* (1983).

GILLINGHAM, JOHN, *Industry and Politics in the Third Reich* (1985).

HANCOCK, W. K., and GOWING, M. M., *British War Economy* (1949).

HANNAH, LESLIE, *The Rise of the Corporate Economy* (2nd edn., 1983).

HARGRAVE, JOHN, *Professor Skinner, alias Montagu Norman* (1940).

HASSELL, ULRICH VON, *The von Hassell Diaries 1938–44* (1948).

HAXEY, SIMON, *Tory M.P.* (1939).

HESS, WOLF-RUDIGER, *My Father Rudolf Hess* (1986).

HESSE, FRITZ, *Hitler and the English* (1954).

HEXNER, ERVIN, *International Cartels* (1946).

HIGHAM, CHARLES, *Trading with the Enemy: How the Allied Multinationals Supplied Nazi Germany Throughout World War Two* (1983).

HOLLAND, R. F., 'The Federation of British Industries and the International Economy 1929–39', *Economic History Review*, 2nd ser., 34 (1981), 287–300.

HOWARD, ANTHONY, *Rab: The Life of R. A. Butler* (1987).

INGHAM, GEOFFREY, *Capitalism Divided? The City and Industry in British Social Development* (Cambridge, 1984).

KAISER, DAVID E., *Economic Diplomacy and the Origins of the Second World War* (Princeton, NJ, 1981).

KEE, ROBERT, *Munich: The Eleventh Hour* (1988).

KENNEDY, PAUL, *The Rise and Fall of the Great Powers: Economic Change and Military Conflict from 1500 to 2000* (1988).

——*Strategy and Diplomacy, 1870–1945* (1983).

KINDLEBERGER, CHARLES P., *The World in Depression, 1929–1939* (1987).

KLEMPERER, KLEMENS VON, *The German Resistance against Hitler* (Oxford, 1992).

KNIGHTLEY, PHILLIP, *The Second Oldest Profession* (1986).

——*Philby: KGB Masterspy* (1988).

LAMB, RICHARD, *The Drift to War, 1922–1939* (1989).

——*The Ghosts of Peace 1935–1945* (Salisbury, 1987).

LAMMERS, D. N., 'Fascism, Communism and the Foreign Office', *Journal of Contemporary History*, 6 (1971), 66–86.

——'From Whitehall after Munich: The Foreign Office and the Future Course of British Policy', *Historical Journal*, 16 (1973), 831–56.

LEITH-ROSS, FREDERICK, *Money Talks* (1968).

LEUTZE, JAMES (ed.), *The London Journal of General Raymond E. Lee, 1940–41* (Boston, 1971).

LUCAS, A. F., *Industrial Reconstruction and the Control of Competition* (1937).

MACDONALD, C. A., 'Economic Appeasement and the German "Moderates" 1937–1939. An Introductory Essay', *Past and Present*, 56 (1972), 105–35.

——'The Venlo Affair', *European Studies Review*, 8 (1978), 443–63.

——*The United States, Britain and Appeasement 1936–1939* (1981).

——'The United States, Appeasement and the Open Door', in W. Mommsen and L. Kettenacker (eds.), *The Fascist Challenge and the Policy of Appeasement* (1983).

——'Deterrent Diplomacy: Roosevelt and the Containment of Germany, 1938–1940', in Boyce and Robertson (eds.), *Paths to War*.

MATHIAS, PETER, *The First Industrial Nation* (1983).

MIDDLEMAS, KEITH, *Politics in Industrial Society: The British Experience since 1911* (1979).

MIDDLETON, ROGER, *Towards the Managed Economy: Keynes, the Treasury and the Fiscal Policy Debate of the 1930s* (1985).

MILWARD, ALAN S., 'Fascism and the Economy', in W. Laqueur (ed.), *Fascism: A Reader's Guide* (1979).

——*War, Economy and Society 1939–1945* (1987).

NEWMAN, SIMON, *March 1939: The British Guarantee to Poland* (Oxford, 1976).

NEWTON, SCOTT, 'Britain, the Sterling area and European Integration 1945–50', *Journal of Imperial and Commonwealth History*, 12 (1985), 164–80.

——'A Who's Who of Appeasement', *Lobster*, 22 (1991), 11–15.

—— 'The "Anglo-German Connection" and the Political Economy of Appeasement', *Diplomacy and Statecraft*, 2 (1991), 178–207.

—— and PORTER, DILWYN, *Modernization Frustrated: The Politics of Industrial Decline in Britain Since 1900* (1988).

OVENDALE, RITCHIE, 'Why the British Dominions declared War', in Boyce and Robertson (eds.), *Paths to War*.

OVERY, RICHARD, 'Hitler's War Plans and the German Economy', in Boyce and Robertson (eds.), *Paths to War*.

PADFIELD, PETER, *Hess: The Führer's Disciple* (1991).

PARKER, R. A. C., 'Economics, Rearmament and Foreign Policy: The United Kingdom Before 1939. A Preliminary Study', *Journal of Contemporary History*, 10 (1975).

—— *Chamberlain and Appeasement* (Basingstoke, 1993).

PEDEN, G. C., *British Rearmament and the Treasury, 1932–9* (Edinburgh, 1979).

—— 'Keynes, the Economics of Rearmament and Appeasement', in W. Mommsen and L. Kettenacker (eds.), *The Fascist Challenge and the Policy of Appeasement* (1983).

—— ' "A Matter of Timing": The Economic Background to British Foreign Policy, 1937–9', *History*, 69 (1984).

—— *Keynes, the Treasury and British Economic Policy* (1988).

PHILBY, KIM, *My Silent War* (1989).

POLLARD, SIDNEY, *The Development of the British Economy, 1914–1990* (1992).

QUIGLEY, CARROL, *The Anglo-American Establishment from Rhodes to Cliveden* (New York, 1981).

RAMSAY, ROBIN, 'Clinton and Quigley: A Strange Tale From the US Elite', *Lobster*, 25 (1993), 14–15.

READ, ANTHONY and FISHER, DAVID, *Colonel Z: The Secret Life of a Master of Spies* (1984).

READER, W. J., *Imperial Chemical Industries: a History*, II: *The First Quarter Century, 1926–1952* (Oxford, 1975).

REDMOND, JOHN, 'An Indicator of the Effective Exchange Rate of the Pound in the 1930s', *Economic History Review*, 2nd ser., 33 (1980), 83–91.

REYNOLDS, DAVID, *The Creation of the Anglo-American Alliance 1937–41: A Study in Competitive Co-operation* (1981).

ROBERTS, ANDREW, *The Holy Fox* (1991).

ROBERTS, RICHARD, 'Tiarks, Frank Cyril', in D. J. Jeremy and Christine Shaw (eds.), *A Dictionary of Business Biography*, 5 (1988).

—— 'The City of London as a Financial Centre in the Years of Depression, the Second World War and Postwar Official Controls, 1931–61', in A. Gorst, L. Johnman, and W. Scott Lucas (eds.), *Contemporary British History 1931–61* (1991).

ROBERTSON, ESMONDE M. (ed.), *The Origins of the Second World War* (London and Basingstoke, 1971).

SAYERS, R. S., *Financial Policy 1939–1945* (1956).

—— *The Bank of England 1891–1944*, III, *Appendices* (Cambridge, 1976).

SCHMITZ, CHRISTOPHER, *The Growth of Big Business in the United States and Western Europe, 1880–1939* (Basingstoke, 1993).

SHAY, RICHARD P. Jnr., *British Rearmament in the Thirties: Politics and Profits* (Princeton, NJ, 1977).

SHOUP, LAURENCE H. and MINTER, WILLIAM, *Imperial Brain Trust: The Council on Foreign Relations and United States Foreign Policy* (New York, 1971).

STAFFORD, PAUL, 'R. A. Butler at the Foreign Office 1938–1939: Political Autobiography and the Art of the Plausible', *Historical Journal*, 28 (1983), 901–22.

'T-124' (RUSSELL GRENFELL), *Seapower* (1940).

TASCA, HENRY J., *World Trading Systems: A Study of American and British Commercial Policies* (Paris, 1939).

TAYLOR, A. J. P., *The Origins of the Second World War* (2nd edn., 1964).

—— *English History 1914–1945* (2nd edn., 1975).

TEICHOVA, ALICE, *An Economic Background to Munich* (Cambridge, 1974).

—— 'Versailles and the Expansion of the Bank of England into Central Europe', in N. Horn and J. Kocka (eds.), *Law and the Formation of the Big Enterprises in the Nineteenth and Early Twentieth Centuries* (Gottingen, 1979).

THOMAS, HUGH, *Hess: A Tale of Two Murders* (1988).

TOLLIDAY, STEPHEN, 'Steel and Rationalization Policies, 1918–1950', in B. Elbaum and W. Lazonick (eds.), *The Decline of the British Economy* (Oxford, 1985).

TOMLINSON, JIM, *Public Policy and the Economy since 1900* (Oxford, 1990).

—— 'Mr Attlee's Supply Side Socialism', *Economic History Review*, 46 (1993), 1–22.

WARK, W. K., *The Ultimate Enemy: British Intelligence and Nazi Germany, 1933–1939* (1985).

WATT, D. C., *How War Came: The Immediate Origins of the Second World War* (1989).

WENDT, B. J., 'Economic Appeasement'—A Crisis Strategy, in W. Mommsen and L. Kettenacker (eds.), *The Fascist Challenge and the Policy of Appeasement* (1983).

Index

Menzies, Robert 186
Menzies, Stewart 141 n., 142, 170, 174–5, 182, 196
Mercedes Benz 197
Middlemas, Keith 1
Midland Bank 58, 61, 66
MI5 (Security Service) 169, 170
Milward, A. S. 3 n.
Mining Association of Great Britain 97–8
Mitchell, Colonel Harold 153
Mond-Turner talks 31–2
Mooney, James 144
Morrison, Herbert 160
Morton, Sir Desmond 170
Mosley, Oswald 4, 32–4, 41, 169–70
Mountain, Sir Edward Mortimer 123
Mowat, C. L. 27
Munich Agreement 58, 85–7, 89
    conference 83, 111
Munitions, Ministry of 17, 19
Mussolini, Benito 53, 81, 108

National Health Service 198, 202
National Joint Advisory Council 135, 163
Nazism 53–5
Newman, Simon 1, 89, 106
New Zealand 39
Nordic League 169
Norman, Montagu 58–60, 62, 65, 89, 90–1, 112, 169
    peace talks 188, 194
    see also Standstill
North Atlantic Treaty Organization (NATO) 200

Operation Barbarossa 185, 191–2
Operation Sealion 177
Oster, Hans 183
Ottawa Conference (1932) 36, 39
Overseas Trade, Department of 94, 96, 99, 124, 155

Parker, R. A. C. 107, 125
Payne-Best, Sigismund 145–8
Peden, George 2, 3, 70–1
Philby, Kim 196 n.
Phillips, Sir Frederick 92
Picture Post 166
Pilcher, Lieutenant-Colonel W. S. 142
Poland 4, 6–7, 104–6, 107, 114, 122, 133, 153, 154
    'indirect aggression' 109
    see also Danzig

Pole, Felix 43
Political and Economic Planning (PEP) 48
Popitz, Johannes 182, 184, 185
Production, Ministry of 164
protection 4, 38, 47
Prytz, Bjorn 173, 175

Raper, Baldwin 142
Radio Corporation of America (RCA) 44
Ramsay, Captain A. H. M. 153
rationalization of industry 4, 40–1, 42–3
    encouraged by Conservative M.P.s and peers 44–5
Reichsbank 59, 60, 125, 197
Reichsgruppe Industrie (RI) 95, 99–101, 126
Renwick, Sir Robert 123, 155–6
Rhenish–Westphalian Coal Syndicate 98
Rhineland, reoccupation of 57
Ribbentrop, Joachim von 83, 105, 122
Right Club 152–3, 169
Robbins, Lionel 43
Roberts, Andrew 173, 202
Rockefeller, Nelson 181
Rolling Stock Manufacturers' Association 155
Romania 88, 103–4, 106, 107
Room, The 181–2
Roosevelt, President F. D. 121, 144, 155, 165, 170, 194–5, 200
Rothschild's (bank) 12, 21
Rommel, General Erwin 186
Royal Dutch Shell 142
Round Table 20–1, 73–4, 142
    journal 85
Royal Institute for International Affairs (RIIA) 20–1, 73–4, 142, 181
Rucker, Arthur 141 n.
Runciman, Walter 96, 99
Rushcliffe, Lord 168

Schacht, Hjalmar 60, 61–3, 65, 75–7, 90
    dismissal 93–4, 98
    peace talks 188, 194
Schellenberg, Walter 145–6, 180, 194, 195
Schlotterer, Gustav 177
Schmidt, Gustav 2
Schroder, J. H. 5, 58, 66, 113, 197
Secret Intelligence Service (SIS or MI6) 86 n., 102, 105, 145–8, 174 n., 180–1, 182, 188
    see also Menzies, Stuart